D0961934

THE BEAGLE

BY MARCIA A. FOY
ANNA KATHERINE NICHOLAS

Featuring special chapters by
Pearl N. Baker
Ray Libby
Kathleen Carling

Front cover photo: Ch. Brantwood's Desperado owned by Anita Tillman.

Back cover photo: Lightnin Ridge White Spot, Sylvia and Victor Lopez's Beagle puppy.

Title page photo: Anna Katherine Nicholas's beloved "Louise"—Ch. Foyscroft True Blue Lou, who gained her title within several months as a puppy and whose wins include a Best of Opposite Sex to Triple Threat at the Bay State Beagle Club Specialty.

ISBN 0-86622-042-9

Distributed in the UNITED STATES by T.F.H. Publications, Inc., 211 West Sylvania Avenue, Neptune City, NJ 07753; in CANADA by H & L Pet Supplies Inc., 27 Kingston Crescent, Kitchener, Ontario N2B 2T6; Rolf C. Hagen Ltd., 3225 Sartelon Street, Montreal 382 Quebec; in ENGLAND by T.F.H. Publications Limited, 4 Kier Park, Ascot, Berkshire SL5 7DS; in AUSTRALIA AND THE SOUTH PACIFIC by T.F.H. (Australia) Pty. Ltd., Box 149, Brookvale 2100 N.S.W., Australia; in NEW ZEALAND by Ross Haines & Son, Ltd., 18 Monmouth Street, Grey Lynn, Auckland 2 New Zealand; in SINGAPORE AND MALAYSIA by MPH Distributors (S) Pte., Ltd., 601 Sims Drive, # 03/07/21, Singapore 1438; in the PHILIPPINES by Bio-Research, 5 Lippay Street, San Lorenzo Village, Makati Rizal; in SOUTH AFRICA by Multipet Pty. Ltd., 30 Turners Avenue, Durban 4001. Published by T.F.H. Publications Inc. Manufactured in the United States of America by T.F.H. Publications, Inc.

Dedication

To Trippe and to Louise,
who will live forever in our thoughts and memory.

"Louise" and Anna K. Nicholas.

"Trippe" and Marcia A. Foy.

Contents

About the Authors

Anna Katherine Nicholas

Since early childhood, Anna Katherine Nicholas has been involved with dogs. Her first pets were a Boston Terrier, an Airedale, and a German Shepherd. Then, in 1925, came the first of the Pekingese—a gift from a friend who raised them. Now her home is shared with a Miniature Poodle and a dozen or so Beagles, including her noted Best in Show dog and National Specialty winner, Champion Rockaplenty's Wild Oats, a Gold Certificate sire (one of the breed's truly great stud dogs), who as a show dog was Top Beagle in the Nation in 1973. She also owns Champion Foyscroft True Blue Lou, Foyscroft Aces Are Wild, and in co-ownership with Marcia Foy, who lives with her, Champion Foyscroft Triple Mitey Migit.

Miss Nicholas is best known throughout the Dog Fancy as a writer and as a judge. Her first magazine article, published in *Dog News* magazine around 1930, was about Pekingese; and this was followed by a widely acclaimed breed column, "Peeking at the Pekingese" which appeared for at least two decades, originally in *Dogdom,* then, following the demise of that publication, in *Popular Dogs.* During the 1940's she was Boxer columnist for *Pure-Bred Dogs/American Kennel Gazette* and for *Boxer Briefs.* More recently many of her articles, geared to interest fanciers of every breed, have appeared in *Popular Dogs, Pure-Bred Dogs/American Kennel Gazette, Show Dogs, Dog Fancy,* and *The World of the Working Dog.* Currently she is a featured regular columnist in *Kennel Review, Dog World, Canine Chronicle* and *The Dog Fancier* (Canadian). Her *Dog World* column, "Here, There and Everywhere," was the Dog Writers Association of America winner of the Best Series in a Dog Magazine Award for 1979.

It was during the late 1930's that Miss Nicholas' first book, *The Pekingese,* appeared, published by and written at the request of the Judy Publishing Company. This book completely sold out and is now a collector's item, as is her *The Skye Terrier Book,* which was published by the Skye Terrier Club of America during the early 1960's.

In 1970 Miss Nicholas won the Dog Writers Association of America award for the Best Technical Book of the Year with her *Nicholas Guide to Dog Judging.* In 1979 the revision of this book again won the Dog Writers Association of America Best Technical Book Award, the first time ever that a revision has been so honored by this association.

In the early 1970's, Miss Nicholas co-authored, with Joan Brearley, five breed books which were published by T.F.H. Publications, Inc. These were *This is the Bichon Frise, The Wonderful World of Beagles and Beagling* (winner of a Dog Writers Association of America Honorable Mention Award), *The Book of the Pekingese, The Book of the Boxer,* and *This is the Skye Terrier.*

During recent years, Miss Nicholas has been writing books consistently for T.F.H. These include *Successful Dog Show Exhibiting, The Book of the Rottweiler, The Book of the Poodle, The Book of the Labrador Retriever, The Book of the English Springer Spaniel, The book of the Golden Retriever, The Book of the German Shepherd, The Book of the Shetland Sheepdog* and in the same series you are now reading, *The Chow Chow, The Keeshond, The Maltese, The Poodle,* and *The Boxer.* In the T.F.H. "KW" series, she has done *Rottweilers, Weimaraners,* and *Norwegian Elkhounds.* She has also supplied the American chapters for two English publications, imported by T.F.H., *The Staffordshire Bull Terrier* and *The Jack Russell Terrier.*

Her judging career began in 1934 at the First Company Governors' Foot Guard in Hartford, Connecticut, drawing the largest Pekingese entry ever assembled to date at this event. Presently she is approved to judge all Hounds, Terriers, Toys, and Non-Sporting Dogs; all Pointers, English and Gordon Setters, Vizslas, Weimaraners, and Wirehaired Pointing Griffons in Sporting breeds, and, in Working Group, Boxers and Doberman Pinschers. In 1970 she became the third woman in history to judge Best in Show at the prestigious Westminster Kennel Club Dog Show, where she has officiated on some sixteen other occasions through the years. In addition to her numerous Westminster assignments, Miss Nicholas has judged at such other outstandingly important events as Santa Barbara, Trenton, Chicago International, the Sportsmans in Canada, the Metropolitan in Canada, and Specialty Shows in several dozen breeds both in the United States and in Canada. She has judged in almost every one of the mainland United States and in four Canadian provinces, and her services are constantly sought in other countries.

Through the years, Miss Nicholas has held important offices in a great many all-breed and Specialty clubs. She still remains an honorary member of several of them.

Marcia A. Foy

Marcia A. Foy was born in Chicago and raised in the suburbs of the North Shore. From early childhood she loved dogs and had many breeds at one time or another as pets, including Pekes, a Basset, a Gordon Setter, and Miniature Poodles.

Her first show dog was a Kerry Blue Terrier, That's Dundel of Delwin, who came from the noted Delwin Kennels of Ed Sayres, Sr. She showed this dog for the first time in 1945, when she was eleven years old.

Marcia moved East in 1960, at which time she acquired her first Beagles. Among those she has owned and shown are the unforgettable Champion Kings Creek Triple Threat; his son Champion Rockaplenty's Wild Oats (who now belongs to A.K.N.); the magnificent bitch, Trippe's daughter, Champion Foyscroft Triple Lena Wor Lo; the multi-Group winners Champion Junior's Foyscroft Wild Kid and the 13″ Champion Jo Mar's Repeat Performance; and many others. Although she has raised only a limited number of litters, she has bred a goodly number of champions, among them dogs who have provided foundation stock for other successful kennels.

Interest in Beagles is shared by a very special love of Poodles, a breed which has long been one of her favorites.

It was in 1976 that Marcia officiated for the first time as a judge, an experience which she has grown to thoroughly enjoy. Her first breeds were Beagles and Dachshunds. Currently she is approved for all Hounds and the Hound Group, the majority of the Terriers, and Best in Show. Her judging assignments take her on a wide course of travel each year, and she has officiated at leading shows throughout the United States and in most of Canada. One of her earliest assignments was that of the National Beagle Club Sweepstakes at Aldie, and she has also judged the Blossom Valley Beagle Club Specialty in California, along with dozens of all-breed shows.

Marcia has been largely instrumental in having persuaded the Southern New York Beagle Club, of which she is an Honorary Member, to hold an annual conformation Specialty, which it now does in conjunction with the Westchester Kennel Club each September—most successfully, we might add!

Chapter 1

Origin of the Beagle

Research reveals reference to the hounds which are without doubt the ancestors of our Beagles coming from the Greeks as far back as 400 B.C. The little dogs were as popular then as they are now, and this popularity helped them to become established in ancient Britain around 200 A.D.

Beagle-type hounds were also known in Italy during this same period, very likely having been brought there from Greece. Some of these almost certainly made their way to the British Isles during the Roman occupation, but who is to say whether the little dogs were introduced there by the Romans or their numbers simply augmented? Indications point to there having been packs of small hounds used for hunting in Britain both prior to and following the Roman invasion.

Predecessors of our Beagles are noted as having been popular in England when the Forest Laws of King Canute were drawn up in 1016 A.D. Dogs which apparently were Beagles had been brought to France when Aquitaine and Guienne were British provinces. By the fourteenth century Beagles had become known in Greece, Britain, Italy, and France.

Talbots, large white hounds brought to England by William the Conqueror, are believed to have played a part in the development of the modern Beagle. These dogs are known to have been forebears of the Southern hound, a dog involved in the development of the Foxhound and thereby of the Beagle.

The name "Beagle" has remained with our little hounds since the latter part of the fourteenth century. It translates "smallest of the hounds."

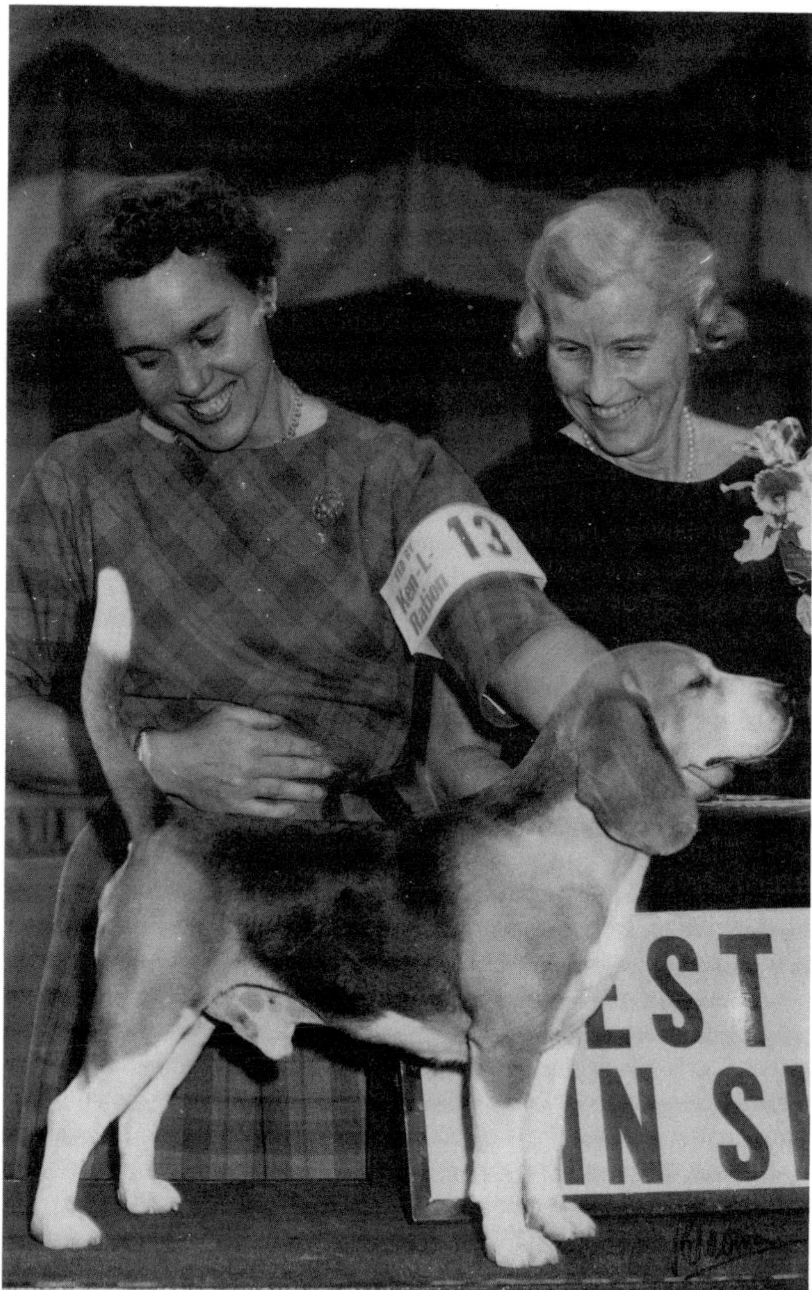

The 15″ Best in Show Beagle, Ch. Gay Boy of Geddesburg, chalked up more than a dozen such honors during his show career for Mr. and Mrs. Willard K. Denton in the early 60's. Handled by Jane K. Forsyth.

Chapter 2

The Beagle in Great Britain

It was in 1890 that the Beagle Club was founded in England, thus it was one of the earliest Specialty Clubs to receive recognition from The Kennel Club. Its first Specialty show was held during 1896, other events following irregularly. The show Beagle did not find it smooth going in England in the period preceding and during World War I, and an upturn did not take place until the early 1950's when a sudden marked increase in activity and interest was noted.

The 1920's make note of only one truly loyal Beagle exhibitor, Mr. Oliver Jones of the Crymmych Kennels. In the 1930's Mrs. Nina Elms was supporting the shows with very good Bassets, Beagles, and Bloodhounds, and her kennel prefix Reynalton earned a niche in hound history. E. Fitch Daglish, Mrs. E. Stockley, Viscount Chelmsford, Miss Wills, and Mr. E.G. Sergeant helped to bring about a rise in the number of registrations and of shows offering Challenge Certificates.

Mrs. Stockley's interest continued following World War II, which was helpful to the breed during the late 1940's. Her bitch Champion Linbourne Violet, born as the war was ending, won fifteen Challenge Certificates and became the dam of the widely admired Champion Linbourne Plunder, these two both bred by Mrs. C.P. Davies. Plunder's litter-brother sired Linbourne Wistful who also was a credit to Mrs. Stockley at the shows.

Grady O'Grady, owned by J.S. Howard, M.R.C.V.S., was a dog who sired some important offspring, among them Mrs. Spowart's Champion Acregreen Why Not; three champions for Mrs. Spowart from her well-admired bitch Champion Woodwren; and Champions Acregreen Whimsey and Wellbred for J.K. Drydens.

Mrs. Wilmshurst and Miss Brucker were two breeders from the 1940's who also contributed well. Champion Solomon of Stanhurst was Mrs. Wilmshurst's best known dog. Bred by Dr. Seward, Solomon sired four splendid champions, and his descendants included an especially important dog of the 1950's, Stanhurst Poacher, who in his turn sired the famed Champion Tavernmews Ranter. Miss Brucker, meanwhile, was making her presence felt with her excellent bitch Champion Twinrivers Mermaid; with Mermaid's dam, Kirby Music; and with Paradox.

As the 1950's were about to get underway, the Appeline Beagles owned by Mr. and Mrs. Douglas Appleton appeared on the Beagle scene. The first of their dogs, and the foundation for the kennel, was the notable Champion Radley Triumph of Appeline, who had been bred by the Radley College Beagles and became the property of the

Ch. Pin Oaks Dynasty's Nugget was exported by the Alderfers to the Appletons in England. He was Best in Show at the Welsh Beagle Club Championship event, and has been excelling in keenest British competition. A son of Best in Show winning Ch. Pin Oaks Ruffles N' Ridges ex Ch. Pin Oaks Kinderkai Sundae, he finished his American championship from the Bred-by Exhibitor classes. Bred by Pin Oaks Beagles, Souderton, Pa.

late Major Courtney Williams, upon whose death the Appletons acquired this dog. A lemon-pied, Triumph won the Peterborough Hound Show and then entered competition at the regular dog shows, where he quickly became a champion. A rare achievement for a Beagle, Triumph truly proved himself a dual-purpose hound par excellence. Later in the 1950's, the Appletons brought over some Beagles from the United States to interbreed with their own stock. These included the 15" dog Appeline Dancer of Camlyn who was from field breeding; and the top-quality show dog American and Canadian Champion Appeline Top Ace, a son of the excellent Gay Fellow of Geddesburg. This dog soon became an English champion.

Around the late 1960's, the Appletons imported from Validay Kennels American Champion Validay Happy Feller, who sired English Champion Dialynne Gamble who became an influential show and stud dog for Marian Spavin.

In the early 1980's, the Appletons purchased a dog of tremendous quality from the Pin Oaks Kennels. This dog, bred by J. Ralph and Helga Alderfer, is already making his presence strongly felt in his new home.

As the 1950's progressed, so did Beagle popularity in the British show ring. While those who had been active in the forties were still involved and active, their ranks were joined by Miss P. Clayton with Lindsey Makeaway, Mr. Wright with various entries from his Rytow Kennels, Mrs. Y. Oldman with the Barsheens, Mrs. Parker with the Towpaths, and by Mrs. Ellis Hughes and Stephen Young with two champions from Lindsey Makeaway.

The first Beagle to win Best in Show at a British all-breed championship event was Champion Barvae Statute, owned by Mr. Watson. To add to his immortality, this remarkable dog sired Champion Derawunda Vixen who in 1959 won Best Bitch in Show at the famous Crufts event. The Barvaes were owned by Mrs. C.M. Clayton, and this kennel certainly did itself proud in the quality of dogs carrying the Barvae prefix. In addition to the aforementioned Statute there was Champion Barvae Paigan whom Mrs. Clayton herself owned. Playful and Pryor belonged to Mrs. Ellis Hughes, for whom Pryor was Best of Breed and won the Hound Group at Crufts in 1962. And Champion Barvar Tangle was winning nicely for Miss E. Wright as the 1950's drew to a close.

Mrs. Ellis Hughes owned Wytchend Kennels, and dogs from this kennel were eventually purchased by Mrs. Crowther-Davies as foundation

Int. Ch. Korwin Concorde, bred by Mrs. C. Watson, Barrhead, Scotland, and now owned by Mr. and Mrs. Eberhard, West Germany. Since going overseas, has had an outstanding career on the Continent, with Seven Bests of Breed, twice Best Hound, and twice Best in Show. Photo by Diane Pearce.

for the Cannybuffs. Other kennels making names for themselves during this period were Elmhurst, Stanhurst, Tavernmews, and Wellshot.

Rozavel Kennels, owned by Mrs. Thelma Gray, and Letton Beagles, owned by Mrs. Beck, were among the earliest to import American show champions into England. Joining forces for the purchase, they acquired a very lovely dog in the 12½" male, American Champion Renoca's Best Showman, following his successful career in the United States.

For her own kennel, Thelma Gray imported American Champion Rozavel Ritter's Sweet Sue, who was a 12½" daughter of the famed American Champion Thornridge Wrinkles, and Sweet Sue's daughter, the 12¾" Champion Ritter's Miss Babe, who was sired by American Champion Johnson's Fancy King. And Mrs. Beck purchased American Champion Letton Wynnstay's Citation.

Another to import a lovely and useful Beagle to England was Mrs. Clayton, hers from Canada, a son of Champion Thornridge Wrinkles. Thus England had both a son and daughter of this dominant sire and magnificent show dog.

Mrs. Gray, a bit later, made an exciting purchase from Mr. and Mrs. W. Stanley Elsy when she acquired English and American Champion Rozavel's Diamond Jerry following a brilliant show career on the Pacific Coast. Had this dog not grown to a bit above the 15" size limit in the United States (which kept him still within England's 16" limit), it is very doubtful that the Elsys ever would have let him go, but as it was, it was a golden opportunity and Jerry's progeny made a vast and beneficial impact on English Beagles.

Other importations to England from the United States have included American Champion Colegren's Little Rebel of Clovergates to Mrs. Pickthall and Page Mill Playboy to Mrs. Ireland.

At the present time, the Rossut Kennels owned by Mrs. Catherine G. Sutton are going great guns with their stunning dog, English and American Champion Graadtree's Hot Pursuit of Rossut. "Corky" has really taken the British Beagle world by storm, and his accomplishments in the show ring and as a sire are, to say the least, impressive.

As of March 1984, Hot Pursuit has won 24 Challenge Certificates, 22 Bests of Breed, three Bests in Show, one Reserve Best in Show, ten firsts in Group, and five Reserves in Group. As Mrs. Sutton points out, this is the only Beagle ever to have attained so spectacular a show record at general championship dog shows in Great Britain. At the end of October 1983, he was second top dog in the Dog World Top Dogs League for 1983. Hot Pursuit was bred by Mary Hammes from whom he was imported by Mrs. Sutton, and he is handled in Britain by Geoff Corish.

As a sire, Hot Pursuit in his first British litters has produced two puppies that have qualified for the Spillers/Dog World Pup of the Year. They are Diana Spavin-Sykes' Dialynne Pedlar, winner of two Reserve Challenge Certificates and Andrew Brace's Too Darn Hot for Tragband, winner of two Challenge Certificates. Mrs. Sutton is very proud of these youngsters who are certainly proving a credit to their sire.

Rossut is the top winning British kennel in Beagles, having a total by late October 1983 of 173 Challenge Certificates won by their hounds!

In addition to Hot Pursuit, the Rossut banner is being kept high by another lovely dog, Champion Rossut Peanuts, who although retired from the ring with seventeen Challenge Certificates, in favor of Hot

Rossut Bluetit, one of the foundation bitches from Linister Beagles and Mistylaw Kennels. A Challenge Certificate winner and a Reserve winner, this was one of the very first *blue* tris ever shown in Great Britain. Bred by Mrs. Cuddiford and owned by Mrs. Betty White and Miss M. Hunter, Linister Beagles.

Eng. Ch. Too Darn Hot for Tragband, owned by Andrew Brace, Uckfield, East Sussex, was Top Winning Beagle Bitch in England for 1983. A daughter of Eng. and Am. Ch. Graadtree's Hot Pursuit of Rossut, she completed her championship in 1983, two days after her first birthday, the age required by the Kennel Club there. Photo courtesy of Mrs. Catherine Sutton.

Ch. Mistylaw Homespun, by Int. Ch. Korwin Concorde ex Linister Damson, is owned by Mr. and Mrs. J.U. Whyte, Howwood, Renfrewshire, U.K.

Linister Harvester, owned by Mistylaw Kennels, Mr. and Mrs. J.U. Whyte, Howwood, Renfrewshire, is behind Int. Ch. Korwin Concorde and Linister Damson. This lovely dog, a son of famous Ch. Deaconfield Rampage, has the beautiful soft expression noted in this line.

Pursuit, is carrying on well as a sire. Another of Mrs. Sutton's Beagles, Champion Rossut Foreman, has 27 Challenge Certificates to his credit.

Mrs. Sutton is a very popular and respected judge, along with being a successful breeder—a lady whose knowledge of dogs is truly tremendous.

Mistylaw Beagles, at Howwood, Renfrewshire, are owned by Mr. and Mrs. J.U. Whyte. Mrs. Whyte, between 1965 and 1976, was co-owner of the Linister Beagles with Miss M. Hunter, but now she and her husband share an active part in breeding Boxers, Toy Poodles, English Setters, and West Highland White Terriers as well.

The foundation bitch at Mistylaw was one from Mrs. Sutton's Rossut Kennels, a very attractive blue/tan/white tricolor; one of the very first such tricolors shown in England. She won a Challenge Certificate and a Reserve Challenge Certificate and is described by her owner as having "strong hunting instincts and a voice that is compelling."

Three littermates of special note from Mistylaw are by International Champion Korwin Concorde (who was bred by Mrs. C. Watson, Barrhead, Scotland, and is now owned by Mr. and Mrs. Eberhard in West Germany, where he is a Group and Best in Show winner) from Linister Damson. Both Concorde and Damson are descended from the Whytes' Linister Harvester (thirteen years of age as we write) who was sired by the famous Champion Deaconfield Rampage bred by Mrs. Dolly Macro. Harvester was out of the Whytes' Barvae Faithful, bred by Mrs. Clayton, and can be traced back to International Champion Thornridge Wrinkles and Canadian Champion Benroe Belle's Babe.

The littermates whose background is described above are, first of all, the highly successful bitch Champion Mistylaw Homespun, born in February 1980, who has to her credit so far four Challenge Certificates and seven Reserve Challenge Certificates including Crufts this year. She is holder of the Scottish Beagle of the Year Challenge Trophy for 1982 and 1983 and has won a Best in show and a Reserve Best in Show at all-breed open events.

Her sister, Mistylaw Helter Skelter, has been a consistent winner at championship shows, and although she is an excellent bitch, she is somewhat in Homespun's shadow.

Their brother is Mistylane Henchman, now in Munich, West Germany, where he is owned by Mrs. Elizabeth Berger. Not shown much, he does have a Reserve Challenge Certificate; and he excels in hunting, which has already earned him a Working Certificate for Hare, Duck and Roebuck.

Chapter 3

Beagles in the United States

There had been Beagles in the United States for many years prior to 1885, the year during which the first to be registered, a dog named Blunder, was assigned number 3188 by the American Kennel Club. Small hounds had been used extensively for fox and hare hunting, particularly in the southern states, even prior to the Civil War. These dogs bore little resemblance to our Beagles of today. Mostly "harepied" in color (white with only slight markings), they are said to have resembled straight-legged Dachshunds except for weaker heads. They were, however, highly respected for their work quality in the field.

It was following the Civil War when American sportsmen started to take note of the appearance of their dogs, and then it became apparent that their looks left much to be desired. Wisely, they turned to some of Britain's best known packs and imported hounds with which to upgrade the beauty of their own.

General Richard Rowett, from Carlinville, Illinois, brought over some of the best looking Beagles seen in America until that time, and it is said that these dogs served as the models for the original Beagle standard in America, which was written around 1887 by General Rowett, Mr. Norman Ellmore, and Dr. L.H. Twaddell. Dr. Twaddell and Mr. Charles Turner, among others, imported some splendid hounds during this period, and the interbreeding of them established both better breed type and the excellence of the Rowett strain.

Beagles were doing well at the dog shows during the 1870's and 1880's, among the important winners being a dog named Rattler and a bitch named Belle, both owned by J.M. Dodge of Detroit, Michigan.

Ch. Page Mill Wildfire, born in 1961, was among the Top Ten Hounds for 1963 and 1964. Her total wins included nine Group Firsts, 42 placements, and approximately 80 Bests of Variety, and seven of the eight Specialty Shows in which she competed. A 13" daughter of Ch. Wandering Wind ex Ch. Oakwood Silky Sue. Owned by Dr. and Mrs. A.C. Musladin, Los Gatos, California.

Following General Rowett's death, his dogs were taken over by Pottinger Dorsey and C. Staley Doud, both from Maryland. These two gentlemen were not interested in bench show activity, so the dogs were seldom if ever shown. Other Rowett descendants were, however, entered in the dog shows, usually with notable success. Dan O'Shea in Canada was one of those who exhibited. And it is interesting that the recently re-established Waldingfield Pack, originally founded in 1886 but inactive for a period of years between then and now, was based on Rowett stock.

Ch. Holmehill's Duke Ebony, by Int. Ch. Chessman of Walnut Hall ex Ch. Holmehill's Fancy Helen, winning the Hound Group at Penn Ridge K.C. in 1963. Frank Ashbey handled for Dr. George F. Roedell, Philadelphia, PA.

The National Beagle Club was founded in 1888. The first field trial for Beagles in the United States was held at Hyannis, Massachusetts, in November 1890 with an entry of eighteen. Three years later the New England Beagle Club became the second to hold a field trial in America.

The first all-breed Best in Show awarded to a Beagle in the United States was won in December 1901 at the Ladies Kennel Association of America, held at Madison Square Garden in New York City. The winner was Champion Windholme's Bangle, a lovely bitch belonging to Mr. Harry T. Peters and bred by M.A. Blaine. Bangle, by Chieftain ex Brunette, was whelped April 10th 1896. It is fitting that this honor should have gone to Windholme Kennels, as Mr. Peters and his son, Harry, Jr., were gentlemen who dedicated much to their hounds and who contributed tremendously to the progress of the breed. Windholme was undoubtedly the leading Beagle kennel and pack of the early part of this century.

In the 1920's among those showing Beagles were Wheatley Kennels, Somerset Kennels, and Mr. C. Oliver Iselin, all active prior to World War I as well. As the 1920's progressed, we find that Louis Batjer was a consistent exhibitor, as were Richard V.N. Gambrill (who had taken over Somerset, which then became known as Vernon-Somerset) and, in 1924 Saddlerock, which was to remain active and famous into the 1980's. Saddlerock is owned by Isabella Hoopes, who is alive and well and as great a Beagle enthusiast as ever. Mrs. Hoopes attended her first dog show in 1901 and was one of four women in a group of 26 handlers to be licensed as such by the American Kennel Club in 1929. The famous Saddlerock dogs have included some of the breed's most prominent winners, and her last homebred champion, Saddlerock Sandman II, finished his title a few years ago for his owners in California; he is also the sire of some exciting young champions.

In 1928 a Beagle won first in the Sporting Group at Westminster (this was before the Hound Group was created in the United States) plus the breed also accounted for Best Brace in Show and Best Team in Show. At this show, also, the Beagles were divided into two separate varieties as is now the custom.

Giralda Farms started showing Beagles in 1929, as did Dan O'Connell.

What an opener for the '30's when Champion Meadowlark Watchman won the James Mortimer Trophy for Best American-bred in Show at Westminster! This was a never-to-be-forgotten thrill, we are certain, for Louis Batjer, owner of the Meadowlarks! And how nice to have seen the decade close with another Batjer-bred dog, Champion Meadowlark Draftsman, owned by Mrs. Harkness Edwards, win the hotly contested award made by the American Kennel Club that year for the Best American-bred Dog of All Breeds during 1939! Draftsman won it on the strength of seven Bests in Show, 42 Hound Groups, and 56 Bests of Breed during 1939 alone.

By the early 1940's, the important Beagle exhibitors were Foxcatcher, Saddlerock, and Walnut Hall. Many new Beagle exhibitors appeared on the scene at this period, but not all of them remained. This was the era of Champion Thornridge Wrinkles, who amassed a notable number of Best in Show and Hound Group victories besides becoming one of the all-time great Beagle sires. Champion Duke Sinatra was another important Beagle of this period. Champion Edgewood Gay Girl was a Best in Show winner of the '40's, and Champion C.S. Sensation did well for himself in the Hound Group.

Chapter 4

Some Well-Known Continental American Kennels

There is no better way to describe the progress of a breed than by telling you of the individual breeders and kennels who have contributed along the way and of those who are currently active. We have selected a cross section of the latter with which to supplement our chapter of breed history in the United States, presenting some of the current leading winners and summarizing the backgrounds from which they have been produced.

A kennel name is important to a breeder, and the name should be selected and used from the time of one's first homebred litter. Kennel names are chosen in many different ways. Sometimes the name of the street on which a breeder is located is the choice, or the name is a form of one's own name or a coined combination of the names of family members. Often a kennel is named for a child who is especially enthusiastic about the dogs. Many use the names, or a combination of the names, of their foundation dogs (either the proper names or call names of these dogs). Whatever strikes your fancy is appropriate, as long as the name does not have an excessive number of letters (remember that the number of letters in a dog's name is limited for registration purposes, and the kennel name is included in the count) and does not infringe on anyone's prior rights. Such a name will identify you and your Beagles through future generations.

A kennel name can be registered with the American Kennel Club, thus becoming exclusively your own for a stated period of time. A kennel name thus registered may not be used by any other person when registering a dog with the American Kennel Club unless, in writing,

Ch. Ledgewood's Timmee's Suzie Q, C.D. winning Best 13" Beagle at Ladies Kennel Ass'n 1980. Owner-handled by Valerie T. Mee.

you specifically permit another person to do so (as would be the case with a puppy you have sold). Information regarding the procedure is available from the American Kennel Club, 51 Madison Avenue, New York, NY 10010. There are specific requirements regarding the type of name eligible for registration as your kennel name, and a fee is to be paid if one chooses this course.

To be of greatest value, kennel names should be applied to all dogs bred by your kennel, as then the dog and its background are immediately identified. A good way of registering each of your dogs is to start each name with your kennel title if the dog is a homebred and to end the dog's name with the addition of the kennel title if it is a dog you have purchased.

On the following pages we pay tribute to some of our long-time breeders and some of the newer ones. On the shoulders of the latter squarely rests the task of carrying on and preserving what has been accomplished and the responsibility for the future well-being of the Beagle breed.

Alpha Centauri

Alpha Centauri Beagles are owned by Robert and Judy Goodfellow at Mason, Illinois. These people have been involved and dedicated Beaglers over quite a period of time now, and some very handsome dogs have been shown bearing their colors.

Champion Alpha Centauri's Crackerjack is the current star here, having won the National Beagle Club Specialty in Houston, Texas, during 1983 and being a Hound Group winner as well.

Back in the mid-1970's Champion Alpha Centauri's Lariat, by Champion Busch's Bonnie Prince Charlie ex Alpha Centauri's Shannon, was doing well for the kennel. A lovely youngster of the late 1970's was Champion Alpha Centauri's Lil Abner, by Champion Busch's Ranch Hand ex Champion Alpha Centauri's Pussy Foot'n, who completed his title in 1977.

Ch. Alpha Centauri's Sam, Jr., by Ch. Alpha Centauri's Sean O'Shea (Ch. Lynnhaven's Gallant Fox—Ch. Limelite Little Toot) ex Alpha Centauri's Zodiab (Ch. Busch's Bonny Prince Charlie—Ch. Alpha Centauri's Pussy Foot'n) was a well-known winning 15″ dog in the 1970's. Bred and owned by Robert E. and Judy Goodfellow. Handled by Bob Goodfellow.

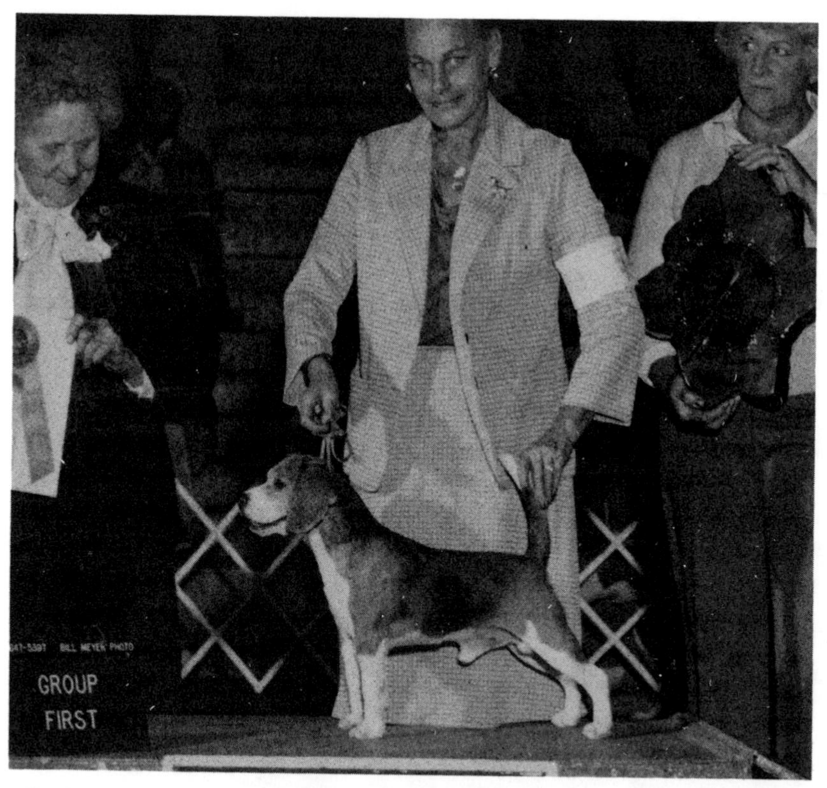

Ch. Jo Mar's Repeat Performance winning a star-studded Hound Group under Doris Wilson on the Florida Circuit in 1983. Marcia Foy owner handling for herself and co-owner William Duguay.

Beagle Chase

Beagle Chase Kennels were founded by Lowell and Fay Mayer back in 1961 at Ft. Lauderdale, Florida, with the purchase of a Beagle puppy for their children.

Their first show dogs were purchased in 1964, when they selected a 15″ dog and a 15″ brood bitch. These were Champion S.K. Rough Rider and Duert Tip Toy Tammy, followed the next year by the pleasure of their first homebred champion, Ruff's Pixie of Beagle Chase.

Beagle Chase has now been the home of twenty or more excellent Beagle champions. The Mayers' lines are to be found in many present-day pedigrees and have surely made a worthy contribution to quality in the breed.

Currently Lowell Mayer has been turning his interests toward judging, so he has not been active as an exhibitor.

Ch. Brendon's Wima Dream Come True, by Ch. Busch's Nuts to You of Brendons ex Yaupon Row Gaiety, handled here by Denny Mounce for S.W. Whitaker, Jr., Yaupon Row Kennels.

Bedlam

Bedlam Beagles, owned by Mandy Cronin at Monroe, Virginia, have the unique distinction of being the only kennel of Group-winning show Beagles that is also a registered pack, member of the National Beagle Club.

It is very interesting that Bedlam's well-known five-couple pack includes six bench-show champions! Among them is the noted multiple Group-winning dog Champion Bedlam Tiger Talk, by Champion Rockaplenty's Wild Oats ex Champion Chillybrook Lemon Fizz, C.D.

Mandy's foundation stock came largely from a Colegren background. One of her early successful winners, Champion Chillybrook Chuckles, C.D., as a puppy won the 15" Sweepstakes at the National Specialty in 1974; then Chuckles became Grand Champion Beagle at the Bryn Mawr Hound Show in 1976 and 1977. Chuckles was sired by Champion Chillybrook Joker out of Champion Colegren Applause, C.D.

Ch. Bedlam Crocus, by Ch. Bedlam Tiger Talk ex Dutchamity Cory of Craigwood, T.D. owned and handled by Mrs. Mandy Cronin to Best of Variety, Roanoke 1982. Judge, Anna K. Nicholas.

The breeding of Champion Chillybrook Lemon Fizz to Wild Oats brought a line to Bedlam which has proven tremendously successful. Not only did the litter itself produce Champion Bedlam Tiger Talk but it also included other champions as well. Even more important, however, has been Tiger's influence as a sire, his champion progeny already proving that Tiger is carrying on in the tradition of his heritage. Among his champions are Champion Bedlam Echo (from Champion Chillybrook Cheerful), Champion Bedlam Sir Sister Wahoo (from Sir Sister Winsome, who is a Group placer and a marvelous hunting bitch, bred by Sir Sister Beagles), Champion Bedlam Raider (from Champion Bedlam Rumor), Champion Bedlam Basil (from Valleymill Gussie, owned by William Bobbitt, formerly owned and finished by Mandy Cronin), Champion Bedlam Crocus (from Dutchamity Cory of Craigwood, T.D., winner of the 13″ Sweepstakes at the National in 1982, finishing with Best of Variety over Specials the following day), the lovely youngster Chillybrook Marvelous (from Chillybrook Spoof), and numerous others.

Beagles at Bedlam include Champion Briarwood Hollyhox Applause, daughter of Champion Jo Mar's Repeat Performance ex Champion Hollyhox Lady T. of Briarwood, who hunts regularly and happily under all weather conditions; Champion Pixshire's Strike Up The Band, who is by Champion Navan's Triple Trouble Rick, thus a Champion Kings Creek Triple Threat grandson; and Champion The Tavern's Double Whammy, by Champion The Whim's Giant Killer ex Champion The Tavern's Gift From Pam, C.D. (a Wild Oats daughter).

Birchwood

Birchwood Beagles were established in 1973 by Linda Lindberg at Cook, Minnesota. Linda started out in obedience, and her first Beagle was Colonel Max Magoo, C.D., followed by Magoo's Happy Valentine, American and Canadian C.D.X.

These two Beagles, shown as a brace and handled by Linda, placed first on many occasions. Happy Valentine became Number One Obedience Beagle and Number Two Obedience Hound in Canada for 1979, competing in Open. Even now, at ten years old and retired, she enjoys being asked to participate in obedience demonstrations.

The first Birchwood litter of show Beagles was bred by Linda from her American and Canadian Champion Meadow-Glo's Birchwoods Holly and sired by American and Canadian Champion Briarpatch Birchwood Guy, a son of Champion Rockaplenty's Wild Oats which Linda had purchased as a show and stud dog from Donna James of Briarpatch Kennels in Winnipeg. She really hit the jackpot with this litter, as one of the puppies, which she sold to Linda Ohman of Thunder Bay, Ontario, turned out to be a most beautiful bitch and came back to Linda to be shown. Betsy accompanied Linda to Linda's first National Specialty in 1980, where Ed Jenner selected her as Best of Winners (and all four of the Birchwood dogs were in the ribbons) and then before returning home Betsy was bred back to her grandsire, Wild Oats. From this breeding Betsy produced two champions which Linda acquired, Linvens Super Star and Linvens Beagle Bailey.

When she came to the 1981 National, Linda brought Super with her. He took Reserve Winners as a puppy there and was purchased, after considering persuasion, by professional handler Jerry Rigden who had been looking for a top Beagle Special for a client. Super Star, a 13″ red and white, has piled up a very impressive record, is a Group winner, and, best of all, is proving to be a sire of tremendous merit with multiple champions in all of his litters.

Currently Linda is winning well with a son and daughter, both blue-tris, by Super Star from Champion Meadow-Glo's Birchwood Holly. Despite the fact that judges are only beginning to appreciate the blues, these two are piling up many successes and so are a source of great pleasure to their breeder-owner.

American and Canadian Champion Briarpatch Birchwood Guy is now a Best in Show dog, a multiple Group winner, and a Specialty winner. He is the sire of, in addition to Champion Birchwood Linven Betsy Ross, the 13" dog American and Canadian Champion Birchwood Stars and Stripes and the 13" male American and Canadian Champion Birchwood Haretrigger, as well as many additional pointed progeny in the United States and Canada.

Ch. Linvens Beagle Bailey, by Ch. Rockaplenty's Wild Oats ex Am. and Can. Ch. Birchwood Linven Betsy Ross, bred by Linda Ohman, is a multi-breed winner owned by Linda Lindberg.

Am. and Can. Ch. Birchwood Linven Betsy Ross, by Am. and Can. Ch. Briarpatch Birchwood Guy ex Am. and Can. Ch. Meado-Glo Birchwoods Holly. Bred and handled by Linda Lindberg. Owned by Linda Ohman. Betsy was from Linda Lindberg's first show litter. She produced two champions in her first litter, sired by Ch. Rockaplenty's Wild Oats; Ch. Linvens Super Star and Ch. Linvens Beagle Bailey. Here taking Best of Winners under Ed Jenner at the 1980 National Beagle Club Specialty.

Linda Lindberg also owns American and Canadian Champion Briarpatch Birchwood Butterkup, a 13" red and white littermate to Guy, by Wild Oats from Canadian Champion Miss Bunty of Briarpatch. Butterkup also has many Best of Variety placements and multi Group placements in Canada. She was Best of Variety at the 1982 Chicago International under Michele Billings.

Another star at Birchwood Beagles is Champion Briarwood Travelin' Man, a son of Champion Jo Mar's Repeat Performance.

Braemoor

Braemoor Kennels, at Kenosha, Wisconsin, are the family project of Wilma and Keaton Plaiss and their daughter Sue. Their interest in Beagles started with their purchase of the handsome 13″ dog Champion Busch's Yosemite Sam from Bill and Cecile Busch, and their interest has continued to grow.

Since then some Chardon stock has been added, plus a Topono bitch.

The Plaisses' first dogs were Scottish Deerhounds, in the breeding and showing of which they are still involved. Sue and Keaton also occasionally handle Rhodesian Ridgehounds for a friend, and they are great admirers of that breed, too.

Ch. Busch's Yosemite Sam, 13″ Group placing Beagle owned by Wilma, Sue and Keaton Plaiss.

Brantwood

Brantwood Beagles, owned by Dr. and Mrs. Arnold Tillman and their daughter Sharai, at Manasquan, New Jersey, began during the summer of 1973 with the fortunate acquisition of a lovely bitch from the Comfort Kennels at Hialeah, Florida. This puppy was co-bred by Lori Norman and Marcia Foy and was destined for the show ring despite having been purchased to be a family pet. At that time the Tillmans were residents of the South, but they sent their bitch, "Meg," out with Jane Forsyth who made her a champion in good order.

Soon thereafter the Tillmans decided to move to Manasquan where they purchased a home with the idea of expanding their Beagle family. Following "Meg's" championship, a stud dog who turned out to be Champion Pin Oaks Gallant Gay Lad, was selected for her. With Gay Lad, owned by the Alderfers, she produced Champion Brantwood's Destini, who was to become the Tillmans' first homebred champion. "Meg," who was officially Champion Lokavi's Double Destini, was by Champion Beaujangles of Beagle Chase from Champion Foyscroft Triple Trollop, a Champion Kings Creek Triple Threat daughter. She had proven herself a successful producer, and again plans were made to breed her. While trying to decide this time on the stud, they saw and fell in love with Champion Pin Oaks Ruffles and Ridges, owned by the Ralph Alderfers, to whom "Meg" was bred.

"Meg" and Ruffles produced three champions, one male and two bitches. The young male, from the day of his birth, became special to the Tillmans, who elected to keep him as their choice from the litter. Named "Brownie" by Sharai, he started his show career at a puppy match, and he won Best in Match at an all-breed event when only four months old. Brown completed his championship with some exciting wins, thrilling his owners as he took Best Puppy in Sweepstakes and Best of Variety 15″ on the same day at the Southern New York Specialty in conjunction with Westchester Kennel Club, at a mere ten and a half months of age. Champion Brentwood's Desperado, "Brown's" official title, became the Tillmans' second homebred champion and their first Hound Group and Best in Show winner. Handled by Ralph Alderfer, he won his first Best in Show at the Twin Brook Kennel Club event despite temperatures in the 90's. Another Best in Show followed at Bald Eagle Kennel Club on July 26th 1981, this time during a torrential downpour.

The next big excitement for the Tillmans was when they traveled to Ohio to show Desperado at the National Specialty under Michele Bill-

Ch. Brantwood's Desperado, Best in Show at Bald Eagle Kennel Club in 1981. Judge, Mrs. Inez Hartley. Handled by J. Ralph Alderfer for owner Anita Tillman.

Ch. Lokavi's Double Destini, Brantwood's foundation bitch, and their famed Best in Show dog Ch. Brantwood's Desperado, *right*, enjoying a quiet evening at home with the Tillmans.

ings, from where he returned with the Best of Variety award to his credit. He achieved Number Three in the Top Ten rating for 15″ Beagles for 1981 and has remained in the Top Ten through 1982 and 1983. He is a Best of Variety winner at Westminster, and his successes as a stud dog have also been notable. Desperado has just retired from the show ring with a record of which to be proud.

For her third breeding, "Meg" came to Champion Rockaplenty's Wild Oats, thus intensifying the Triple Threat line in her own pedigree. She and Wild Oats produced three lovely puppies, the one selected by the Tillmans for themselves growing up to become Champion Brantwood Semi Tuff, who achieved a Best of Variety award at his first dog show and a four-point major at Trenton en route to his title. He is now top stud dog for a young couple in Florida, and his first litter for them provided two fine young hounds about to make their debuts at this time.

The mating of Champion Brantwood's Desperado to Champion Craigwood's Shannon produced six puppies, a male from which was purchased by the Buglair Kennels owned by Garland and Karen Moore at Atwater, California. The success of this dog has been written of in the Buglair Kennel story; a fast friendship has grown between his breeders and his owners. The puppy has become the important winner whom the Moores are presently campaigning.

From this litter, the Tillmans selected future Champion Brantwood's Notorious to keep for themselves. "Tiger" swept through to his title in short order and, now as an owner-handled Special, already has a Hound Group placement to his credit.

The third to finish from this litter was Champion Brantwood's Shadow, who has become both house pet and show dog for the Tillmans after his return to them when the family to whom he had been sold was no longer able to keep him. The fourth to finish from the litter was Champion Brantwood's Samantha Bonnie who, two months after the birth of her first litter, was Winners Bitch for a five-point major at the 1983 Southern New York Specialty.

Understandably, the Tillmans are much elated over the addition to their family and breeding program of the dam of these four champions, Champion Craigwood's Shannon. She is listed by the Fall *Canine Chronicle* report as Number Two Beagle Dam and was ranked Number Three Top Producing Beagle Dam for 1982.

Shannon has been bred to Desperado for a second time as we are writing.

Ch. Buglair Topper winning Best 15″ Beagle and Best in Specialty at the Beaglers of San Joaquin Specialty. Topper was 13 years old at the time, making this an especially noteworthy achievement and win! A most handsome Beagle owned by Buglair Beagles, Garland, Karen and Carol Moore.

Buglair

Buglair Beagles, located at Atwater, California, were founded in 1957 by Garland Moore, following a search to replace the family dog that "looked like a Beagle." Admiration and interest in the breed blossomed into showing, breeding, and eventually handling dogs for others. Garland became an all-breed licensed handler in 1965. The breed gained another fancier when Garland married Karen in 1969. Karen was also licensed to handle dogs (Sporting, Hounds, and Toys). Their daughter Carol also shares her parents' love of the breed and the sport. In 1976 the Moores retired their handlers' licenses to pursue their goal of judging, and both are currently licensed by the American Kennel Club.

Garland Moore's original Beagle was Fritzi O'Yodling Acres, whose lineage traced back to the famous Pine Lane Beagles. In the early years, frequent crosses were made back to Lee Wade's Kinsman dogs. Champion Garland's Ginger II, the first homebred champion, was named the Top Producing Beagle Dam for 1965, based on a litter sired by Champion Kinsman Hullabaloo.

One of the breeding program's first major successes came when a bitch from Kinsman breeding, Champion Buglair Candy, was bred to Champion Double Jac Texas Taxes. The result was a litter of five champions, including Champion Buglair Topper, and saw Candy named as the Top Producing Hound Dam for 1966, *Kennel Review* System. Topper was ranked among the top winning 15″ Beagles from 1966 through 1970. He followed in his dam's footsteps by being named Top Producing Beagle Sire in 1971 and 1974. A Topper son, Champion Buglair Top of the Mark, carried top producing honors to a third generation when he was named a Top Producing Beagle Sire in 1975. Mark was also ranked among the top winning 13″ Beagles in 1972 and 1973. Topper's litter-brother, Champion Buglair Tex, was also a Group winner on both coasts.

In the past few years, additional stock has been brought in to help maintain the quality of the line. One bitch, Champion Buglair Echo Valley Sunrise, won the Southern California Beagle Specialty from the Open Class. Just under eighteen months of age, Sunrise also had been Best in Sweepstakes earlier that same day. While the majority of her pedigree is Johjean, she is also a Topper great-granddaughter. Her daughter, Danish and American Champion Buglair Sun Flare, was exported to Denmark in April 1981, becoming "Gold Bitch" or top winning Beagle bitch in that country by the end of 1981, following less than half a year's showing. Flare's sire, Champion Buglair The President, a Topper grandson, was recently exported to Denmark and is much in demand as a stud. His first crop of puppies will be competing in 1984, and they should make him a top producing sire in that country by the end of 1984.

Another Buglair acquisition is Champion Brantwood Buglair Bandit, whose lineage is primarily Pin Oaks and who also goes back to Topper in the fifth generation. His first litters show much promise.

In July 1982, Garland Moore was invited to Denmark to judge Beagles and Basset Hounds. There he found an excellent 13″ bitch who he brought back with him, Magic Noire Wilma. She started her show career in October 1982 gaining a major, and then she won back-to-back majors at the Southern California Specialty and Pasadena.

Between 1957 and through 1983 there have been 75 owned or bred Buglair champions, not including those sired by Buglair dogs for other people. The Moores continue to enjoy breeding and showing on a limited basis, and they look forward to their daughter taking over the program one day.

Multiple Best in Show winning 15″ Beagle, Ch. Busch's Nuts to You of Brendons, with Bill Busch. This sire of 79 champions to date is by Ch. Busch's Bonny Prince Charlie ex Ch. Lawndale's Gusty Wind. Wm. and Cecile Busch, breeders. Cecile Busch and Brenda Gentry, owners.

Busch's

Busch's Beagles were established back in 1959 when Cecile and William Busch of Cape Girardeau, Missouri, purchased their first show Beagle and foundation dog, Champion Clark's Lackawanna Tony, the last champion sired by the great Champion Thornridge Wrinkles. The foundation bitches were a daughter and some granddaughters of Tony. Hoffman's Maggie, one of them, produced five champions; her daughter, Busch's Little Dixie, produced ten.

In 1964 the breeding program got under way in earnest, with the first homebred champion born in 1965.

Champion Johjean Joker of Do Mor was the Busches' first Special, purchased from William and Dorothy Moore of the noted Do Mor prefix. This dog earned himself a place on the Top Ten 15″ Beagle list for 1966, but even more important he seemed to nick perfectly with their Tony daughters, providing the foundation of the Busches' breeding program. This dog sired in the area of 30 champions and was the Number One Beagle Sire in 1968 and 1970.

Champion Busch's Bonnie Prince Charlie was sired by Joker. He was winner of the Stud Dog Class at the National in 1972, and among his champion progeny is Champion Busch's Nuts To You of Brendons, multiple Best in Show and Specialty winner. "Barney," in turn,

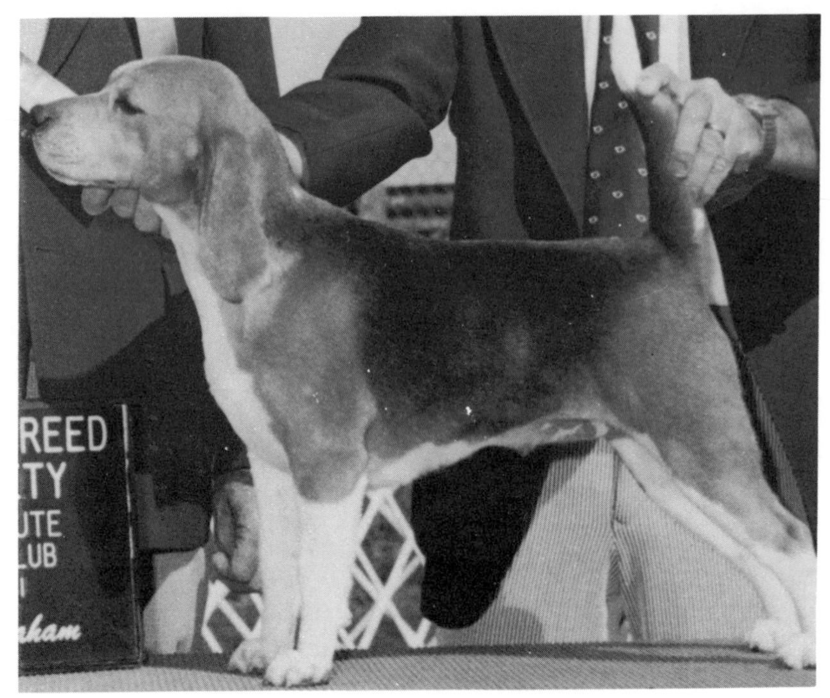

Best in Show 15″ bitch, Ch. Busch's Easy to Remember, by Ch. Busch's Nuts to You of Brendons ex Ch. Busch's Easy to Love. Bred and owned by Wm. and Cecile Busch.

is the sire of Champion Busch's Gin Rickey, a Hound Group winner at his very first show when only seven months of age and a multiple Best in Show dog.

One of the most valuable assets of the Busches' breeding program has been their great bitches, such as the all girl litter by Joker from Busch's Little Dixie. These included Champions Busch's Dixie Debutante, Busch's Dixie Dynamo, Busch's Dixie Doll, Busch's Dixie Duplicator, and Busch's Dixie Daisy, who have produced a formidable list of champions between them.

Among the memorable winners owned by Bill and "Fitzi" Busch, one thinks of the 13″ dog Champion Busch's Ranch Hand (Champion Busch's Nuts To You of Brendons ex Champion Busch's Dixie Dynamo), Champion Busch's Flash Back of Eljon (Champion Busch's Dynamatic ex Champion Busch's Back Talk of Brendon); 15″ Champion Busch's Jam Session (Nuts To You—Champion Busch's Easy To Remember, a 15″ Best in Show Bitch by Nuts To You ex Champion Busch's Easy To Love; and many others who have distinguished themselves in the ring and/or as producers.

Cad-Mar

Cad-Mar Kennels, owned by Jim and Rosalie Lisano at Pasadena, Texas, added the sound of Beagle bugling to their lives and the lives of their three children, Cathy, Christy, and Tommy, in 1975. Their first Beagle was purchased as a pet for their son's second birthday. He fell in love with a red and white female puppy and promptly named her "Lucky Charm" after his favorite cereal.

The Lisanos had been showing mostly Poodles for years and had intended to keep the Beagle just to love and be a pet for the youngsters in the family. They soon, however, started watching the breed at the shows, tried Charm out in the ring a few times, and then retired her to the whelping box with championship points to her credit. She indeed proved herself to be a "lucky charm." Her first litter produced three champions from among four puppies, Champion Cad-Mar's Apple Jack, Champion Cad-Mar's Sugar Pop, and Champion Cad-Mar's Cap'n Crunch. The fourth puppy, Cad-Mar's Raisin Bran, had major points before being sold and getting loose in the country never to again be seen.

Cad-Mar's Mighty Tonka, co-owned by Nancy Haines and the Jim Lisanos, Cad-Mar Beagles, now close to the title.

Ch. Cad-Mar's Country Morn owned by Cad-Mar Beagles, Rosalie and Jim Lisano.

The "Beagle bug" had added lots of "snap, crackle and pop" to Cad-Mar. Charm's first litter put her on the Top Producer list, so it seemed only natural to continue the trend of cereal names, adding to those already mentioned Champion Cad-Mar's Tota-Le Pickadilly, Champion Cad-Mar's Trix of Starcrest, Champion Cad-Mar's Country Morn, and Champion Cad-Mar's Co Co Puff, among others. Later the names of kid's "favorites" was started and Cad-Mar's Mighty Tonka and Cad-Mar's Barbie Doll, among others, were added.

A trip to the National Beagle Club Specialty held at Santa Barbara a few years ago and visits to the kennels in California caused the Lisanos to purchase two Beagles from Starcrest Kennels which came to Texas and were shown to top honors of a Specialty Best of Breed, several Group placements, and many Best of Variety wins. Both Champion Mystic Mint of Starcrest and Champion Cad-Mar's Trix of Starcrest have brought much pleasure to the Lisanos with having Top Ten ratings.

Chardon

Chardon Beagles, owned by Donna and Charles Kitchell at Davenport, Iowa, flashed into prominence when their Champion Chardon Kentucky Derby, a fine son of Champion Starbuck's Hang 'Em High, started attracting the admiration of the judges for some very important winning. This handsome young dog started his career under the ownership of his breeders; then as his career progressed, the Kitchells joined forces with Charles and Catherine Most as co-owners. It was under this joint ownership and the very capable handling of Derby's good friend B.J. Orseno that he really hit the big-time, winning five Bests in Show, the first of which had been at Minneapolis in 1981, plus an imposing Group record in stiff and fearless competition. In the breed, he won Best of Variety on five occasions at Chicago International, and he was Best 15″ at Westminster in 1981.

Am. and Can. Ch. Chardon Triple Crown, 13″, by Am. and Can. Ch. Chardon Kentucky Derby ex Am. and Can. Ch. Chardon Match Point, winning Best of Variety over entry of 52. Owners Charles and Donna Kitchall.

Am. and Can. Ch. Chardon Magnific Marathoner winning Best in Show at Winnipeg, Canada, under judge Robert Nutbeam.

As a sire, Derby has also distinguished himself. One of his daughters, the 13″ red and white bitch American and Canadian Champion Chardon Triple Crown was among the Top Ten 13″ Beagles for 1981, 1982, and 1983 and was Number One 13″ bitch in 1983. She has two Hound Group firsts to her credit and was Best of Opposite Sex at Westminster in 1983.

Another Derby daughter, American, Canadian, and Mexican Champion Chardon Krystal K Jamtime, is a Best in Show winner and was Number One Beagle in Mexico for 1983.

There are many more winners by Derby, including American and Canadian Champion Chardon Restive Recruit, who finished with four majors, owned by Bette Edwards and Caryl Swanson in Illinois; American and Canadian Champion Chardon Texas Leaguer, a Best Puppy in Show winner in Canada, owned by Vicky Schulte in Minnesota; American, Canadian, and Brazilian Champion Chardon Upset, now in Brazil, owned by Armando Natali; and Champion Chardon Arch Rival, now in the Dominican Republic.

There is another Hang 'Em High son who has also contributed well to Chardon Kennels. This is American and Canadian Champion Chardon Magnific Marathoner, from Chardon Festive Occasion, who was Best in Show at Manitoba in 1981 and has fifteen Group Placements and five Group firsts to his credit, plus having been Best of Variety at the Chicago International. This dog, too, has made his presence felt as a sire, among his progeny being American and Canadian Champion Chardon Yankee Clipper, now owned by Bill Vaughan in Brisbane, Australia; American and Mexican Champion

Chardon Love Forty, owned by Sergio Balcazar in Mexico; American and Canadian Champion Chardon Gideon Gold Medalist, still at home with the Kitchells; and their young 13″ bitch, Champion Chardon Yegorova, Best of Variety at the 1983 Wisconsin Beagle Club Specialty, who finished with seven consecutive wins from the Puppy Classes.

Chrisette

Chrisette Beagles, at Templeton, Massachusetts, were established in 1973 with Sandra Robichaud's purchase from Marcia Foy of the beautiful puppy who grew up to become Champion Foyscroft Red Barn. A son of Champion Rockaplenty's Wild Oats ex Champion Foyscroft Triple Lina Wor-Lo, "Barney" finished quickly despite being red and white, a color not at that time being seen frequently in

Ch. Chrisette's Pride n Joy, by Ch. Rockaplenty's Wild Oats ex Ch. Junior's Charm of Chrisette. Bred, owned, and handled by Sandy Robichaud, Chrisette's Beagles, finished in five straight shows.

Eastern show rings. "Barney" died in March 1983, leaving some wonderful memories and several champion progeny as well.

Sandy next acquired a sweet daughter of Champion Kings Creek Triple Threat, Gay Day's Look Out For Me, which gave the Robichauds their first taste of breeding Beagles.

A 13″ tri bitch from Dick Johnson, Champion Junior's Black Pearl, came to Chrisette and was bred several times. Champion Junior's Charm of Chrisette, a daughter of the all-time top producing Beagle bitch Champion J's Bonnie V of Beagle Chase, sired by Champion Jana Pageant, also came from Dick Johnson. Charm was bred to Champion Merry Song's Pooh Bear, from which two puppies were sold to show homes and both died tragically.

It was from American and Canadian Champion Pin Oaks Royal Delight, an elderly 13″ bitch with lots of quality, that Chrisette Beagles bred their first champion, sired by Champion Junior's Gold Spike. This was Champion Chrisette's Yankee Drummer, not only a champion himself but also an excellent stud dog who has sired half a dozen or more champions.

Champion Junior's Charm of Chrisette bred to Champion Rockaplenty's Wild Oats gave Sandy Robichaud three champions in one litter, one being her second homebred champion, the lovely Chrisette's Pride 'n' Joy, a beautiful 13″ bitch who finished in five consecutive shows, taking back to back five-point majors and Best of Opposite Sex at a Specialty along the way.

Pride 'n' Joy was in due time bred to Yankee Drummer, and they produced 13″ American and Canadian Champion Chrisette's Macho Man, Number One 13″ Beagle for 1983; and 15″ Champion Chrisette's Joshua who, although shown sparingly, has distinguished himself with Group placements and was 15″ Best of Variety at the 1983 Southern New York Specialty under Ed Jenner. Both dogs are producing well. Macho Man's first litter, from Champion Junior's Fun Machine, includes five champions with the sixth on the way to the title as we write. Among them are the Group-placing Champion Junior's Macho Grande and the bitch, 15″ Champion Junior's Tess of Chrisette, who was Best of Variety and Best of Opposite Sex to Best in Show to Macho Man at the 1983 Bay State Specialty, twelve months old and handled by the Robichauds' daughter Nannette.

The Robichauds can well take pride in their very special little hounds and in the fact that in only ten years of breeding and limited showing they have had the fun of finishing or breeding 23 champions.

Colegren

Colegren Kennels were founded by Mrs. William O. Coleman, III, at that time a resident of Greenwich, Connecticut, in 1963 when she purchased three young Beagles from the Johjean Kennels belonging to Edward Jenner at La Grange, Illinois. Mrs. Coleman's intense interest and devotion to the breed led to the development of a highly successful breeding kennel, for awhile at Greenwich and then later at Durham, North Carolina, where the family moved in 1970 and where they still are living.

Over the years, many very famous and beautiful Beagles have been bred at Colegren. In the earlier days, both Mrs. Coleman's son Bill and her daughter Louise actively shared her interest in the dogs. Now, however, the youngsters all are married and living on the Pacific Coast —still fond of dogs although presently not active with them.

At her beautiful estate in Durham, Ginny Coleman divided her interest until just recently between her thoroughbred hunters and her Beagles. For the past few years other activities have taken much of her time, and she and Mr. Coleman are fond of traveling, so the "kennel" now consists of just one "family Beagle."

Ch. Colegren's Heir To Fame, consistent winning 15" Beagle dog bred by Colegren Kennels, Mrs. William O. Coleman, III, owned by Mr. and Mrs. James A. Farrell, Jr. "Billy" was a Group winning dog of the mid-1970's in keenest eastern competition.

The great foundation bitch from Colegren's Kennels, Ch. Johjean's Bill Jamboree Jubal.

Colegren's outstanding foundation bitch was Champion Johjean's Bill Jamboree Jubal, who produced fourteen champions, a record-breaking number which made her at the time the nation's all-time Top Producing Beagle Dam, and *Kennel Review's* third Top Producing Dam of All Breeds in 1971, with five champions to her credit that year.

During one five-year period, Colegren produced twenty champions, and more have finished since then. The stars have been such dogs as "Jubie" herself; a son of hers, Champion Colegren's Duke Devil, who was a Top Ten Beagle in 1971; the fabulous 13″ bitch who Jack White owned and handled to multiple Group and Best in Show victories, Champion Colegren Sonnet of Briarwood; and the noted 15″ dog, Champion Colegren's Heir to Fame, with whom Mr. and Mrs. James A. Farrell, Jr., made a very big Best of Variety and Group record in stiffest Eastern competition toward the mid-1970's under Bob Forsyth's handling.

Daisyrun

Daisyrun Beagles, at Waldorf, Maryland, are owned by Mr. and Mrs. George (Nadine) Eaton and Rene Chicoine, whom we first met as Beagle exhibitors early in the 1970's.

At that time they were represented by American and Canadian Champion Ravenswood Piping Hot, sired by Champion Jana Raider ex Champion Ravenswood Touch of Midas, bred by Stevie Barnes and co-owned by Nadine Eaton and Rene Chicoine. On her only appearance as a Special this bitch took Best of Opposite Sex to Best of Breed at a Bay State Specialty on which occasion her daughter, Daisyrun's Christmas Mouse, shared the honors by going Winners Bitch and Best Puppy in Show from the 6-9 month class. In subsequent litters, "Piper" produced Champion Daisyrun's Pooh Bear, by Champion Buttonwood's Bold Bomber, Winners Bitch at a National

Ch. Daisyrun's Flower Power, consistent winner, bred, owned and handled by Nadine Eaton.

Ch. Daisyrun's Prunedale Paddy winning the Hound Group at Durham K.C. 1979 for Nadine Eaton, Waldorf, Maryland. George Alston handling.

Specialty; and Champion Daisyrun's Flower Power, a Group winner and Number Five among 13″ bitches in 1980, she sired by Champion Starbuck's Hang 'Em High.

"Piper," as we write, at twelve years of age still is hale and hearty and still moves beautifully.

While living in California, Nadine acquired, from Tony and Judy Musladin, a daugther of Champion The Whim's Buckeye ex Champion The Whim's Comeuppance. She is Champion The Whim's Daisyrun, and she was Number Six among the 13″ Variety in 1979.

Champion Daisyrun Prunedale Paddy, a 15″ dog by Champion The Whim's Spirit of Seventy Six ex American and Canadian Champion Ravenswood Cinnamon, is a Group-winning dog and an excellent stud. It is interesting that he, a Buckeye son, and Champion Briarwood Day Tripper, a daughter of Champion Kings Creek Triple Threat and owned by the Lincolns, have in two litters produced ten champions—a nice blending of famous bloodlines! Day Tripper was the only daughter of that great 13″ bitch Champion Draper's Lemon Drop Daisy Mae.

Champion Hollypines Daisyrun Sun, a 15″ dog from Paddy and Day Tripper, was, among other important wins, Best of Variety for Nadine at Westminster in 1983, where he was enormously admired.

D'Capri

D'Capri Beagles are owned by Ella Mae De Capri, formerly of Pennsylvania but now living at Lenoir City, Tennessee.

Ella Mae is one of the several breeders who got their start through Tarr Hill Kennels, basing their breeding program principally on the Champion Kings Creek Triple Threat lines. She has been very successful with her dogs despite illness having limited her showing and breeding of them in years past, and she has a most impressive collection of champions to her credit. She is back in the ring again now, so we shall expect to see still more of her lovely Beagles adding titles to their names shortly.

The 15" tri bitch Ch. Tarr Hill Triplette, by Ch. King's Creek Triple Threat ex Ch. Lo Na's Gaiety, was bred by Jim and Liz Hendricks, Tarr Hill Beagles, and is owned by Ella Mae De Capri.

Echo Run

Echo Run Beagles, located at New Brighton, Pennsylvania, are owned by Kathleen Carling, who is a comparatively new breeder enjoying her hounds to the utmost.

Her foundation bitches were Champion Timberlost's Once Is Not Enough, purchased in 1981 from Barb Youngberg, and Showboat's Freebie, who is a daughter of Champion Junior's Foyscroft Wild Kid ex Champion Lo Na's Gay Girl. Thus both bitches are strong in the bloodlines of Champion Kings Creek Triple Threat.

Kathleen Carling also owns Champion Touchstone's Smokey Bear, C.D., a handsome blue-tri dog who has recently finished his conformation title. Her latest show bitch is Echo Lane's Heartbreaker, a fine blend of two top bloodlines.

Handled by Robert Double for owner Diana Connolly, Portersville, PA, Ch. Echo Run's Sky Blue Commotion taking Best of Variety 15″ at Trumbull County 1981. This bitch is of the blue color being seen more frequently nowadays than formerly in the show ring.

The gun dog trials have lately started to interest Kathleen, who is becoming quite involved with them and finds them extremely exciting. You will find more from her on this subject in the field dog section of this book. Kathleen hunts over all her Beagles, and she speaks of doing so as follows (we are providing you with this information in Kathleen's own words since there is so wide a belief that show and house Beagles are not successful in the field):

> My hunting started in 1976. I had a field Beagle years before, but I ran her only for my husband. When I acquired Smokey (Champion Touchstone's Smokey Bear, C.D.) I couldn't wait to show him. When he was four months old I was told not to bother trying to field break him because a 'sissy' show dog who lived in the house could never make it in the field. Well, although he isn't Gun Trial material, he is a pleasure to watch and to hear in the field. I showed those guys that a house dog made as good or better hunter because he hunted for me not for himself. After that I started running all of them, Tazi (Champion Timberlost's Once Is Not Enough) at a year and a half, which was a little late, but I had been told that she might get scarred and become unshowable. That was not the case, though, because after she finished her championship in the ring I did not have any great trouble with the dogs getting out in the briars.
>
> Field breaking should begin between four months and six months of age. Running around, having fun, and letting the pup's natural curiosity take over are very important. I never had a chance to break any of mine that early except Smokey.
>
> My young bitch Katie, Smokey's daughter and pointed, is doing the best. On a recent hunting trip a cottontail was wounded and she found it for us. That began her hunting career. She is a joy to watch, with her beautiful movement, running effortlessly across creeks and hills.
>
> I feel that hunting also provides an excellent test for temperament. Nothing could be more revealing than shooting over them. I especially enjoy it because I 'sometimes' miss my target and the dogs know it's time to run the lucky rabbit. I hope that I can spend more time in the field this year. I could use some advice on breaking, and they are very helpful in the local gundog clubs (one of which I have joined) to us show people. My first love, tho', is hunting privately with my own dogs.

Foyscroft

Foyscroft Beagles are situated at Danbury, Connecticut, enjoying life as family dogs with their owner, Marcia A. Foy. Although she continues to show on a limited basis, Ms. Foy's interests now lean more toward her judging activities, but Beagles will always remain a very real part of her life.

When one thinks of Foyscroft, one's thoughts immediately turn toward that incomparable great, Champion Kings Creek Triple Threat. "Trippe" was born on September 3rd 1964 at the Kings Creek Kennels in Georgia, one of a litter of three puppies by Champion Kings Creek Stagerlee ex Security Susie Black Flash, his breeder Michele Leathers Billings. He died on October 15, 1976.

The incomparable Ch. Kings Creek Triple Threat owned by Marcia Foy. Trippe is a Diamond Certificate sire of more than 75 Champions, and his progeny include Top Hound and Best in Show winners.

Ch. Rockaplenty's Wild Oats, by Ch. Kings Creek Triple Threat ex Ch. Page Mill Call Girl, multiple Group winner; National Specialty winner; multiple Best in Show winner; the sire of 56 champions, early in his career winning a Hound Group handled by Marcia Foy. Owned by Anna Katherine Nicholas.

By the time he had reached seven and a half months of age, "Trippe" was a champion. Michele sold him to Mrs. William Pym, for whom he won well as a young dog under Jane Kay's handling.

Triple Threat was offered to the Foys for sale at Westminster in 1968, as Mrs. Pym was not well at that time and was planning to go out of dogs. Right then, Marcia Foy made up her mind that this was to be *her* dog, and despite the fact that "Trippe" was then three and a half years old, an age at which many Beagles are considered ready for retirement, she insisted on having him. At the time, Triple Threat's show record stood at 131 times Best of Variety, twelve times Best Hound, and a goodly number of Group placements.

What Triple Threat and Marcia Foy accomplished together is a matter of history. Upon his retirement from active competition, "Trippe" had won Best of Variety 396 times (still the breed record for any dog of any breed in the United States); and he had been Best Hound 84 times, with 177 additional Group placements bringing his total Group placements to 261. He had been Best in Show at all-breed events eight times, and he had been Best of Breed at three Specialty Shows, including the first one held by the National Beagle Club in 1970, judged by John P. Murphy.

Champion Kings Creek Triple Threat was on the Top Ten Beagles in America in 1965, 1966, 1967, 1968, 1969, 1970, and 1971. He was the second Top Hound in America in 1970, fifth in 1969, and tenth in 1971, all on the *Kennel Review* System. He was one of the Top Ten Hounds, with more than 10,000 points, for 1969.

Triple Threat's Westminster record is another outstanding achievement, for he is the only Beagle to have four times won Best of Variety there; and in 1970 he was second in the Hound Group, which so far as we can recall is the highest place won by a Beagle in a Westminster Group since the A.K.C. divided the Hounds from the Sporting dogs more than several decades previously.

As a sire, Triple Threat produced close to 80 champions. His grandchildren are uncounted!

Champion Rockaplenty's Wild Oats, who is Triple Threat's son and owned by Anna Katherine Nicholas, has carried on well the family tradition as a sire of quality. His 56th American champion has recently finished, and he has many Group- and Best in Show-winning champions in Canada and in South America, along with champion progeny in Australia.

As a show dog, Wild Oats had been campaigned only for slightly over a year when he was purchased by A.K.N., after which he has made very infrequent appearances, mostly owner-handled in the Veterans and Stud Dog Class at the Specialty shows where he has numerous firsts to his credit, including Best of Opposite Sex to Champion Plain and Fancy's Clover from the Veterans Class a few years back. "Tuffy" is thirteen years old now. He was the Number One Beagle, both varieties and all systems, of 1973 and on the Top Ten list in 1974. He has won the National Specialty (in 1974), the Bay State Specialty, back-to-back all-breed Bests in Show, and multiple Hound Groups despite the briefness of his career.

Wild Oats is a Gold Certificate Sire (Irene Schlintz) and has been on

Ch. Jo Mar's Repeat Performance on the first occasion of his winning Best 13″ Beagle at Westminster. Marcia Foy, co-owner and handler.

the Top Ten Stud Dog list for some half dozen years.

For the third generation at Foyscroft, there is the handsome 15″ tri dog, Champion Juniors Foyscroft Wild Kid, who is by Wild Oats from the top producing Beagle bitch of all time, Champion J's Bonnie V of Beagle Chase. Kid's progeny are only now beginning to appear in the show rings. He was campaigned from mid-1975 through 1977 and was on the Top Ten Beagles of those years. A multiple Group winner, he has close to 75 Bests of Variety to his credit.

The 13″ dog, Champion Jo Mar's Repeat Performance, by Champion Carwood Capasa Amigo ex Champion Lokavi's Sure Shot of Jo Mar, is co-owned by Marcia Foy and the son of his breeder, William Duguay. From the day he stepped into the show ring, "A.J." has been a winner, completing his championship while still a puppy. A multi-Group winner, he has won numerous Best of Breed awards (two at Bay State Specialties, several at Southern New York Specialties, and Best of Variety and Opposite Sex to Best of Breed at the National). "A.J." has also twice won the Variety at Westminster, among his

Ch. Foyscroft Triple Lina Wor Lo is handled by her breeder, Judy Colan, to Best of Opposite Sex, at the Bay State Beagle Club Specialty. Owned by Marcia Foy.

Ch. Pixshire's One and Only, the dam of 11 champions, here is winning Best of Variety 13″ at the National Specialty in 1975. Owned by Marcia Foy, "Pixie," now 13 years old, is going strong as this is written.

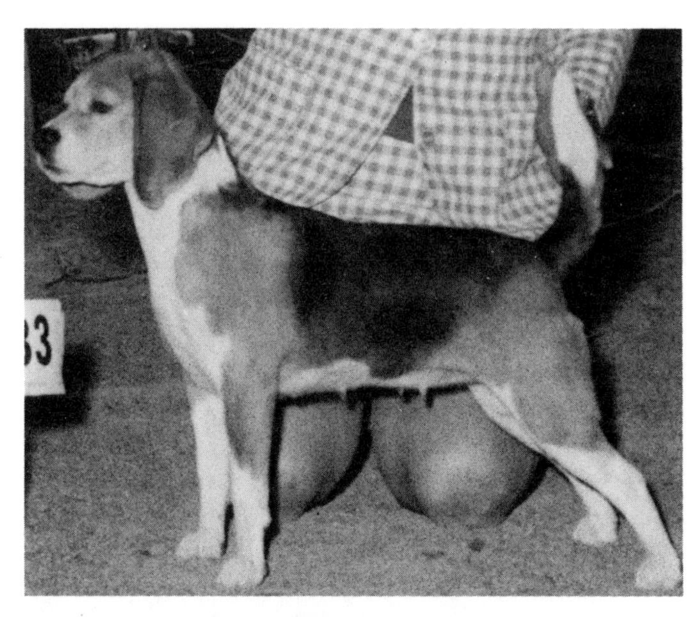

other Best of Variety wins. He has been a Top Ten Beagle in 1977, 1978, 1979, 1980, 1981, 1982, and 1983 and although it is early in the year as we write, he is already on the list for 1984. At the present time, he has been Best of Variety on 171 occasions, with a very satisfactory ratio of Group placements. He is the sire, so far, of about a dozen champions and is, of course, a Triple Threat descendant.

Two other Triple Threat sons, from his last litter at Foyscroft, are Champion Foyscroft I'm Triple Tiger (Best of Variety 15″ at a Southern New York Specialty) and Champion Foyscroft I'm Triple Terrific, who completed his championship with only five times shown.

The girls at Foyscroft are the magnificent bitch, Champion Foyscroft Triple Lina Wor Lo, a Trippe daughter from a Lawndale bitch, who during 1971 and 1972 was Best of Variety 63 times, won first in three Hound Groups (very unusual in those days for a Beagle bitch), has 30 Group placements, and has Best of Opposite Sex awards to her credit from both the National and Westminster. Lina, in her only litter by Wild Oats, produced Champion Foyscroft Red Barn, founder of the Chrisette Beagles, and Champion Foyscroft Wild Flower, who was Number One 13″ bitch during her show campaign in the mid-1970's.

Top producing bitch at Foyscroft is Champion Pixshire's One and Only, the dam of 11 champions (all by Triple Threat), who was Best 13″ Beagle and Best of Opposite Sex to Best of Breed at the National in 1975.

Franticia Wild Justin taking one of his majors, handled by co-owner Pat Moscaritola. A son of Ch. Jo Mar's Repeat Performance ex Franticia's Wild Shaded Sadie. Frank and Pat Moscaritola, owners, Franticia Kennels.

Franticia

Franticia is the kennel name of two dedicated Beagle breeders who have some very excellent champions to their credit. These are Frank and Patricia Moscaritola who live at Warwick, Rhode Island, and they have been associated with Beagles for some fifteen years.

Pat and Frank's dogs are based mostly on the descendants of Champion Kings Creek Triple Threat and his son Champion Rockaplenty's Wild Oats. Their earliest champions include Champion Foyscroft Wild Is The Wind, who was the very first champion sired by Wild Oats, and Champion Foyscroft Triple Mini Archer, who was by Champion Kings Creek Triple Threat ex Lawndale's Mini Skirt. They also own the gorgeous red and white bitch, Champion Foyscroft Sweet Triffles, who is a litter-sister to Champion Foyscroft Triple Line Wor Lo.

From these dogs, and their descendants, Pat and Frank have been producing a steady succession of very lovely Beagles, including several champions and several more who are "knocking on the door." Their one outside breeding within the past few years was to Champion Jo Mar's Repeat Performance; a young son so produced needs but one major as we write.

Fulmont

Fulmont Beagles are owned by William and Julie Fulkerson and situated on a most beautiful mountain at Lenoir City, Tennessee.

Their first Beagle was acquired as a pet, back in 1960 while Mr. Fulkerson still was in graduate school, with breeding in earnest starting about 1963. Their foundation stock was purchased from Stephanie Kennedy whose dogs represented a cross between the old C.S. Beagles and the Do Mor line. From her the Fulkersons acquired Champion S.K. Trooper, Champion S.K. Pollyanna, and Do Mor Flapper. The latter gave the Fulkersons their first homebred champion, sired by Trooper, in 1965.

In 1964 the Fulkersons made a trip to California, where they visited Page Mill Kennels owned by Carroll Diaz. They were filled with admiration for the Beagles they saw there and as a result sent all of their best bitches for breeding to Carroll's stud dogs. The result was ten Fulmont champions within a few years.

Page Mill still figures strongly in the Fulmont breeding program, and Carroll Diaz and Julie Fulkerson have become fast friends over the years, co-owning some of the dogs. Among the latter is the 13″ dog Champion Jana Ace In The Hole, owned by Carroll and Julie and Arlen Hoobler. He came to Fulmont following the death of his breeder, Aletha Harvey, and in his first four litters since then, he has sired seven champions including a Group winner, plus some lovely

Ch. Fulmont's Flash Cube, 13″ dog, by Ch. Fulmont's Pub Crawler ex Ch. Fulmont's Fable, a homebred owned by William and Julie Fulkerson. Flash is the only red and white Beagle of either Variety who is a Best in Show winner. Handled here by Julie Fulkerson.

puppies waiting in the wings. Another Fulkerson-Diaz co-owned Beagle is Champion Page Mill Fulmont Lady Diana, and her dam, Champion Page Mill Star Struck.

A very noteworthy little 13″ red and white dog, Champion Fulmont's Flash Cube, by Champion Fulmont's Pub Crawler ex Champion Fulmont's Fable, bred, owned, and handled by the Fulkersons, has created a well-deserved sensation as the only 13″ red dog Beagle to go Best in Show; and he did it owner-handled! He is a handsome little dog with many admirers among those who have seen him.

Champion Fulmont's Friend Of A Friend, 15″, by Champion Jana's Nassau of Page Mill ex Fulmont's Face Card, is another owned and bred by the Fulkersons; Friend is doing quite well, as is a full brother, Champion Fulmont's Face in The Crowd.

One of the current principal stars from Fulmont is the gorgeous bitch Champion Tarr Hill Classical Jazz, a 15″ daughter of Champion Pixshire's The Entertainer ex Champion Tarr Hill's Triple Tina. A granddaughter of Champion Kings Creek Triple Threat, this bitch has piled up a formidable list of wins in many shows. She is handled by Sharon Clark, of Swan Lake Beagles, who co-owns her with Julie Fulkerson. Jazz was bred by Liz Hendricks and Terry and Barbara Youngberg.

A baby on the Fulmont scene, 15″, Fulmont Swan Lake Fairy Tale, by Face in the Crowd from Classical Jazz, is creating excitement at this time and needs just a major to finish as we go to press.

Graadtre

Graadtre Kennels, owned by Charles and Mary Hammes at Boones Mill, Virginia, was established in the late 1960's with Norwegian Elkhounds.

The first of their Beagles was purchased in 1974, from Robert and Sylvia Felix. She is Champion Plain and Fancy's Delilah who at present holds a Gold Certificate as an outstanding producer for six consecutive years and who has produced a total of 21 champions, with still more close to finishing as this is written, from a total of twenty-four puppies! All of these were sired by the noted winner and producer, Champion Starbuck's Hang Em High.

Delilah's first puppy to be exhibited was Champion Graadtre's Tom Dooley, Winners Dog in the 13″ Variety at the National Specialty in 1977; he completed his title while still a puppy. Champion Graadtre's L'il Night Music was Reserve Winners Bitch as a puppy at the 1982

National. A granddaughter, Champion Graadtre's Double Exposure, was 13″ Winners Bitch and Sweepstakes winner as a puppy at the 1980 National in Aldie. All three are Group placers, as are Delilah's sons, Champion Graadtre's Peppercorn and Champion Graadtre's Master Copy, and grandson, Champion Graadtre's Free Flight.

One son in whom the Hammes take special pride is Champion Graadtre's Hot Pursuit of Rossut, now owned by Mrs. Sutton and written of in the British chapter. He is enjoying an outstanding career in England, which started four days out of quarantine when he won Best in Show at Border Union, the first of three all-breed Best in Show victories. At present he holds the all-time Beagle record in England, with 24 Challenge Certificates, 22 Bests of Breed, ten Groups, five Reserve Groups, one Reserve Best in Show, and several Specialty Bests in Show. His achievements as a producer are keeping pace with his wins as a show dog, his first champion daughter having been Best of Breed at Crufts in 1984. For 1983, "Corky," as Hot Pursuit is known, garnered the Number One position among Hounds and Number Two dog of any breed in the United Kingdom. His daughter, Champion Too Darn Hot for Tragband, was Top Winning Beagle Bitch and Top Winning Beagle Puppy for 1983. Mary Hammes comments, "We are pleased with the love and guidance Mrs. Sutton has given to this beautiful, gentle hound."

In the past ten years, Charles and Mary Hammes have finished more than 30 Beagles. With Delilah as their foundation bitch, the tradition of quality is continuing. One of Delilah's daughters, Champion Graadtre's Reflection, has four champions to her credit and numerous grandchildren are presently being exhibited.

Harnett

Hounds of Harnett belong to Richard and Ann Roth at Wilmington, North Carolina. At the present time this is a new kennel for Beagles; but they are working on a very solid background, and the future should see them attaining prominence with some splendid dogs.

The kennel is strongly based on the bloodlines of Champion Rockaplenty's Wild Oats, with most of the Roths' dogs descended from them. "Pride of place" probably goes to the pretty tricolor bitch Champion Kamelot's Queen Anne's Lace, by Wild Oats from Champion Plain and Fancy's Bumble Bee, who finished in June 1983.

Then there is American and Canadian Champion Densom's Ruff 'N Tuff, another Wild Oats daughter, this one from American and Cana-

Ch. Ju-Dee's Genuine Risk of Harnett, 15″ tri, by Ch. Bedlam Tiger Talk ex Ju-Dee's San Lee Petunia, completing title here, age 14 months, taking Winners Bitch and Best Opposite Sex for 4-point major at Piedmont, July 1983. Owned by Ann H. Roth and handled by Richard Roth.

dian Champion Foyscroft's Little Trouble (Champion Kings Creek Triple Threat ex Champion Pixshire's One and Only). These two are truly lovely bitches, great assets to any kennel.

Densom's Playin' Possum, 15″ tricolor by Canada's Top Winning Beagle, Champion Wagon Wheels Wisecrack from Little Trouble, gained Group placements during her Canadian career.

Queen Anne's Lace came to the Roths from Ray and Ginger Scott, "Ruffie" and Possum from Dennis Sommers.

The Roths are interested in obedience work with their hounds, too. Among those with whom they have been successful are Sure Luv's Mist-er Beau Jangles, C.D., and Roth's Henry of Harnett, C.D.

Hollyhox

Hollyhox Beagles, owned by Curtis and Mary Sease at Waynesboro, Pennsylvania, got into the breeding of show Beagles when they sent their lovely bitch Champion Wagon Wheels Winter Holly to be bred for the first time to Champion Kings Creek Triple Threat. In the past Curt had been interested in field Beagles, but this was a whole new ball game, one which turned out most successfully.

From this first litter came Mary Sease's first homebred champion, the beautiful bitch Champion Hollyhox Gypsy Queen O'Trip. From that and other breedings to Triple Threat, Champion Hollyhox Lady T of Briarwood, Champion Hollyhox Hope of Wagon Wheels, Champion Hollyhox Triple Velvet Lady, Champion Hollyhox Triple Lady Tammy, Champion Hollyhox Kelly of Trippe, Champion Hollyhox Shadow of Trippe, and Champion Hollyhox Triple Pink Lady also were produced.

Ch. Hollyhox Kelly of Trippe with his breeder Mary Sease; co-owned by Mary Sease.

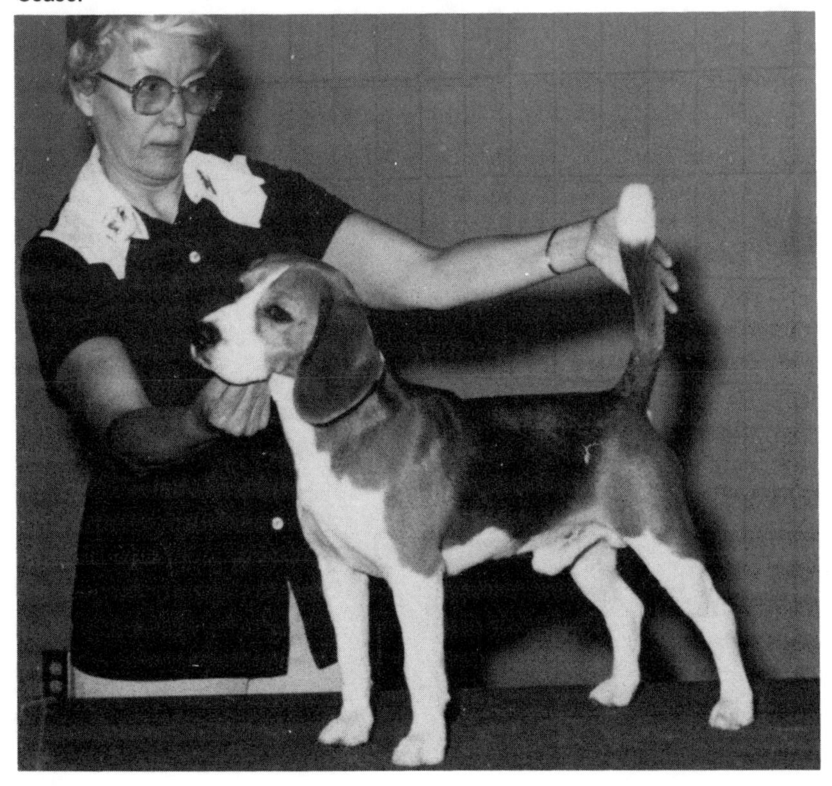

Ch. Kings Creek Triple Threat winning one of his 8 All Breed Bests in Show in top Eastern competition, this one at Holyoke Kennel Club in July 1970. Owner-handled by Marcia Foy.

Most of the above are now producers of champions, too. Mary subsequently sent other bitches to Triple Threat and to his son Champion Rockaplenty's Wild Oats, the latter being the sire of Champion Hollyhox Bird of Rockaplenty, Hollyhox Pinky's Wild Laurel, and Hollyhox Lee's Wild Pink Minx.

The stunning 13″ bitch Champion Hollyhox Pinky's Wild Laurel was bred to Champion Jo Mar's Repeat Performance, from which came a very exciting Group-winning 13″ dog, Champion Hollyhox Urban Cowboy, owned by Mary Sease and Eddie Dzuik. Cowboy had at least several Groups to his credit before his sudden death, which cut short what seemed on the way to becoming an especially outstanding career.

Hollypines

Hollypines Beagles, at Tijeras, New Mexico, are the hobby of William (Dick) and Lillian Lincoln, who met Jane Green Corbett while attending an obedience class in 1965 and from her obtained their first Beagle, Champion Adobe's Little Kechina. Bred to Champion Elsy's Portland Punch, Kechina gave the Lincolns one puppy, Lincoln's Bright Penny, who was the first champion bred by what was to become Hollypines Kennels.

So deeply involved with their Beagles did the Lincolns become that they now have bred 31 champions as we write this in February 1984. Two of these are international champions, one an American-Canadian champion, and two have earned Companion Dog degrees.

Among the Beagles who have contributed to Hollypines' success along the way have been Champion Elsy's Storm Trooper (Champion Elsy's Rumboat ex Elsy's Joyful Judy), Champion Draper's Lemon Drop Lil Abner (Champion Wagon Wheels Winter's Tale ex Draper's Peg O'My Heart), Champion Briarwood Bearcat (Champion Johjean Jentle John Janzoom ex Champion Wagon Wheels Dilly), Champion Alice of Eremarck (Champion Buglair Top of the Mark ex Champion Jana Jody of Eremarck), Champion Briarwood Catkin O'Hollypine (Champion Kings Creek Triple Threat ex Champion Briarwood Bearcat), and Champion Briarwood Day Tripper (Champion Kings Creek Triple Threat ex Champion Draper's Lemon Drop Daisy Mae).

Ch. Briarwood Day Tripper and Ch. Draper's Lemon Drop Lil Abner winning Best Hound Brace from judge Mrs. Wm. W. Wimer, III at Rio Grande in 1977. Owned by Hollypines Kennel.

Am. and Can. Ch. Hollypines Briarwood Spike, by Ch. Daisyrun's Prunedale Paddy ex Ch. Briarwood Day Tripper, Hollypines Beagles, Dick and Lillian Lincoln.

Bitches were sent for breeding to a number of the noted stud dogs, with at least one champion resulting from each litter. Hollypines' most successful breeding to date has been between Champion Daisyrun's Prunedale Paddy and Champion Briarwood Day Tripper. Of their eleven puppies from two litters, ten have completed their championships; they have included Champion Hollypines Briarwood Ellie, 15″ Winners Bitch at the 1981 National Specialty; Champion Hollypines Briarwood Spike, 15″ Best of Variety at the October 1983 Arizona Beagle Specialty; and Champion Hollypine's Daisyrun's Sun, owned by Nadine Eaton, who was 15″ Best of Variety at Westminster in 1983.

Champion Briarwood's Day Tripper lost her life during the birth of her last litter of six puppies. She was the 1982 Dam of the Year according to the National Beagle Club awards. Her fourteen champion get are her legacy to Beagledom and a tribute to her excellence as the daughter of those two magnificent Beagles, Champion Kings Creek Triple Threat and Champion Draper's Lemon Drop Daisy Mae who were winners of the top awards at the National Beagle Club's very first Specialty show.

Holmehill

Holmehill Beagles, at Philadelphia, Pennsylvania, originated in 1957 when Dr. George Roedell and his father John Roedell acquired their first 15″ Beagle, a dog from the bloodlines of Nick Rubino's Champion Rubino's Question Mark and Ed Johnson's Champion Johnson's Fancy King. Next a 13″ bitch was acquired from Nick Rubino, Champion Holmehill's Fancy Helen, who, upon completion of her championship, was bred to International Champion Chessman of Walnut Hall, who was a son of International Champion Thornridge Wrinkles. From this litter only one dog was campaigned, Champion Holmehill's Duke Ebony, who had a successful show career with Group wins and placements.

Owing to lack of time because of Dr. Roedell's profession and a growing family, in 1967 the Roedells discontinued showing their Beagles although they continued to own a few of the breed for the pleasure of their companionship.

Ch. Holmehill's Rusty Jones, by Ch. Holmehill's Maximum ex Ch. Holmehill's Great Performer, taking Best of Winners for a major on the way to his title under Mrs. Daniell-Jenkins at Lackawanna K.C. Bred and owned by Dr. George F. and Jeffrey J. Roedell.

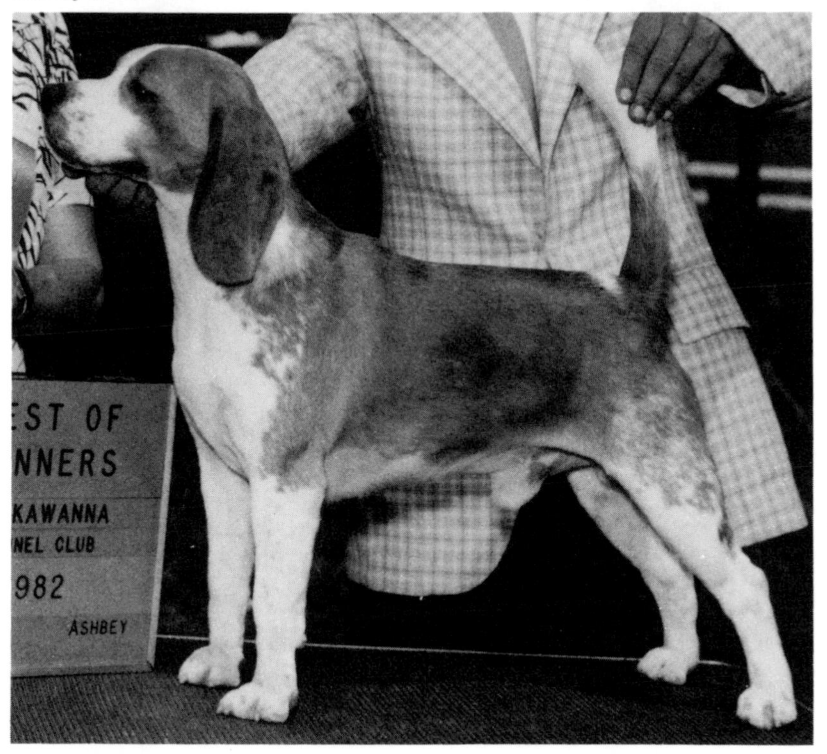

Ch. Holmehill's Golden Dream, by Ch. Holmehill's Duke Ebony ex Ch. Holmehill's Jolly Dolly completing title in May 1966 at Bryn Mawr. Bred by John J. Roedell, owned by John J. Roedell and Dr. George F. Roedell, the latter handling.

In the fall of 1979, Dr. Roedell's youngest son Jeff expressed interest in resuming the breeding and showing of Beagles. So it was that again a father and son Roedel team are back in Beagle competition, this time started with the purchase of a male and a female puppy from Helga and Ralph Alderfer. Since then Holmehill Beagles have finished four champions to date, with a number more, I feel sure, to follow. Jeff has proven a most proficient handler of his dogs, and both he and Dr. Roedell are obviously taking genuine pleasure in their hobby.

Hy-Rollin

Hy-Rollin Beagles, at Oneonta, New York have long been the hobby of K. Nick Leonard who thoroughly enjoys participation in field trial activities and also in the dog show end of Beagling.

Nick recently completed the championship of his pretty red and white bitch Hy-Rollin Cinnamon Candy, a daughter of Champion Englandale's Sundance Kid ex Lee's Lady Tangier, and we predict that it will not be too long before we are seeing him back in the ring again with another one to enjoy taking to the title.

Ch. Hy-Rollin Cinnamon Candy, by Ch. Englandale's Sundance Kid ex Lee's Lady Tangier, was bred by Joseph F. Kaminski, Jr., and is owned by K. Nick Leonard.

Jo Hill's

Jo Hill's Beagles are the hobby of Hildegarde and Joseph Del Campo who live at Baldwin, New York. All her life Hildegarde has loved animals; and so, when they moved from Brooklyn to Baldwin "to the country" naturally her first thought was "now I can have a dog." Once they were settled, a dear friend of Hildegarde's decided that the time had come, so she proceeded to present Hildegarde with two Beagles, both bitches, one seven months old and the other three years old, as it seemed to her that since the Del Campos had two children, they also should have two dogs.

Hildegarde's friend who gave her the Beagles was a breeder whose dogs were descended from Clint Callahan's Sogo line. It took several years to accomplish it, but eventually she persuaded Hildegarde to breed Mona Lisa back to Mr. Callahan's stud, Sogo Small Talk II. Sad to relate, the puppies were born dead; and not long thereafter Mona Lisa was discovered to have cancer and had to be put to sleep. They tried breeding the other bitch, Betsy, who had one dead puppy, and Hildegarde decided that was *it*—no more breeding. When Betsy finally left them, though, at age thirteen, the Del Campos soon found the loneliness in the house more than they could bear, and so another Beagle joined the family—this time from Alice Johnson's kennel, who was registered as Jo Hill's Diamond Lil and was by Champion Bown's Star Knight from Johnson's Fancy Daisy Ann. This was in 1973, and it started the Del Campos attending dog shows. Their little bitch did not really enjoy the shows, and Hildegarde started again to become discouraged; but at about that time they became acquainted with Dick and Maureen Reynolds who invited them to join their local Beagle club, and so the Del Campos started becoming more involved. The Del Campos, in co-ownership with Tony Rizzo (a Dachshund breeder who was a friend, also belonged to the club, and wanted to have a share in the breed), purchased a dog puppy, Englandale's Lord Buffington, from the Reynolds. This dog, who finished his title and became the sire of many champions, is a senior citizen now at eleven years old. When Buffy was close to the title, Hildegarde and Joe purchased another puppy from the Reynolds, Englandale's Top Choice, who was a joy to show, truly loving to be in the ring. He shares the household now with Buffy, being just about a year younger.

At Dick Reynolds's suggestion (and with his encouragement), the Del Campos were finally persuaded to breed their Johnson-bred bitch, and they selected the stud dog Dick had recommended, Champion

Ch. Jo Hill's Joyful Treasure, by Ch. Rockaplenty's Wild Oats ex Jo Hill's Diamond Lil taking Best of Variety at Northwestern Connecticut in 1979. Bred and owned by Jo Hill's Beagles, Joseph and Hildegarde Del Campo. Mrs. Del Campo handling.

Rockaplenty's Wild Oats. Things now took a turn for the better, and a litter of six handsome, healthy pups duly arrived. The pick of the litter became Champion Jo Hill's Joyful Treasure, and through her progeny she has made a very real contribution to her breed.

Along about now, Joe Del Campo, who had been until then tolerant of his wife's hobby and dearly loved the dogs, started to take an interest in the breeding and showing of the Beagles. He came across a magazine advertisement one day on Champion Lawndale's Jovan, owned by Mrs. Pat Hardt. A good deal of corresponding and telephoning followed, the upshot of which was that Joe purchased Jovan for Hildegarde, and he has, indeed, proven a valuable asset and a delight to own.

Ch. Lawndale's Jovan, by Ch. Lawndale's Chaz ex Pixshire's Dainty Doll, owned by Joseph and Hildegarde Del Campo. Jovan finished undefeated in eight shows handled by Pat and Herbie Hardt. The Del Campos purchased him in 1979, and he has brought them great joy as well as some wonderful puppies.

At about this same time, the Del Campos also added several other Beagles to their family, including a Busch-bred bitch from Earl Gribben of Alabama, Wynnwood Hi Hopes of Jo Hill; a 13″ bitch, Lawndale's Heaven Scent, from Pat Hardt; and a male pup, Chardon's Merry Medalist (by Hang 'Em High), from the Kitchells.

Joyful Treasure was bred to Jovan and produced four red and white males. Lee McGurrin promptly purchased the one who became Champion Jo Hill's Lee Red Jason, a Bay State Specialty winner who is consistently in the Best of Variety and frequently in the Hound Group winners circle.

This same breeding was repeated, and now there is a lovely bitch en route to her title, a tri, who will be Champion Jo Hill's Jewel of Jovan as she already has both majors.

Johjean

For many years the Johjean Beagles at La Grange, Illinois, were one of the strongest influences in the entire Beagle world. Many leading breeders have acquired foundation stock and outcrosses to their breeding programs from here, and the quality of the breed has benefited by this fact.

Now owned by Edward B. Jenner and John Refieuna, along with John's son Jay Refieuna, Johjean was originally the project of John Refieuna and his late wife Jean. Early in its history it merged with Ed Jenner's Forest Beagles, and the combination has been entirely successful through the years.

Ed Jenner started with Beagles ahead of the Refieunas, having founded his kennel, Forest, some four decades ago. Named for the street on which he then lived, his kennel soon became noted due to the unusually high quality of his dogs.

Ch. Johjean's Yellow Kernel winning Best of Breed at Blossom Valley Beagle Club Specialty Show in 1977, handled by J. Refieuna and E. Jenner. who are long time Beagle breeders and have owned some of the breed's greatest. This lovely red and white 15" dog has done considerable winning for these noted fanciers.

Junior's

Junior's Beagles are owned by Dick Johnson of Miami, Florida, who has made considerable impact as a breeder.

This is the home of those two great producing bitches, Champion J's Bonnie V of Beagle Chase, the dam of eighteen champions, and Champion Junior's Belle Starr, who is not far behind her in numbers of champions.

Then there is Champion Junior's Fun Machine, who is the dam of twelve champions in three litters, seven of which (and possibly eight by the time the figures are in) finished during 1983.

Dick Johnson, whose kennel is named for his first Beagle, Junior, started out primarily with Page Mill, Beagle Chase, and Hi Spirit bloodlines. Early in his breeding program, he used Champion Rockaplenty's Wild Oats three times, getting Champions Junior's Secret

Two outstanding producers among Beagles. *Left,* Ch. J's Bonnie V of Beagle Chase, all-time Top Producing Beagle Dam with a total of 18 champions. *Right,* Ch. Junior's Belle Starr, C.D.X., dam of 15 champions. These two are the foundation of Dick Johnson's Junior's Beagles.

Ch. Junior's Macho Grande, by Ch. Chrisette's Macho Man ex Ch. Junior's Fun Machine, taking Group Second at Venice K.C. 1983. Dick Johnson, breeder-owner-handler, Junior's Beagles.

Love, Junior's Score Two, Junior's Champagne Mame, Junior's Foyscroft Wild Kid, Junior's Fall Fashion, Junior's Gypsy Jen, and Junior's Dandy Man from these breedings.

The current champions at Junior's Kennels are many, as Dick has seemed to have a "green thumb" for producing them. Champion Junior's Macho Grande finished at eight and a half months of age and is one of six in his litter to finish! Champion Junior's Crown Jewels is among the littermates with whom Dick is especially pleased, as she has taken Best of Variety on each appearance so far as a Special.

Champion Junior's Commander is the present top stud dog at this kennel, producing some very pleasing puppies, and the young Macho will soon be joining him.

Dick Johnson has, on a couple of occasions, introduced outcrosses to his program by leasing stud dogs, each for a period of time.

Ch. Plain and Fancy's Bumble Bee, Winners Bitch at the Southern New York Beagle Specialty 1979, is the dam of the Best in Show 13" bitch Ch. Kamelot's Queen Bee. Bumble Bee is by Ch. Starbuck's Hang Em High ex Ch. Plain and Fancy's Clover.

Kamelot

Kamelot Beagles, at Central Square, New York, came about as the result of young Mike Scott, son of Ray and Ginger Scott, wanting one with which to compete in Junior Showmanship. The 13" bitch, Champion Hobbytime Curtain Call, joined the family, as did a red and white bitch who became Champion Lyn Mar Acres T.N.T. Mike was extremely successful with them in Junior Showmanship, and soon the entire family was actively participating in the Beagle world.

As Beagle owners, the Scotts are famous for two great bitches: the magnificent 15" Champion Plain and Fancy's Clover and her granddaughter, the lovely and consistent 13" bitch Champion Kamelot's Queen Bee. Both of these have scored brilliant records in the Beagle world, but they have not been alone in keeping the Kamelot banner high!

Champion Plain and Fancy's Clover, by Champion Mitey Cute Just Like Daddy ex Plain and Fancy's Miss Muffett, started her show

Ginger Scott with Ch. Kamelot's Playboy, 13″ son of Ch. Rockaplenty's Wild Oats and Ch. Plain and Fancy's Clover.

Ch. Kamelot's Queen Anne's Lace, 55th champion by Ch. Rockaplenty's Wild Oats, is one of three whom he sired from Ch. Plain and Fancy's Bumble Bee. Owned by Ann Roth, handled by Ginger Scott.

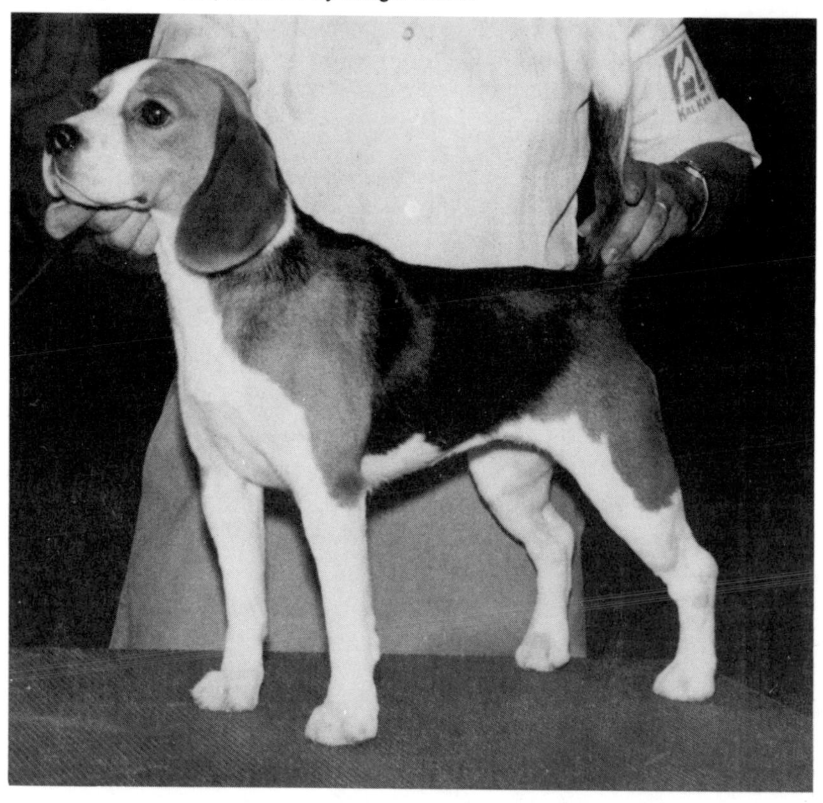

career in the mid 1970's, owner-handled by Ray Scott. In keenest Eastern competition she amassed an impressive array of Best of Variety and Group placement awards. She is a bitch who drew admiration from our most respected judges. When she was retired (except for occasional appearances as a veteran) she had become a Best in Show winner, a multiple Hound Group winner, and the only bitch in history (and one of only two Beagles ever to have done so) to have *twice* won the National Specialty, which she did in 1978 and 1980. Clover had numerous other Specialty wins as well.

In between all this, Clover took time off on several occasions to have puppies. For her first litter she was bred to Champion Starbuck's Hang Em High, producing the lovely bitch Champion Kamelot's Bumble Bee. Next she was bred to Champion Rockaplenty's Wild Oats to produce the 13″ dog Champion Kamelot's Playboy and the 15″ dog Champion Kamelot's Kountry Squire. Later Clover was bred to Champion Plain and Fancy's Duke Gemini, again producing champions.

Meanwhile Champion Kamelot's Bumble Bee was bred to Champion Rockaplenty's Wild Oats, which gave the Scotts the 13″ bitch Champion Kamelot's Queen Bee. "Polly" became Number One 13″ Beagle for 1981, won several all-breed Bests in Show, was Best 13″ at the National in 1981, and was a multiple Group winner. Another lovely bitch in this same litter, Kamelot's Honey Bee, swept through to a sensational fourteen points, beating the Specials as a puppy nearly every time in the ring; then she tragically was killed by a car just one point short of her title. Had she lived, there is no telling what heights she might have reached, as she was truly most outstanding.

The breeding of Bumble Bee to Wild Oats was later repeated, this time producing Champion Kamelot Queen Anne's Lace.

Champion Camelot's Playboy has proven a highly successful sire of champions with quality youngsters winning well and adding to his credit, coast to coast.

As this book goes to press, Ray Scott has just accepted a position as American Kennel Club Field Representative for the MidWest, where he and Ginger are in the midst of moving. Appropriately, son Mike, who started the interest in Beagles, is now a professional handler and taking over his parents' kennel in upper New York State, from where he will be handling dogs as a career and, it is hoped, doing a bit of Beagle breeding. Clover and Polly are among the special ones who are accompanying Ray and Ginger to their new home.

Laurhel

Laurhel Beagles, at Oakham, Massachusetts, are owned by Helen and Laurie Johnson, who are breeders with some very fine Beagles to their credit.

Their lovely bitch, Champion Laurhel's Sweet Pea, who is a daughter of Champion The Whim's Buckeye from a Colegren bitch, started the Johnsons off in Beagles with some very steady and consistent winning, owner-handled by Mrs. Johnson.

Sweet Pea was not only a credit to them in the ring but she has also proven to be a great producer; bred to Champion Rockaplenty's Wild Oats, she gave her owners the multiple Group-winning 15″ dog Champion Laurhel's Freddie Freeloader, born in 1980, in a litter which also included a Group placing 13″ bitch, Champion Laurhel's Buttercup, and another beautiful bitch whom I believe has also finished.

Freddie is carrying on in the tradition of his family as a producer, his children now beginning to reach the ring. At least several of them are obviously slated for championship, so Laurhel clearly has more bright stars in the future.

The multiple Group winning 15″ dog, Ch. Laurhel's Freddie Freeloader, by Ch. Rockaplenty's Wild Oats ex Ch. Laurhel's Sweet Pea, owned, bred, and handled by Helen and Laurie Johnson who have bred and shown many outstanding Beagles.

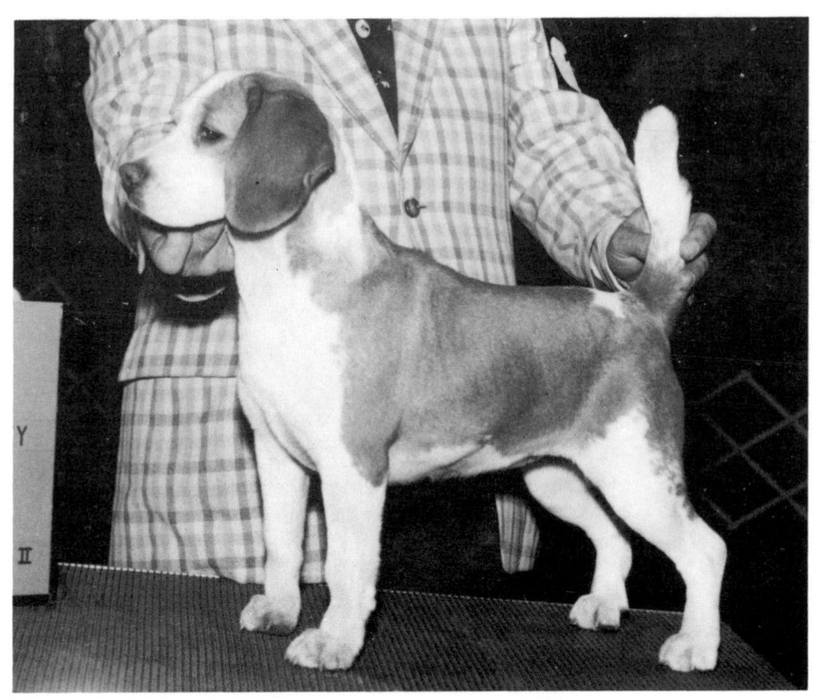

Ch. Hollyhox Lee's Wild Pink Minx with owner, Lee McGurrin, completing title at Windham County in 1980. A Wild Oats daughter.

Lee's Red Beagles

Lee's Red Beagles are owned by Lee W. McGurrin at Uniondale, Pennsylvania; and, as their name indicates, this kennel places particular emphasis on the red and white Beagles in preference to the tricolors.

Lee's original Beagle was purchased from Mary Sease of Hollyhox fame during the 1970's. Since then he has bred, owned, sold, and handled some very handsome dogs; and there is no question that his enthusiasm for this color has resulted in a good deal of popularity for it.

Lee's best known dog is the handsome and famous Champion Jo Hill's Lee's Red Jason. Bred by Hildegarde Del Campo, Jason is by Champion Lawndale's Jovan ex Champion Jo Hill's Joyful Treasure (a daughter of Champion Rockaplenty's Wild Oats); he was born in November 1980. He has won Best of Variety well over one hundred times as we write, was Best of Breed at a Bay State Specialty, and has numerous Hound Group placements to his credit. Thus he has scored a true breakthrough for consistent winning in a Beagle of his color.

Jason also is proving a highly successful sire; and one of his daughters, Lee's Red Dolly of Jason, took Best of Variety as a puppy her very first time in the ring, was Best of Winners and Best of Opposite Sex a few weeks later at the Bay State Specialty, and also won Best Puppy in Sweepstakes that same day. She was close to her title at less than seven months of age.

Just to prove that he has an open mind on the subject, Lee has recently brought out a very nice tricolored daughter of Jason from Champion Felty's Andrea of Frantz, appropriately named Lee's Tri A Tri, who he has been handling for Joyce Paver and who recently became a champion, having finished with a five-point major at the Bay State Beagle Club Specialty, and who we understand he will Special. But don't be fooled for one moment! Lee McGurrin's heart, and primary involvement with Beagles, always will remain with the red and whites to which his breeding program has contributed so well.

Ch. Lee's Try A Tri, daughter of Ch. Johill Lee's Red Jason ex Ch. Felty's Andrea of Frantz, owned by Joyce Paver and handled by Lee McGurrin finished by taking her second 5-point major at the Bay State Specialty 1983.

Lightninridge

Lightninridge Beagles are fairly new to our fancy, but they would seem to have a very bright future in the Beagle world based on the enthusiasm of owners Victor and Sylvia Lopez who live at Katonah, New York.

Sylvia and Victor have long been members of the Southern New York Beagle Club and were field enthusiasts. Then, from Charles Dalton, they purchased a bitch who was sired by a Wild Oats son (Champion Sandilly Gentleman Jim) from a field bitch. Although they had been thinking only about the field aspects of Beagle ownership, from Charlie Dalton they started to pick up an interest in the show world.

Victor soon found out that his original bitch was not quite good enough to win, so he retired her to breeding and set out to collect some good foundation bitches. He did! Two lovely red and white bitches, Champion Brantwood's Lee's Daisy Be Red and Champion Holiday's April Showers, moved to Lightninridge, both finished quickly, and both are producing well.

Victor and Sylvia Lopez now have several homebred champions to their credit from these two bitches and from the earlier one who has proven herself nicely as a producer.

The latest Lightninridge champion as we write is the 13″ dog Short N'Sweet, by Champion Jo Mar's Repeat Performance ex Daisy Be Red.

Am. and Can. Ch. Brantwood Lee's Daisy Be Red, by Ch. Rockaplenty's Wild Oats ex Ch. Lokavi's Double Destiny, owner-handled by Vic Lopez, to Best of Opposite Sex, Saw Mill 1983.

Ch. Beau-A-Buffet taking Best of Variety at the International in 1964 at eight years of age. The judge was Hollis Wilson. Owned by Brendan and Neil Holloran, handled by the latter.

Lohenbru

Lohenbru Beagles were first registered with the American Kennel Club in 1975 by the Holloran family of Chicago, Illinois, but for many years before then these folks had owned and been involved with Beagles.

All Shook Up of Park Lane, their first Beagle to be shown, was purchased by Pat Holloran from William and Marion Suffern in 1957. Although never finished, this little dog instilled in the Hollorans a love for dog shows and the breed.

Following the International in 1962, where he had seen her take a five-point major, Pat Holloran purchased a 13″ bitch, future Champion Beau-A-Buffet, from the Beaumonts, Beau-A-Beagles. She became a multiple Best of Variety winner with Group placements, one of her Varieties gained under Hollis Wilson at the International in 1964. Unfortunately, although bred on two separate occasions, this bitch never conceived. However, she remained a household pet and companion to the Holloran brothers, Brendan and Neil, until her death at six years of age from leukemia.

It was awhile before the Hollorans replaced Buffet. Then early in 1972 Neil saw an advertisement for a litter by Champion The Whim's Buckeye, and they went to look at the puppies, bringing home with them the bitch who became the grand matriarch of the present-day Lohenbru Kennels, future Champion Mil-Bran Blissful Whim.

Ch. Pixshire's Gentle Breeze, 15", taking Winners Bitch at Terre Haute 1980. Owned by Neil and Judy Holloran, Lohenbru Beagles.

When it came time to breed their new bitch, Neil selected a stud dog close to her sire's own breeding, the 13" dog Champion Wilpat Desperado of Franbee, who, like Blissful, had some nice wins to his credit, including a Best 13" Variety award at Westminster. Neil co-owned this dog with Ronice Brown, and the litter from Blissful and Desperado gave Lohenbru its first homebred champion, Lohenbru's Pride 'N' Prejudice.

Next Blissful was bred, in 1976, to Champion Starbuck's Hang 'Em High, from which came the Hollorans' second homebred champion, Lohenbru's Sweet Surrender.

In May 1976 Neil Holloran purchased a puppy by Champion The Whim's Buckeye ex Champion The Whim's Comeuppence from Tony and Judy Musladin, the future Champion The Whim's Stemwinder who has become a well-known winner and successful sire. Blissful was bred to Stemwinder producing their third homebred champion, 15" Lohenbru's Close Encounter.

The most recent addition to the kennel is a 15″ bitch, Champion Pixshire's Gentle Breeze, a double granddaughter of Champion Kings Creek Triple Threat who, bred to Stemwinder, in 1982, produced the 15″ tricolor dog, Champion Lohenbru's The Honeymoon's Over, finished at eleven months with five majors and a Best of Variety and Group third from the classes.

The Hollorans thoroughly enjoy their Beagles, and their pride in the dogs' success at the shows is equalled by their pleasure in them at home as family members.

Londonderry

Londonderry Beagles, now a busy and successful project of Lee Cord at Sayville, New York, really came about very unexpectedly. As Lee says, "never in my wildest imagination did I ever think of becoming a breeder or of showing dogs. I did not know dog shows existed. There were always pups in my formative years, but not any specific breed." Ironically, Beagles always were very special to Lee, however, and in her teenage years she collected statues of them, feeling someday she would own a live one.

Her first Beagle was given to the Cords by a farmer in the mountains where the family spent their summers following Lee's graduation from nursing school. She was a beautiful liver and white, but because she wasn't a tri, Lee kept telling everyone she was not a true Beagle. Her markings were perfect from Lee's description—white muzzle, blaze, and the most beautiful collar around her deep red neck.

The Cords lost this well-loved bitch at ten years of age, just two weeks before they moved into their present home at Sayville. Once settled, they purchased a German Shepherd puppy and then began thinking of a playmate for her. Talking with a patient one day while working at the hospital, Lee told him about her Beagle and found that he bred and hunted them. The next day when his wife came to visit him she had a gift for Lee—an adorable tiny Beagle puppy which she had smuggled in, concealed in her handbag.

Cindy and the Shepherd grew to be great friends; and when the Shepherd died at six years of age, the little Beagle was inconsolable, so a Brittany Spaniel pup came to join the family.

Lee's first love remained the Beagle, and when hers succumbed to kidney failure, she was taken by a co-worker to visit Maureen and Dick Reynolds to see the Beagles they owned and raised. This was her first introduction to "bench Beagles" and it was definitely love at first

Ch. Londonderry's Breath of Spring, by Ch. Colegren's Heir to Fame ex Ch. Englandale's Bonnie Sue, taking her first major at Westminster K.C. 1977. Owner-handled by Lee Cord.

sight. A puppy was reserved for Lee from the litter the Reynolds' expected from Champion Johjean July Jeanne. This turned out to be Champion Englandale's Bonnie Sue—and Lee Cord with her Beagles was on the way to a thoroughly rewarding future. Interestingly, this little bitch was also the Reynolds' first homebred champion.

At eighteen months of age, Bonnie was bred to Champion Dunken Hill's Duke of Colegren, and thus it was that Londonderry Beagles became a reality. Bonnie had three champions in the litter: Champion Londonderry's Lady Cynthia Sue, Champion Londonderry's Lord Oliver, and Champion Londonderry's April Mist. For her second litter, Bonnie was bred to Champion Colegren's Heir to Fame, producing Champion Londonderry's Cavalier, Champion Londonderry's Curtain Call, Champion Londonderry's Breath of Spring, and Champion Londonderry's Friar Tuck. Two litters—eleven puppies—seven champions.

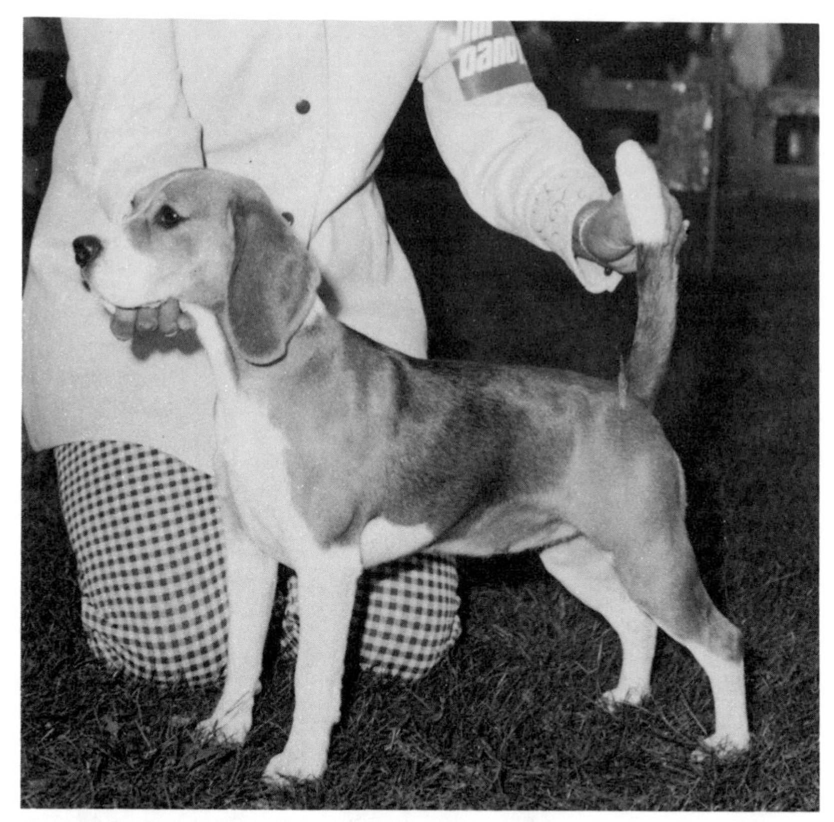

Ch. Londonderry's Curtain Call, by Ch. Colegren's Heir to Fame ex Ch. Englandale's Bonnie Sue, the dam of Chs. Londonderry's Aladdin and Londonderry's Gentleman Jim. All owner-handled by Lee Cord.

Cynthia Sue bred to Cavalier produced Champion Londonderry's Beth of Mac Vic, owned by Eric Del Buono. "Cindy" also produced Champion Jon and Londonderry's Drummer Boy. Lord Oliver bred to Curtain Call produced Champion Londonderry's Alladin and Champion Londonderry's Gentleman Jim.

As we write in early 1984 Lee is showing two young pups who are both pointed, and it is hoped they will finish this year. They are Londonderry's Physician and Londonderry's Debutante, by Alladin ex Breath of Spring. Two other Aladdin puppies are also doing well, owner-handled by Jeannette Durand.

Feeling the need for an outcross, in 1983 the Cords bred Champion Londonderry's Love Me Tender to Champion Whiskey Creek's Racer's Edge owned by Michele Sager and Tony Castellano. Five beautiful girls were included in the litter—watch for several of them about the time this book comes out!

Meadow Crest

Meadow Crest Beagles, owned by Annette M. Didier of Fort Wayne, Indiana, came about in the fall of 1977 when she acquired Starbuck's Meadow Song (Champion The Whim's Buckeye ex American and Canadian Champion Elsy's Shooting Star) from the Hiltzes. "Amy" easily finished her American and Canadian titles, owner-handled, en route to becoming Meadow Crest's foundation bitch. A few of her outstanding wins include Best Puppy in Sweepstakes at the 1978 National Beagle Specialty, and Best of Winners at the Central Ontario Beagle Club Specialty in 1978 and again in 1981 (to finish).

The Meadow Crest name was established in May 1979 with the arrival of Champion Starbuck's Meadow Song's first litter, sired by Champion Hickorynuts Hangman (Champion Starbuck's Hang 'Em High ex Champion Colegren's Hickorynut Spring), which reintroduced the Colegren line into the existing Whim-Elsy combination. This breeding produced three 15″ males: Champion Meadow Crest's Grand Slam, who was Meadow Crest's first home bred and Group-winning champion; American and Canadian Champion Meadow Crest's Top O'The Ninth, a multiple Hound Group winner in Canada and Reserve Winners Dog at the 1980 National Beagle Club Specialty Show, owned and handled by Ray Hornbostel; and Champion Starbuck's Full Count, Hound Group winner and the first Beagle owned and handled by Harry and Jo Ann Schoo.

Champion Meadow Crest's Grand Slam's growing list of accomplishments include Best of Variety at the September 1981 Southern New York Beagle Club Specialty in conjunction with Westchester. Also, "Chip" ranked among the Top Ten 15″ Beagles in 1981, sharing this honor with his litter-brother, Champion Starbuck's Full Count. In 1983, "Chip" won Best Stud Dog at the National, and he is currently ranked a *Kennel Review* and *Canine Chronicle* Top Producer for 1983. To date his offspring include eleven champions, two of them all-breed Best in Show winners and two additional Hound Group winners, along with numerous others close to finishing their titles.

In 1981 the breeding between Meadow Song and Hangman was repeated with the hope of producing an outstanding bitch. Again, a litter of 15″ males was whelped (this time five) which produced Champion Meadow Crest's Masterpiece, multiple Best in Specialty winner and multiple Hound Group placer, owned by Mrs. Lois Lambert;

Ch. Meadow Crest's Grand Slam, 15″ dog, by Ch. Hickorynuts Hangman ex Am. and Can. Ch. Starbuck's Meadow Song, the No. 8 15″ Beagle for 1981, *Kennel Review* and *Canine Chronicle* systems. Owned and handled by Annette Didier, Meadow Crest Beagles.

Champion Meadow Crest's Winjammer, multiple Hound Group placer owned by Richard and Sylvia Lingenfelter; Champion Meadow Crest's Showdown owned by White Acres Kennels; Champion Meadow Crest Whispering Wind owned by E. Phillips and D. Nierman; and Champion Meadow Crest's Deuces Wild, breeder-owned.

For Meadow Song's third litter, she was bred to Champion Sunbriar Lucky Star (Champion Starbuck's Hang 'Em High ex Canadian Champion Buttonwood's Broker's Tip), again in anticipation of producing bitch puppies. At last! Out of this litter came not only another 15″ male, Champion Meadow Crest's Nik of Thyme, multiple Best of Variety winner and Hound Group placer from the classes, but also Meadow Crest's first and second 15″ homebred bitches, Meadow Crest's Lucky Charm and Meadow Crest's Triple Charm, the latter a multiple Best of Variety winner needing just one major to finish as we write.

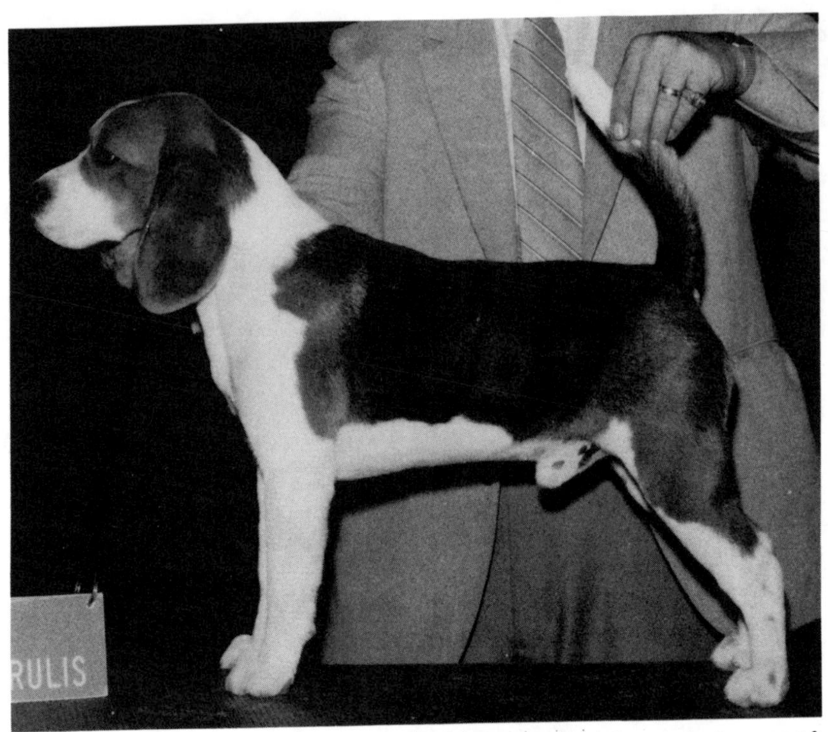

Ch. Meadow Crest's Windjammer, 15" dog. Multiple Hound Group-placing son of Ch. Hickorynuts Hangman and Am. and Can. Ch. Starbuck's Meadow Song. Owned by Richard and Sylvia Lingenfelter, handled by Harry L. Schoo, and bred by Annette M. Didier.

Lucky Charm caught the eye of Baroness Ottoline van der Borch tot Verwolde (Sergeant Pepper Beagles in the Netherlands) who purchased her in June 1983. Lucky Charm is already a Hound Group placer from the classes in the Netherlands. She will be bred to Sergeant Pepper's Trademark (Dutch Champion Clovergates Fancy Pants ex English and Dutch Champion Wembury Anna) at a later date, and a bitch puppy from this combination will be brought back to be re-introduced into the Meadow Crest Lines.

Champion Starbuck's Meadow Song has already produced nine champions (including two Specialty winners, three Hound Group winners, and four additional Hound Group placers). She was also named a *Kennel Review* Top Producer in 1980—quite a *foundation* she turned out to be! Further breedings are planned for this valuable bitch.

Merry Song

Merry Song Beagles came into being when Dr. Mara M. Baun and Dr. Nancy Bergstrom, of Elkhorn, Nebraska, purchased their first show Beagle, Champion Sun Valley's Honey Bear, in San Francisco in 1975. She was out of the last of Alice Jeffries's breeding and she was purchased from Robert Hanson. Dr. Baun and Dr. Bergstrom derived great satisfaction from Bear's companionship and from learning to show dogs.

The ladies moved to Michigan shortly after Honey bear had completed her championship, during 1975, where they bred her to American and Canadian Champion Starbuck's Hang 'Em High. Perhaps the highlight of Honey Bear's show career was taking Win-

Am. and Can. Ch. Merry Song's Uppity Ms., by Am. and Can. Ch. Starbuck's Hang 'Em High ex Ch. Sun Valley's Honey Bear, taking Best of Breed at the Southern California Beagle Club Specialty in 1982. "Belle" also won the National in '83. Owned by Drs. Mara M. Baun and Nancy Bergstrom.

ners Bitch at the Blossom Valley Beagle Club 1975 in her second show. Her first litter produced American and Canadian Champion Merry Song's Pooh Bear, Uppity Ms., and Nutcracker. They won Best Litter in Match in tough competition the second time they were shown.

When their show careers started in earnest, many exciting wins followed. Nutcracker finished her title after gaining her second major with a Best of Variety from the classes and a Hound Group first. She is a multiple Group winner, ranking among the Top Ten 13″ Beagles in 1978 and 1979. She was Best of Opposite Sex at the National Beagle Club Specialty in 1983 at six and a half years of age. As a producer, four of her five puppies from two litters have finished or are close to doing so. A son, American and Canadian Champion Merry Song's High and Mighty, is a multiple Group winner, while a daughter, Canadian Champion Merry Song's Free Spirit, is a multiple Best Puppy in Show winner in Canada, and Champion Merry Song's Husker is a multiple Group placer.

American and Canadian Champion Merry Song's Uppity Ms. was Winners Bitch at the National Specialty in 1977, Best of Breed at the same event in 1982, a multiple Group winner and placer, and an all-breed Best in Show winner. She was ranked among the Top Ten 15″ Beagles in 1980. She was also an integral part of Merry Song's Brace showmanship, and with American and Canadian Champion Merry Song's Pooh Bear she took Best Brace at the National in 1977, while with American and Canadian Champion Merry Song's High and Mighty she has won multiple breed and Group Brace competitions and a Best Brace in Show.

Uppity Ms. has produced two litters with High and Mighty. All four of the first pups went on to finish quickly, two going on to win and place in Groups. The second litter is now eight months old.

Dr. Baun and Dr. Bergstrom are currently showing Champion Merry Song's Exclamation as a Special and starting out some of the puppies. It is their policy only to breed when they wish to produce a new Special, and they are pleased that 75% of their first four litters finished championship.

Currently the doctors are engaged in the studies of Pet Person Interaction, including studies of the physiological effects of petting dogs. Exclamation is the control in their petting studies, and Uppity Ms. will be the pet in their studies of pets and the elderly nursing home resident, to begin soon.

Navan

Navan Beagles are owned by Nancy Vanstrum of Oxford, Florida, who bought her first Beagle in 1956 as a pet and companion. Obviously the personality won her over, since now, 28 years later, she is still one of the biggest Beagle fans.

Nancy was not able to breed her first litter until 1965. From this breeding she kept a female to train and show in obedience. While showing Suzy to her C.D. title, Nancy had the opportunity of seeing and learning other aspects of the dog show world. By observing and

Jenny's Sweet Suzie, U.D. 1965-1978. Bred and owned by Nancy Vanstrum, Navan Beagles. She is described by her owner as "my best friend ever." She not only accomplished much in obedience, but was a challenge and joy to train and show, and will be forever missed by her owner despite the many lovely Beagles still at Navan.

Ch. Navan's Triple Trouble Rick, co-owned by his breeder Nancy Vanstrum and Virginia Flowers, is a multiple Best in Show dog who won the National Specialty in 1975 and 1976 and has sired more than 50 champions. He is a son of Ch. Kings Creek Triple Threat.

studying the breed, she found that Champion Kings Creek Triple Threat offered the qualities she most admired; therefore, she decided to make this her foundation line.

Since 1967 this has been the foundation on which Navan Beagles have been built. The bitch Navan's Penny A Go Go, bred to Triple Threat, produced two Best in Show winners: Champion Navan's Triple Trouble C.D., a consistent winner in the United States and Best in Show in South America; and Champion Navan's Triple Trouble Rick, a multiple Best in Show winner in the United States, a double National Specialty winner, and a Top Beagle. In addition to these, Navan Beagles have produced several Group winners and placers and Variety winners too numerous to list.

From her very limited and selective breeding program, Nancy Vanstrum has herself, as breeder-owner, trained and shown seventeen champions to their titles. More are almost finished, and some lovely puppies are waiting their turn.

Page Mill

Never in all Beagle history has there been a more influential kennel than Page Mill owned by Carroll Gordon Diaz at Los Gatos, California. Right from its inception in 1956 until the present day, Page Mill dogs are in the rings winning and in the backgrounds and pedigrees of all our most successful present strains.

Going back to the earliest days, Champion Page Mill Downbeat was the sire of Champion Page Mill Whirlwind who was the sire of Champion Wandering Wind (from Champion White Acres Lady Slipper) who in turn sired 35 or more champions. Another son of Whirlwind was Champion Page Mill Trademark, sire of Champion Page Mill Hallmark (Top Beagle of 1967, Best in Show at Orange Empire, and Best of Variety at Westminster), plus Champion Page Mill Celebrity, Champion White Acres Page Boy, and Champion Page Mill Landmark.

Ch. Page Mill Fulmont Lady Diana, 13″ bitch, by Ch. Fulmont Friend of a Friend ex Ch. Page Mill Star Struck, bred and owned by Julie Fulkerson and Carroll G. Diaz.

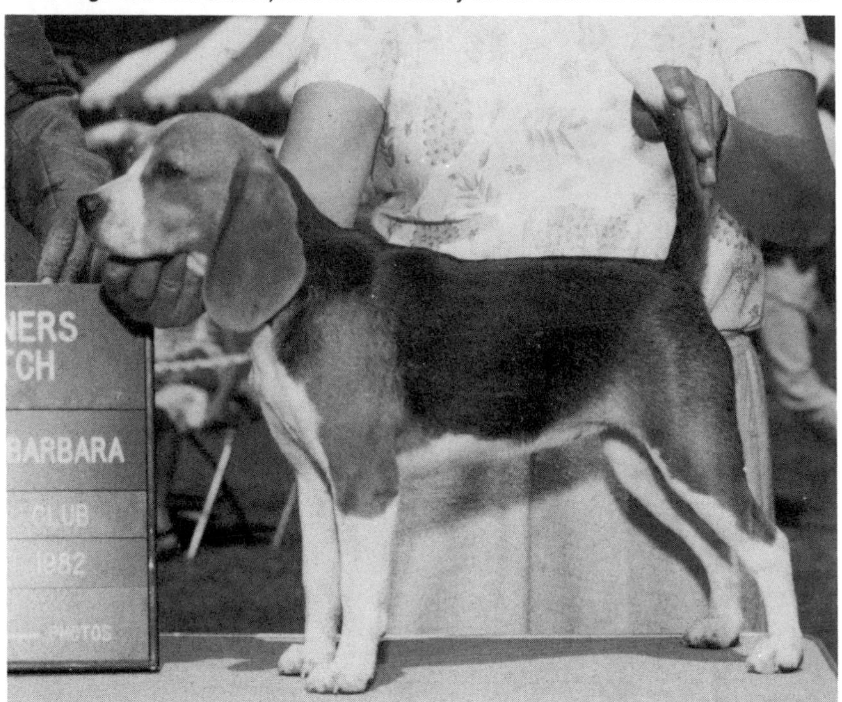

Ch. Page Mill Krystal, 15″ bitch, bred, owned, and handled by Carroll Diaz, Page Mill Beagles. She is a daughter of Ch. Fulmont's Flash Cube ex Ch. Page Mill Winnie The Pooh.

Champion Page Mill Hallmark, through his daughter Champion Page Mill Call Girl, is a grandsire of Champion Rockaplenty's Wild Oats whose champion offspring in the United States alone number 55, with a dozen or so more between Canada, South America, and Australia.

The early Page Mill dogs are behind the Whims, Starbuck, Fulmont, and literally dozens of other kennels in various sections of the United States. Champion Wandering Wind and Champion Page Mill Wildfire are behind The Whims and Starbuck. Champion Page Mill Blue Chip was sent to Dick Johnson when he was gathering foundation for his kennel. Champion Page Mill Lone Star and Champion Page Mill Barnstorm went to the David Arnolds in Texas where they have had a very dominant effect on many kennels. In many other cases owners of current winning dogs, looking back in their pedigrees, will find the Page Mill influence behind them.

Although inactive with the kennel over a short period of time, Carroll has been as engrossed as ever with her dogs during recent years. And there are Page Mill stars on the horizon to prove it.

Patches

Patches Beagles, owned by Patsy A. and Charles D. Grant at Pensacola, Florida, have a very select kennel with some truly lovely dogs. Among them are Champion Teloca Cookie Too of Belbravo, 15″ son of Champion Teloca Cookie Monster from Champion Teloca Sue Carolyn B Belbravo, a consistent winning bitch in the late 1970's; Champion Teloca Puddin' An' Tame, C.D., 13″ winning dog of the early 1980's; and Champion Teloca Upstage Bann'D 'N Boston, 13″ daughter of Puddin ex Champion Teloca Red's Middle Child, C.D., another successful campaigner of the late 1970's. The Grants are co-breeders with Marie Shuart of the new Best in Show winner Champion Teloca Patches Littl' Dickens, owned by Wade Burns and Marie Shuart.

Ch. Teloca Patches Littl' Dickens, 13″, by Ch. Teloca Patches On Target, C.D. ex Ch. Teloca Upstage Bann's in Boston, C.D., shown taking Hound Group One 1983. Co-owned by Wade S. Burns, handling, and Marie Shuart, Miami, Florida.

Pickadilly

Pickadilly Beagles were founded at the beginning of the 1960's with the purchase, by Mr. and Mrs. Robert (Jean and Bob) Dills, of a young show and breeding prospect bitch sired by the John Refieunas' then top stud dog, Champion Do Mor Dictator, from a litter-sister to Hollis Wilson's grand dog, Champion End O'Maine Ridge Runner. This impressively bred youngster became Pickadilly Penny.

Shortly after Penny joined the family, the Dills, who were Midwesterners at the time, moved East to Wilton, Connecticut, to the lovely home which they occupied for more than twenty years, until

Ch. Pickadilly High Priority was bred, owned, and handled by Jean Dills to become one of three champion daughters in a litter by Ch. Rockaplenty's Wild Oats ex Ch. Pickadilly Triplicate.

1982 when Bob retired from his position with General Foods in White Plains, New York. He and Jean decided to relocate to Oregon to join their children, who were already living there. That is where the Pickadilly Beagles, some Dachshunds, and Jean and Bob now are to be found.

Soon after settling at Wilton, Pickadilly was underway. For her first litter, Penny was bred to Mrs. William Coleman's Johjean Judd, and on the day that Judd became a champion, Penny's puppies by him were born. Mrs. Coleman bought the best dog, who became Champion Pickadilly Peter and was the first champion bred by Jean Dills. First choice bitch in the litter, who remained with the Dills, became Champion Pickadilly Party Girl, who in turn produced two litters for them, from one of which came Champion Pickadilly Party Punch. Another Penny daughter, Pickadilly Double Direct (who in her first litter by Champion Johjean Jabat produced four puppies of which two were American and Canadian champions), was next bred to Champion King's Creek Triple Threat producing Champion Pickadilly Triplicate.

Triplicate was bred back into her sire's line to the Triple Threat son Champion Rockaplenty's Wild Oats. A litter of three champion bitches resulted, among them Champion Pickadilly Prima Donna who became the foundation bitch of Ed Nelson's Ledgewood Kennels, winning consistently as a Special over champion dogs and producing a number of champions as well.

Important dogs along the way at Pickadilly have been the handsome and successful male Champion Pickadilly Doctor Do Mor and the lovely Champion Pickadilly Petticoat Fever (Champion Pickadilly Peter ex Colegren Carolina Fore), who produced at least several champions.

Champion Colegren's Heir To Fame was the sire of Champion Pickadilly Petticoat Chaser, who did well as a Special and as a sire.

Two dogs with whom Mrs. Dills had considerable success in the United States were both sold to Brazil where they have contributed well to the breed. They are Champion Pickadilly Wild Card, by Wild Oats from Champion Pickadilly Doctor Sunshine, who was widely admired a few years back and helped create the "red and white breakthrough" in the United States in stiffest Eastern competition with Best of Variety and Group placements.

Pickadilly has an impressive list of homebred champions to its credit, and we hope it will continue to grow in its new Pacific Coast location.

Pin Oaks

Pin Oaks Kennels, owned by Ralph and Helga Alderfer at Souderton, Pennsylvania, point with pride to the fact that they have bred or owned a total of 52 champion Beagles, 38 of which have finished between 1975 and 1983.

Prior to their marriage, in 1961, Ralph had owned and worked with some excellent field Beagles, running them in trials and making titles with some. Sadly, as so frequently happened in the past when preventive measures had not been so well perfected, taking in a dog for a "friend" brought distemper to his dogs, wiping out the entire pack. For awhile Ralph did not have the heart to resume activity in the breed, which is surely understandable.

Since, when one is fond of dogs, getting along without them is difficult, Ralph and Helga decided to try another breed and started to raise Pekingese which Helga had always loved. But then came a house on an acre of ground—and Ralph's interest in Beagles started to revive. Meeting Bob Felty, and visiting his kennel of show Beagles, was an exciting experience for the Alderfers, as these were the first of this type of Beagle they had known. Soon afterwards the first of their show-type Beagles joined the family, purchased from Ed Johnson whose Fancy Beagles were among the finest of their day.

Now Pin Oaks Kennels is a going operation and famous around the world, represented by winners in the United States (including Hawaii), Canada, England, Australia, and South America. Ralph and Helga handle the dogs themselves, traveling to the shows in their motor home, and are two of Beagledom's most enthusiastic members.

As previously mentioned, the Pin Oaks foundation stock was based on dogs from Johnson's Fancy Beagles, some of Mr. Felty's, and in addition stock carrying Gaycroft, Sogo, and other bloodlines active in that day. A little dog Champion Windmans Tom Thumb, by Champion Nottawa's Amigo ex Champion Char Mar Becky Sharp and bred by Mrs. Mary Louise Marks, was purchased from Robert Trimpey quite early in the breeding program, and he is still to be found in many current Pin Oaks pedigrees, the Alderfers respecting him highly for his beneficial influence. Another purchase from Mr. Trimpey was the bitch Hi Spirit Jin, by Champion South Paw Senor Amigo. Both of these were 15″ Beagles.

Pin Oaks started hitting the really big time winning in the mid-1970's when they brought out a splendid 15″ dog, Champion Pin Oaks Mr. Chips. They took him through to his title and then sold him

The handsome 15″ dog, Ch. Pin Oaks Ruffles N' Ridges, bred, owned, and handled by J. Ralph Alderfer here winning Best in Show at Thousand Islands Kennel Club in the early 1980's. Born December 1978, Ruffles has been a consistent winner and is the sire of champions for Pin Oaks Kennels.

Ch. Hearthside Lovely Talisman, 15″ bitch, by Pin Oaks Lucky Marksman ex Pin Oaks Bright Topaz, finished at four shows in a row and has been an outstanding producing bitch for Pin Oak Kennels.

to Long Island fanciers who had been seeking a top quality show dog; for his new owners he became a consistent and important winner and stud dog with numerous champions to his credit. Mr. Chips was followed by a neat little 13″ dog, Champion Pin Oaks Knicks and Chips, who won the Variety at a Southern New York Specialty, was consistent in the breed ring, and brought home some Group placements as well. At the height of his success here, "Nickie" was sold, following much persuasion on the part of the new owner, to Eduardo Quinteiro of Brazil. In his new home he became a Group and Best in Show dog and has benefited the breed as a worthy sire as well.

Champion Pin Oaks Ruffles N' Ridges was the next to meet with success. This handsome dog is a Best in Show winner, a multiple Group winner, and a really superb stud. Among his progeny is another Best in Show dog, Anita Tillman's Champion Brantwood's Desperado.

Champion Hearthside Lovely Talisman, the dam of Ruffles, was sent to be bred to Champion Rockaplenty's Wild Oats, giving the Alderfers another of their current winners. This one is Champion Pin Oaks Mello Maverick, who also is a consistent Best of Variety dog with Group placements. Also in this same litter was a red and white who went to Canada where she became Canadian Champion Pin Oaks Fire N' Ice, owned by Louise French. "Tally" was a most beautiful bitch and a great producer—the kind every kennel likes to own!

Recently the Alderfers sold a very handsome dog to England, to the Douglas Appletons, where he is scoring spectacular success. Also there is a Hawaiian kennel which is now very strong in Pin Oaks and which is breeding some quality dogs.

Ch. J's Jolly Dolly of Beagle Chase, 15" bitch by Ch. Hi Spirit J.C. ex Beagle Chase Kate, owned by Pin Oaks Beagles.

Powveiras

Powveiras Beagles, at Sunnyvale, California, started in 1966, the result of a little Beagle who wandered to their door, "his owner lost," whom Mary Powell and Trudi Reveira invited to move in and who stayed.

Next came Sam, who had been tied up for a year when the Humane Society forced the owners to surrender him for cruelty. Mary and Trudie bailed him out, managed to get his papers, and then showed him in breed and obedience until he gained C.D. and C.D.X. degrees.

While showing Sam, the two ladies saw and fell in love with a pup called Jana Inka being shown by Aletha Harvey. Two weeks later she joined the family, to become a champion in four shows.

Next a little pup called Jana Malia was purchased, now a champion with a C.D., C.D.X., and two legs towards her U.D. degree. After that Powveiras's own breeding program was established, with Champion Powveiras Popo'Ele', Powveiras Menehune (just 9 7/8″ tall) and Champion Powveiras Kini Keoki, C.D.

Trudie Reveira with the first of the Beagles shown in obedience by Powveiras Kennel which she co-owns with Mary Powell. This is Sam, by Guy X111 ex Patricia V111, who distinguished himself with both C.D. and C.D.X. degrees.

Ch. Powveiras Princess Kaiulani, handsome daughter of Ch. Saddlerock Sandman ex Ch. Jana Inka, bred and owned by Mary Powell and Trudie Reveira.

When Mary and Trudie saw Champion Saddlerock Sandman, the gorgeous gold and white son of Champion Kings Creek Triple Threat owned by Marcia Foy and Isabella Hoopes, nothing would do until he had moved in and joined the family. He and Champion Jana Inka produced those two beautiful "golden girls," Champion Madame Pele and Champion Powveiras Princess Kaiulani. Then Princess Keoki and he were mated, producing the latest champion, Powveiras Kini Kamehameha, who finished in six shows with four majors, the last one going Best of Variety from the classes over five Specials!

Since their first two Beagles had needed homes, Mary and Trudie became interested in rescue work. In 1977 they started the Northern Beagle Rescue; since then they have placed over 140 rescued Beagles. This is due to their deep love for the breed and the fact that every Beagle needs a family, both champions and pets alike.

Ranrob

Ranrob Kennels began in 1974 when Mrs. Robin Zieske of Cambridge, Minnesota, purchased a Beagle from Jenny Whitcomb of Jade-Court Kennel for her son. At Mrs. Whitcomb's urging, Robin took this first Beagle, later to become Group-placing Elexandra Elite of Jade-Court, to a match show and was promptly "hooked" on the world of show dogs. Later that year she obtained a second Jade-Court bitch, the future Champion Eve's Enchantress of Jade-Court.

In 1977 Robin was fortunate to acquire Champion Starbuck's Buckshot from Linda and David Hiltz. A littermate to Champion Starbuck's Hang 'Em High, "Bucky" was already finished when he came to live with the Zieskes. Owned by Robin Zieske and David Hiltz, Robin campaigned him to an all-breed Best in Show and Number Four 15″ Beagle in 1979.

"Bucky" was subsequently bred to Champion Eva's Enchantress of Jade-Court to produce Champion Ranrob's Intrepid Lad owned by Carolyn Vance. A multiple Group winner, "Bud" was campaigned by Robin to a position in the Top Ten Beagles for 1981. A repeat of this breeding produced Champion Ranrob's On Target.

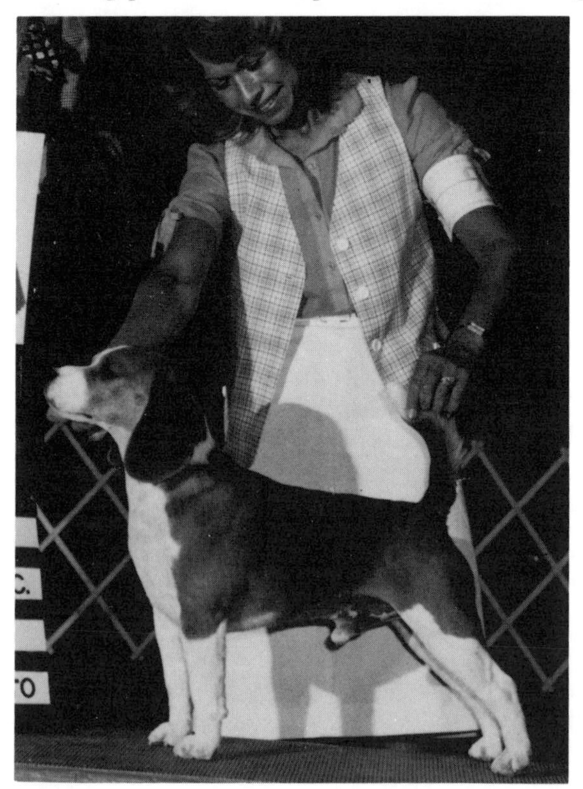

Ch. Ranrob's Intrepid Lad, by Ch. Starbuck's Buckshot ex Ch. Eve's Enchantress of Jade-Court, is a multiple Group winner and was a Top Ten 15″ Beagle in 1981. Breeder Mrs. Robin Zieske, owner, Mrs. Carolyn Vance.

Ch. Starbuck's Buckshot, 15″, by Ch. The Whim's Buckeye ex Ch. Elsy's Shooting Star, Best in Show winning dog bred by David and Linda Hiltz. Owned and handled by Mrs. Robin Zieske and co-owned with David Hiltz. Buckshot was No. 4 among 15″ Beagles in 1979.

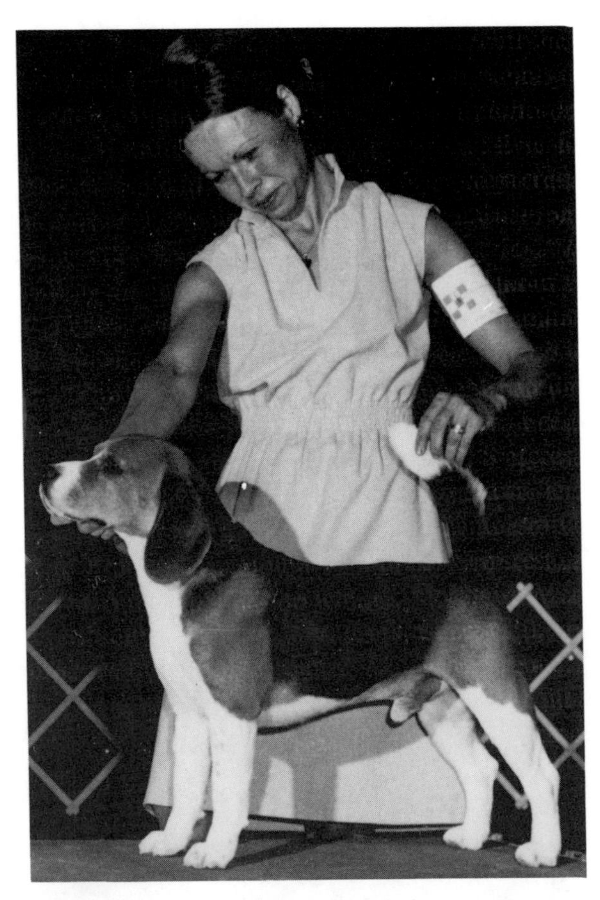

In 1980 Robin purchased a puppy which was to become group-placing Champion The Whim's Hot To Trot, co-owned with Judith Musladin. This bitch was bred to Champion Starbuck's Hang 'Em High to produce Champion Ranrob's A Little Bit of Hot.

The year 1981 also saw two more Starbuck bitches taking up residence in the Zieske household. One bitch, Champion Starbuck Promises To Keep, was bred to Champion Ranrob's Intrepid Lad to produce Champion Ranrob's Hooligan of Brueacre, owned by John Bell of Scotland. The other bitch was to become Champion Starbuck's Fair Warning, owned by Robin Zieske and David Hiltz. Although a diminutive 15″ bitch, there was certainly nothing small about her charismatic fire and spirit in the show ring. Capturing her first Hound Group at seven months of age, she went on to become a two-time all-breed Best in Show winner. She was Number Two 15″ Beagle in 1982 and Number One Beagle in both Varieties in 1983.

Rayana

Rayana Beagles combine the names of their owner Diana Connolly and her daughter Rachel Connolly Corbin, at Portersville, Pennsylvania. Rachel is very keen on Junior Showmanship, and both mother and daughter are great Beagle enthusiasts.

The foundation bitch here is Champion Echo Run's Sky Blue Commotion, who shares honors with the dog Champion Touchstone Smokey Bear. Commotion is a granddaughter of Champion Starbuck's Hang 'Em High and of Champion Junior's Foyscroft Wild Kid.

Ch. Echo Runs Sky Blue Commotion, granddaughter of Ch. Starbuck's Hang 'Em High and of Ch. Junior's Foyscroft Wild Kid, a lovely example of the increasingly seen blue color in Beagles. Diana Connolly, owner.

Ch. RD's Rhinestone Cowboy, by Ch. The Whim's Buckeye ex Ch. RD's Highland Heather, No. 5 13" Beagle 1978; No. 10 13" Beagle 1977. This sire of six champions was defeated only once in the show ring. Owned by Ardie Haydon, RD's Beagles.

RD's Beagles

Ardie Haydon acquired the first of her RD's Beagles, located in the Denver area of Colorado, in April of 1965 for her twelve-year-old son, who wanted to show. As it turned out, it was actually for her, as her son's interest diminished but hers continued to grow; and soon she was studying and reading everything she could lay hands on about the breed.

From Marion Jeffers a bitch was leased to breed to Ravenswood Marksman, a product of a half-brother and sister breeding by Champion Page Mill Whirlwind whom Ardie had admired. The puppies arrived during June 1967, and a bitch was kept who matured to become Champion RD's Highland Mist.

"Misty" was bred three times: first to Champion Page Mill Hallmark in 1969, producing Champion RD's Flash Point; then to Champion Jana Raider in July 1971, from which Champion RD's Highland Heather and Champion RD's Joe Cool finished within a week of one another; and then to Champion Jana Buddy in 1973, resulting in Champion RD's Ms. Mignon.

RD's High Plains Drifter, by Ch. Jana Saberano ex Pegaway's Just Plain Jane, is owned by Ardie Haydon.

The next step was to breed Champion RD's Highland Heather to Champion The Whim's Buckeye in February 1975. Champion RD's Rhinestone Cowboy was in their resulting litter, a Top Ten Beagle in 1977 and Number Five in the 13″ Variety in 1978.

Rhinestone Cowboy was bred in July 1977 to a bitch of Wildcreek, Buglair, and Kinsman on the sire's side with a few field champions on her dam's. Ardie purchased a male from this litter, who became Champion RD's High Country Cowboy. Shown just once in the Puppy Class, he was switched into open although hardly past six months of age, and he swept through undefeated to his championship. He went on to obtain thirteen Group placements before being retired at the age of three years. Rhinestone Cowboy was then bred to Champion Hill's Sweet Sue in April 1979, Sue being a daughter of Champion RD's Joe Cool. The Haydons took a bitch from this litter, Pegaway's Just Plain Jane, whom Ardie bred to Champion Jana Soberano for her first litter, keeping a bitch, Champion RD's Spittin Image, for herself. Following this first litter, Jane was bred to Champion Brighton's Playboy II; in that litter there was a male who became Champion RD's Little Deuce Coupe and is now co-owned by Jennifer Harris who is showing him in Junior Showmanship. Ardie has found it great fun watching Jennifer and Deuce work together, as Deuce lives to show and to please Jennifer.

"Misty's" first breeding was to Champion Meadow Creek's Grand Slam, producing one bitch and six males! The bitch is now Champion RD's Lucky Draw, and one of the males has become Champion RD's Aces 'N' Eights, owned by Peggy and Julie Steward. Three more from this litter are major-pointed.

For her second breeding, Champion Misty went to Champion RD's Rhinestone Cowboy. These pups are only four and a half months old now, and they look extremely promising as we write.

As there are not a great many shows in the Denver area, Ardie points out that to make a champion one must do a bit of traveling. Her travels are somewhat limited owing to a job that is very demanding. Nonetheless she has done extremely well with her lovely Beagles, and we wish her lots more of the same in the future.

Ch. RD's Little Deuce Coupe, by Ch. Brighton's Playboy II ex Pegaway's Just Plain Jane, is co-owned by Ardie Haydon and Jennifer Harris.

Ch. Timberlost's Three Way Split, 15″ dog, finished title at Licking River, Oct. 1981. Son of Ch. Starbuck's Hang 'Em High ex Ch. Tarr Hill Triple Tina, handled here by David Hiltz for owners Barb Angus and Barb and Terry Youngberg.

Starbuck

Starbuck Beagles are owned in Plymouth, Michigan, by David and Linda Hiltz, who have the distinction of being the breeders as well as owners of that great multiple Best in Show and Group winner, Champion Starbuck's Hang 'Em High. Always owner-handled, this handsome dog has attained more Bests in Show and Group firsts than any other Beagle so far, and he has, as well, a siring record that is growing almost daily.

Hang 'Em High was born on April 29th 1974, by Champion The Whim's Buckeye ex Champion Elsy's Shooting Star. Through the pages of this book you will find details on many of his Best in Show and Group winning offspring from their owners. He is a dog whose contributions to the breed will never be forgotten.

There have been other great winners in the Starbuck history as well; however, I hesitate to use information which does not come direct from the owner. Currently David Hiltz and John Savory have been showing Champion Starbuck Tradition with considerable success. He is a handsome son of Champion Meadow Crest Grand Slam ex Champion Starbuck Carry Nation who has been doing well in Group and Variety competition. Champion Starbuck Fair Warning, co-owned by David Hiltz and Robin Zieske, has also been staying in the limelight.

Starbuck dogs are behind many of the important current kennels, as our readers will note throughout the pages of this book.

Starcrest

Starcrest Kennels, owned by Robert and Louise Merrill and their daughter at Los Gatos, California, had their beginning when, in 1959, a purebred Beagle puppy was purchased as a hunting dog for Bob Merrill. His pedigree stated him to be a grandson of Champion Kinsman High Jinx ex Thornridge Betty. The puppy became Van Wrinkle, C.D., and he was highly successful in the field.

In 1965 the Merrills had the opportunity to purchase a Beagle bitch from E.G. and Dorothy Johnson. She had been born on Christmas eve, and the Merrills named her Isle Royal's Hokulami (which means "heavenly star" in Hawaiian). She became the first of the Merrill champions.

In 1968, following the move to the hills of Los Gatos, six Afghan Hounds and five adult Beagles, plus a litter by Champion Page Mill Hallmark from Hokulani, added up to "the family." The first homebred champion was a puppy by Tip from Hokulani, Champion Isle Royal's Kanoa. By this time the "dog show bug" was taking over,

Am. and Can. Ch. Ms Mac Muffin of Starcrest, 13″ bitch, by Am. and Can. Ch. Jet's Gremlin of Starcrest ex Page Mill Dawn of Starcrest. Bred by Carroll Diaz and Louise Merrill, owned by R. and L. Merrill, and handled by D. Merrill.

with the Merrills showing both Afghans and Beagles and Bob Merrill having succeeded in helping Tip to his C.D. Diana Merrill was taking both points and a C.D. on her Afghan about then, too.

The first Starcrest champions were Champion Summer Storm of Starcrest and a litter-sister Champion Summer Breeze of Starcrest, by Champion Seven Hills Gold Toke ex Isle Royal's Carousel.

In 1970 a male puppy was purchased who became Starcrest's foundation stud. This was American and Canadian Champion Jet's Gremlin of Starcrest. Bred to a bitch Louise Merrill co-owned with Carroll Gordon Diaz, he sired American, Canadian, and Mexican Champion Pacific Casper of Starcrest, a multiple Group and Specialty winner. The Merrills have his litter-sister, Champion Page Mill Billie J of Starcrest. This breeding was later repeated, and it produced American and Canadian Champion Ms Mac Muffin of Starcrest, Champion The Bonus Jack of Starcrest, Champion Wilkeeps Tutsie of Starcrest, and Champion Page Mill Pamela of Starcrest.

Louise Merrill feels that for them line-breeding has been extremely successful, keeping in mind to outcross occasionally. The latest litter at the kennel is out of Champion BJ's Lorna Doone of Starcrest sired by Page Mill Semi Tuff, a son of Champion Rockaplenty's Wild Oats, thereby bringing in some new blood.

Suntree

With their Suntree Beagles at Albuquerque, New Mexico, Bill and Susan Dooley in their years as breeders have succeeded in producing the very nice number of 25 champions, not counting the many produced by sires or dams from their kennel, which is surely very good going.

The Dooleys' interest in the breed began not in show Beagles but just a family pet. She led, however, to their encountering the dog show world when it was decided to breed her to a local champion.

Next came a puppy purchased through an ad from a reputable kennel. She did not turn out as they had hoped, but in training her the Dooleys met Dick and Lillian Lincoln of the Hollypine Kennels. From them came the Dooleys' first to achieve championship, Champion Hollypines Peter Pan, C.D.

A leased bitch, Champion Blue Chip Molly S, bred to Peter Pan, produced the Dooleys' first homebred to gain the title, the red and white bitch Champion Suntree's Mother Lode, who has been the dam of five champions.

Ch. Suntree's Hocus Pocus, 15″ male, by Ch. The Whim's Buckeye ex Ch. Hollypine's Rage-O Sierra Sun, C.D., bred and owned by Bill and Susan Dooley.

Around this same time, the Dooleys were deeply impressed by a bitch the Lincolns brought back from Michigan, a daughter of Peter Pan's litter-sister bred to Champion Starbuck's Hang 'Em High. They were successful in acquiring this bitch for themselves, and she became Champion Hollypines Rage O Sierra Sun, C.D., the foundation of Suntree Beagles.

Rage was a Group winner and had multiple Group placements. She completed her obedience degree on the same day she first placed in a Group, and she was in the Top Ten Beagles for two years. She produced eleven puppies in three litters before the Dooleys lost her to cancer, and ten of these puppies became champions, including four with multiple Group placements.

Ch. Suntree's Fear No Evil, 15″ male by Ch. The Whim's Rule the Roost ex Ch. Suntree Out of Order, making a good Hound Group placement. Dr. William Houpt, judge. Bred and owned by Bill and Susan Dooley.

Eight of Rage's puppies have in their turn produced champion offspring. One male from her litter sired by Champion The Whim's Buckeye became an eight-champion Top Producer; this was Champion Suntree's Hocus Pocus. His litter-mate, Champion Suntree's Outrage, did a lot of winning and has produced several champions. Rage was twice Best of Opposite Sex to her sire's Best of Breed at the Phoenix Arizona Beagle Club Specialty.

The Dooleys have been breeding Rage's offspring to their first champion Suntree's Mother Lode and to her progeny with very satisfactory results. One lovely bitch was Champion Suntree's Out of Order. Her first pup is Champion Suntree's Fear No Evil, Winners Dog at the 1983 National Beagle Club Specialty, who finished in three shows and has two Group placements at one year of age.

Swan Lake

The Swan Lake Beagles are owned by Sharon L. and Herbert F. Clark and are located at Simpsonville, South Carolina. Sharon is both a breeder and a handler of Beagles, and her success in both fields has been well deserved.

Outstanding among even all these other handsome Beagles is that marvelous little 13″ bitch Champion Swan Lake's Gingersnap, whom Swan Lake bred and Sharon handled and who is the adored favorite of owners Pamela and Betsy Powell. Really a *quality* bitch, "Ginger" has brought glory to all concerned, although she was shown on a limited basis; one of her most important wins was that of Best of Breed, the first time ever at the National for a 13″, when the National Specialty took place at Ravenna, Ohio, in 1981 with Michele Billings as the judge.

Gingersnap's dam, Champion Swan Lake's Big Bad Mama, was Number One among 15″ bitches on the Beagle ratings for 1976. A

The exquisite 13″ bitch Ch. Swan Lake's Ginger Snap, by Ch. Craigwood's Tic Tac ex Ch. Swan Lake's Big Bad Mama, winning Best of Breed at the National Beagle Club Specialty, August 1981, at Ravenna, Ohio. Ginger Snap is the only 13″ Beagle to have won Best in Show at the National.

Ch. Swan Lake's Spirit O'Craigwood, by Ch. Small Talk of Beagle Chase ex Ch. Funny Face of Beagle Chase, a multi Group placing 15″ dog. Bred by Sharon L. and Herbert F. Clark. Owned by Luck Campbell and Sharon Clark.

daughter of Champion Small Talk of Beagle Chase ex Champion Funny Face of Beagle Chase, she, too, was bred by the Clarks.

Another of the important dogs at Swan Lake is Champion Swan Lake's I Declare, by Colegren's Peter of Craigwood from Champion Funny Face of Beagle Chase. A multiple Best of Variety winning bitch, she was Number Two Top Producer in 1982. She was bred and owned by the Clarks and handled by Sharon.

Others of note are Champion Swan Lake's Luke of Craigwood, by Champion Swan Lake's Spirit O'Craigwood ex Champion Craigwood's Shannon, a multiple Group placing 15″ dog owned by Sharon L. Clark and Sandra Campbell and handled by Wade S. Burns; and Champion Keowee Jared of Swan Lake, by Champion Hickorynuts Hangman ex Champion Swan Lake's I Declare, who finished with four majors in 1982. Jared was bred by the Clarks, is handled by Sharon, and is owned by Don and Betty Castle.

Tarr Hill

The Tarr Hill Beagles, owned by Jim and Liz Hendricks, were located at Mingo Junction, Ohio; and although they were not established until the 1970's, they made a very lasting and worthwhile contribution to the breed.

Throughout most of the past decade, Tarr Hill was extremely active, doing considerable well-planned breeding and producing many outstanding dogs. Their foundation was based on Champion Kings Creek Triple Threat through his sons and daughters, with a touch of Page Mill.

One cannot help but feel respect in contemplating the number of champions from Tarr Hill and the quality of these dogs. The impact of Tarr Hill on the breed can be noted in many pedigrees, and an imposing number of these dogs have been the foundation cornerstones for some highly successful younger kennels.

Ch. Tarr Hill's Triple Tina winning the Brood Bitch Class with two of her daughters at the National Beagle Club Specialty 1982, Aldie, Virginia. Winning for Tina, who is owned by Terry and Barb Youngberg, are Ch. Tarr Hills Final Curtain and Ch. Tarr Hills Classical Jazz. Tina was not only top producing Beagle bitch of 1981, but her seven champions finished during that year made her the *Top Producing Bitch of all breeds, Kennel Review* system, plus giving her the record of finished champions for any bitch in any one year. The judge pictured is Mrs. James Edward Clark.

The Tavern's

The Tavern's Beagles were established early in the 1970's when Linda Forrest of Bordentown, New Jersey, purchased the lovely 13" daughter of Champion Rockaplenty's Wild Oats who became Champion The Tavern's Gift From Pam. This was the start of a whole series of winning Beagles for Linda, who has bred trained, owned, and shown an imposing list of winners to their championships in conformation and to important honors in obedience competition.

Soon after "Pammie" had finished, Linda purchased a daughter of Champion Kings Creek Triple Threat and Champion Pixshire's One and Only. This lovely bitch grew up to become Champion Foyscroft Wild Goose, an American, Canadian, and Bermudian champion with Companion Dog Excellent and Utility Dog titles in America, Canada, and Bermuda as well.

Ch. The Tavern's Gift To Pam, a Ch. Rockaplenty's Wild Oats daughter, with owner Linda Forrest. "Pammie" was the first of Linda's many champions, and a foundation bitch for her The Tavern's Beagles.

Am. and Can. Ch. The Tavern's Tom Collins, by Am., Can., Braz. Ch. The Whim's Giant Killer ex Am. and Can. Ch. Foyscroft's Wild Goose, Am., Can., Bda. C.D.X., T.D. One of the splendid Beagles owned by The Tavern Kennels.

Linda purchased a puppy, future Champion The Whim's Giant Killer, from the Musladins to use as an outcross on her bitches. Combined with her Triple Threat bloodlines, the results have been excellent, with several generations of homebred champions bearing The Tavern's as their kennel prefix.

A number of dogs from Linda's kennel also have been sold to fanciers in Brazil, where they have met with very satisfactory success.

Teloca

Teloca Beagles, owned by Mrs. Marie Shuart and located at Miami, Florida, stand among the foremost in the breed today. Mrs. Shuart can well take pride in the fact that her kennels have produced more than 100 champions at the close of 1983, with lots more to follow as her interest and enthusiasm seem to grow each year.

It all began with the purchase, back in the early 1960's, of a well-bred bitch intended to be a family pet. This was Lady Susan of Camelot, C.D., who, two years after joining the Shuart family, was bred and produced a total of four litters for them which included six champions and two Group winners. It was not until she was past her eighth birthday (she lived to be sixteen years old) that Susan earned her obedience C.D. Many of the Teloca champions now sport obedience letters following their names, as Marie Shuart has always enjoyed training her Beagles in this work and they have done well by her there.

13" Ch. Teloca Navan Pruf O'The Puddin, taking Hound Group Fourth. "Pru" finished undefeated at age seven months. Co-owned by Jose M. dePoo, III and Marie Shuart.

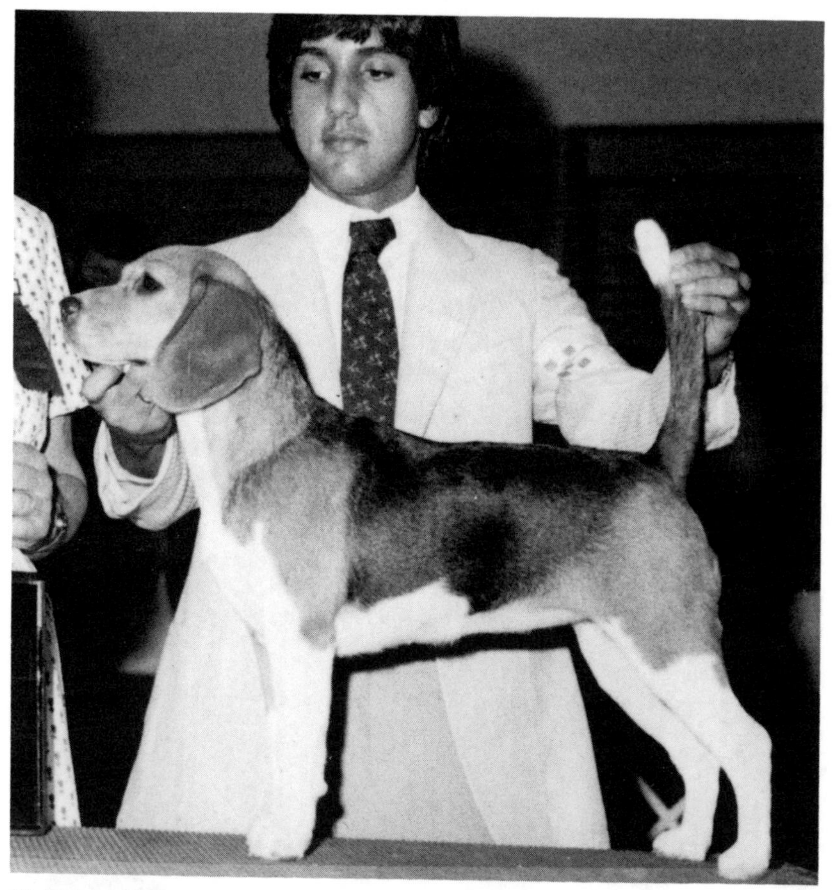

Ch. Teloca Florence of Arabia, C.D., by Ch. Teloca Gettum Up Scout, C.D. ex Ch. Teloca Florence Might'n Gale, 15" bitch, handled by Andres Gil Del Real for owner, Jose M. dePoo, III, Coral Gables, Florida.

Champion's Robin's Red of Honey Hill, C.D., and Champion Robin's Luv, C.D., were born in 1966 and lived to be fifteen years and sixteen years of age respectively. These are the background behind the Teloca winners of today.

Early breedings of the Teloca bitches included Champion Robin's Red of Honey Hill, C.D., to Champion Kings Creek Triple Threat in 1971. Bitches were also sent to California, to some of the famous Whim's stud dogs.

Throughout the 1970's right up until the present the Teloca dogs have been keeping themselves well in the limelight with Group winning and other important victories.

Timberlost

Timberlost Beagles came into being in 1976 after Terry and Barb Youngberg had raised a couple of litters of Miniature Schnauzers and Doberman Pinschers. Their time had been spent prior to then in the sport of obedience competition, but they had reached a plateau where they wanted to show in conformation. After many lengthy discussions and much research it was decided that a Beagle would make the ideal show dog and house pet.

In 1976 they purchased, from Liz Hendricks, a puppy sired by Champion Rockaplenty's Wild Oats from Champion Pixshire Fancy Free. She became Tarr Hill's Li'l Miss Gidget. Gidget never made it in the show ring as she was a bit too tall to be a 13″ and not heavy enough in bone to make it against the big 15″ bitches. So, on the ad-

Ch. Tarr Hill's Triple Tina, 13″ bitch, owned and handled by Barb and Terry Youngberg, is one of the last daughters of Ch. Kings Creek Triple Threat and was from Ch. Lo Na's Gaiety. Tina became the *Top Producing Dam of all breeds* in 1981 with some outstanding Beagles to her credit. Owned by Timberlost Kennels, Barb and Terry Youngberg, Rochester, PA.

Ch. Tarr Hill Final Curtain, daughter of Top Producing Dam of 1981, takes Best of Variety over six Specials and on to win the Hound Group at Western Reserve, K.C. in 1981. Owned by Barb Youngberg, Timberlost Beagles. Final Curtain is by Ch. Pixshire's The Entertainer ex Ch. Tarr Hill's Triple Tina, both Triple Threat children.

vice of Liz and Jim Hendricks, Gidget was retired and another puppy, who grew up to become Champion Tarr Hill Triple Tina, replaced her in the ring. Tina was by Champion Kings Creek Triple Threat from Champion Lo Na's Gaity, and she finished at ten months of age in just one month of showing.

Meanwhile, Li'l Miss Gidget was bred to Champion Pixshire's Triple Sec and produced four black-tri-puppies, two of which became Timberlost's first two homebreds. A pay-back puppy went back to Tarr Hill Kennels, hence that name as a prefix. Champion Tarr Hill's Barbie Sec Spot and Champion Timberlost's Beau Jangles were Gidget's "claim to fame," and Beau Jangles won a Group placement back in Timberlost's early days.

Tina, for her first litter, was bred to Champion Pixshire's The Entertainer, producing a litter of three black-tri bitches. Two of these went back to Tarr Hill Kennels as part of the breeding arrangements, again the reason some of the Timberlost "kids" carry the Tarr Hill prefix. Through time, one of the bitches that had gone to Tarr Hill changed hands in ownership, bringing future Champion Tarr Hill's Final Curtain back to Timberlost, while Champion Tarr Hill's Classical Jazz is co-owned by Liz Hendricks and Julie Fulkerson. Final Curtain brought great pleasure to the Youngbergs when, shortly after gaining her title, she won the Hound Group at the Western Reserve Kennel Club Dog Show in 1981. Jazz, heavily campaigned by Sharon Clark for Liz Hendricks and Julie Fulkerson, had many Group placements and wins prior to retiring for breeding.

In 1980 Champion Tarr Hill's Triple Tina was bred to Champion Starbuck's Hang 'Em High owned by David and Linda Hiltz. This produced five black-tris, all of which finished during the following year.

Tina was accidentally poisoned in her kennel through a neighborhood mishap; and although she recovered from renal failure, her breeding days were over. "Now all the great bitches that she produced for us will have to be the ones to carry on," to quote Barb Youngberg. Thanks to Tina, Timberlost Kennels became the owner of the Top Producing Dam of 1981. Also, according to the National Beagle Club annual awards, Tina is a record-breaking dam, and she also took the Brood Bitch Class at the National at Aldie under Mrs. James Edward Clark.

Timmee's

Timmee's Beagles, owned by Valerie D. Mee at Smithtown, New York, had its beginning in the breed with the purchase of an eight-week-old tricolored Beagle puppy who grew up to become Champion Ledgewood Timmee's Suzie Q, C.D. Although never thrilled at showing in the conformation or junior showmanship rings, she did distinguish herself in the obedience ring where she received her C.D. degree in three straight shows with scores in the 190's. From there she went into show business. Her trainability and huge appetite were the only requirements for magazine and television commercials, and hers is a well-known face in *Vogue* and as salesman for products made by Gaines. She was even flown to California with her owner for one job. Suzie Q is a daughter of Champion Jo Mar's Repeat Performance

Ch. Timmee's Joyeux Noel, owner-handled by Valerie T. Mee, taking Best of Winners at Tuxedo Park Kennel Club 1982.

from Champion Pickadilly Prima Donna (Champion Rockaplenty's Wild Oats ex Champion Pickadilly Triplicate).

Suzie was bred to Champion Londonderry's Aladdin and the litter was so nice that it was repeated the following year. This litter produced two champions, Timmee's Joyous Noel who finished at eight and a half months and Champion Timmee's Christmas Spirit who finished shortly thereafter. "Holly" (Joyous Noel) has followed in her mother's vocational footsteps by starting to appear in commercials also.

Validay

Validay Beagles are owned by Mrs. Valentine Davies of California and Mrs. Mildred Loew of New York, the kennels located on the Pacific Coast.

The first of these Beagles was purchased by Mrs. Davies and her late husband as a replacement for a dearly loved Pointer they had recently lost at the time. The four-month-old pick of litter puppy with whom they fell in love could be purchased only with the understanding that he be shown. This seemed like fun to Mr. and Mrs. Davies, and so he was brought home to become, in quite short order, Champion Jubilee Gay Cinders, sired by Champion Gay Blade of Vi-Jo ex a daughter of Champion Craftsman of Walnut Hall. In 1952 Mr. and Mrs. Davies purchased the bitch who became Champion Validay First Lady, the first of the many champions carrying this now very famous prefix. She, too, was by Champion Gay Blade of Vi-Jo, her dam Champion Del Ray Delight.

First Lady was a 13″ bitch, Cinders a 15″ dog.

1953 was the year in which Validay's first litter was born, three puppies which included the future champions Validay Artful and Validay Artist, both 13″.

During the following few years, Mr. and Mrs. Davies finished Champions Validay Commodore, Courtley, Fashion, and Heather.

In 1959 the next of Validay's truly important winners finished to become Champion Validay Jupiter, who was by Thelma Brown's noted dog, Champion Opus Tubac Trumpeter from Champion Validay Courtly. A multiple Group winner, this dog also sired an impressive number of champions. His untimely loss at only seven years of age was a sad one.

Mr. Davies passed away in 1962, following which Mrs. Davies went off on a trip while her cousin, Mildred Loew, came from New York to oversee the kennel. Almost inevitably Mildred fell in love with the Beagles and by the time Mrs. Davies had returned, her cousin wanted partnership, thus creating Validay East and Validay West. Upon her return East, Mrs. Loew took along the last puppy sired by Cinders, winning Best of Variety with him at Westminster in 1965, and he also attained Group firsts and placements on both coasts.

Some of the bloodlines added over the years to Validay have included Champion Del Ray Queen of Spades, dam of seven champions, who traces back to Clint Callahan's Sogo dogs, so prominent in the East; and Champion Herold's Prince Charles, a popular and consis-

Validay Beagles' Ch. Herold's Prince Charles, noted winner of the 1960's, owned by Validay Beagles and handled by Robert S. Forsyth.

Ch. Junior's Fun Machine, 12 ¾", by Ch. Jana Pageant ex Ch. J.'s Bonnie V of Beagle Chase, has produced 12 champions in three litters, continuing her mother's tradition, as Bonnie is Top Beagle Dam of all time. Dick Johnson, breeder-owner, Junior's Beagles, Miami, Florida.

tent Group dog, who also came from the East, having been purchased from Ed Johnson's Fancy Beagles. Champion Bento's Corky, sired by Champion Validay Happy Feller, through his dam brought Florida's Hi Spirit lines to the kennel. Validay bitches have been bred out to Sun Valley, Kinsman, and Johjean lines and to Murray's Merry Man, a short-time resident of the kennel.

Currently, Validay has been winning well with the 13" dog Champion Junior's Fun Machine, purchased from Dick Johnson in Florida. Another 13" dog which carried the Validay banner proudly a few years back was Champion Validay Neiland's Amos.

Champion Validay Happy Feller was sold to England in the 1970's, to the Appletons, where he distinguished himself both in the show ring and as a sire. Validay Beagles are also to be found in Italy, Mexico, and South America.

The Whim's

The Whim's Beagles were begun by Dr. and Mrs. Anton C. Musladin of Los Gatos, California, when Mandy joined their family. She was a baby Beagle from a litter of three belonging to a young intern at the hospital where, in 1959, Dr. Musladin was completing his residency. Despite the fact that Dr. Musladin had two more months to go at the hospital, and Mrs. Musladin was putting in a full 80-hour week with her own practice, Mandy joined the family—an event which we are sure the Musladins have never regretted, as this led to a whole series of exciting developments and the creation of a most successful line of Beagles.

Ch. The Whim's Fuzz Buster, 15″ dog by Ch. The Whim's Buckeye ex Ch. The Whim's Cocked Hat. Bred by Pati Mathews and owned by Jeri Cates, Fuzz Buster is a Specialty and Group winner.

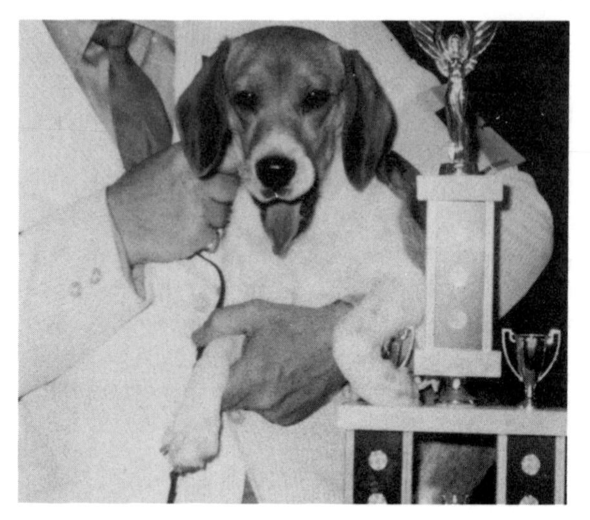

The great Ch. The Whim's Buckeye winning his first Best in Show in 1970 for breeder-owners Dr. and Mrs. A.C. Musladin, Los Gatos, California. This famous 13″ dog is by Ch. Wandering Wind ex The Whim's Firecracker.

Mandy was strictly field type and did not in the least relish her "lonely dog" existence, so she taught her owners the charms of her breed, and it was not long before she was joined by more of them. Mandy lived to be thirteen. She was bred once, to a 13″ dog owned by the Gillettes of Rancho Gabriel Borzoi fame. Through this association the Musladins started attending dog shows and becoming acquainted with the Beagle Fancy.

Page Mill Wildfire, born in 1961, came to live with the Musladins at three months old. When she won a Beagle Specialty, under Thelma Brown, by going straight through from the classes, Tony Musladin promptly became hooked on the "the show thing." Judy took a bit longer; but with Wildfire's first Hound Group in 1963, she, too, was thoroughly inducted into the ranks of "dog show people." Wildfire did all concerned proud, becoming a Top Ten Hound in both 1963 and 1964. Her complete show record was nine Group firsts, 42 placements, and about 80 times Best of Variety. She also won seven of the eight Beagle Specialties in which she competed. Wildfire was a daughter of Champion Wandering Wind ex Champion Oakwood Silky Sue, one of three sisters by Champion Pine Lane Powerhouse.

Bred to Champion Page Mill Trademark in 1965, Wildfire produced The Whim's Firecracker, a 13″ bitch who has taken her place as an outstanding producer and has been highly influential in the progress of the breeding program at The Whim's. On four occasions bred back to Champion Wandering Wind, her grandsire, Firecracker became the dam of seven American champions and a Danish champion, the latter the first Beagle to attain a Best in Show award in Denmark, the Whim's Pilgrim's Progress.

Ch. The Whim's Too Hot to Handle, 13″ dog, winning Best of Variety at the Southern California Beagle Specialty in 1983 at six months. A son of Ch. The Whim's Rule the Roost ex Ch. The Whim's Hot to Trot, this outstanding youngster is handled by breeder Judy Musladin who co-owns him with Robin Zieske.

Among the famed winners produced from Wandering Wind and Firecracker is that great little 13″ dog Champion The Whim's Buckeye, who was Top 13″ Beagle in 1970, Top Beagle, both Varieties, in 1971 and 1972, and Top Hound in 1972. He is the sire of 97 champions, including Ten Best in Show winners, fifteen Group winners, six Specialty Best of Breed winners, and ten Top Producing Beagles.

Fulfilling a long-standing wish of Dr. Musladin's, Champion Wandering Wind joined their family in 1967. In a rather limited stud career, Windy sired 35 champions, and Irene Schlintz has rated him one of the top producers of all time. His influence on the Beagle breed has certainly been widespread and admired!

During the 1970's and early 1980's, dogs owned and/or bred by Tony and Judy Musladin have continued to make history. Champion The Whim's Touch Me Not, a Priscilla Mullins daughter, was Top Beagle, both Varieties, for 1974 and 1975. Champion The Whim's Cock of the Walk, by Buckeye ex Champion The Whim's Chatterbox, is a Specialty and all-breed Best in Show winner and was Top 13″ Beagle in 1976 along with being a Top Producer. Champion The Whim's Tooth Fairy, by Buckeye from Priscilla Mullins, was Top 13″ Beagle for 1979 and 1980. Champion The Whim's Rule the Roost was Top 13″ Beagle of 1981.

Champion The Whim's Priscilla Mullins, full sister to Buckeye, has, like her brother, played a great producing role in the development of The Whim as we know these lovely dogs today.

Whiskey Creek

Whiskey Creek Beagles were established in 1974 when Whiskey Creek's Mint Julep was purchased from Bob Felty. In 1976, two months after whelping Julep's first litter, the owners, Michelle Sager and Tony Castellano, moved to Montville, New Jersey, where they built a kennel, planning to raise Beagles and Dalmatians, in both of which breeds they have since been successfully active.

From Julep's first litter came Whiskey Creek's First Edition, known as "Cricket," who was never shown but who has produced some very nice dogs. She was first bred to Champion The Whim's Buck Stops Here, C.D., who had been purchased as a puppy from Judy Musladin and who became their first champion, finishing quickly, and then going on to earn his C.D. degree. From this litter came the 13″ Champion Whiskey Creek's Chug-A-Lug and the 15″ Champion Whiskey

Ch. The Whim's Buck Stops Here, C.D., going Winners Dog to finish under Gayle Bontecou. Bred by Judy Musladin, owned by Michelle Sager and Tony Castellano.

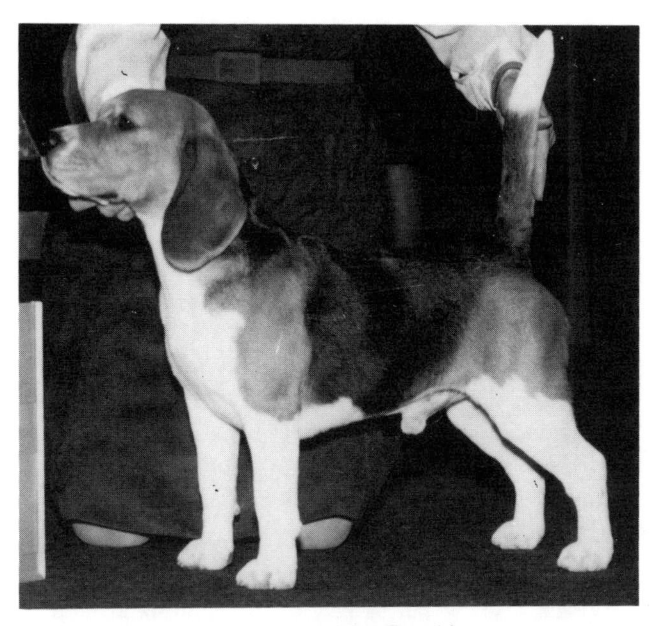

Ch. Whiskey Creek's Racer's Edge, Best of Variety 15″ Beagle at Westminster 1984. Owned and bred by Michelle Sager and Tony Castellano.

Creek's Racer's Edge. The latter has been Whiskey Creek's most successful show dog to date, being a multiple Group winner with numerous other placements who most recently took Best of Variety at the Westminster Kennel Club's 1984 dog show.

Michelle and Tony are also quite proud of the accomplishments of their little 13″ bitch, Champion The Whim's Demon Rum, purchased from the Musladins. Demon finished with three five-point majors, two of them back-to-back at the two shows following the National Specialty in Ravenna, Ohio, in 1981, and she finished later that year by going Best of Winners at the Bay State Specialty.

Unfortunately, all but one of the puppies in Cricket's second litter, sired by Champion The Tavern's Tom Collins, were lost. The remaining puppy, however, grew up to become Champion Whiskey Creek's Tam O'Shanter, who finished at eleven months from the Puppy Class. She is a truly gorgeous bitch, and the plan is to Special her in 1984.

Michelle and Tony are looking forward to a good future with several fine bitches to work with and their two stud dogs, The Buck Stops Here and Racer's Edge. These enthusiastic fanciers are, as we write, in the process of buying some land in New Jersey where they plan to build a new house and kennel.

Chapter 5

Beagles in Hawaii

Recently it was our pleasure to meet a Beagle fancier from Hawaii, back visiting her family on the mainland, and we were delighted to learn from this lady that there is considerable activity there within our breed. She is Karen Merrill, whose visit to see our dogs we thoroughly enjoyed and who is now anticipating a litter by Champion Jo Mar's Repeat Performance from one of her very lovely bitches.

Hawaii has a busy, active Beagle Specialty Club, the Beagle Club of Hawaii, which maintains a full schedule of happenings to interest fanciers of this breed. Meetings are held the first Sunday of each month, and we understand that the A.K.C. has just granted the group permission to hold "B" matches for conformation, obedience, and tracking. The club publishes a very well-presented newsletter, *Hawaiian Beaglers Bay,* and we note sponsors handling classes as one of its activities. President of the club is Jeannie Bromley of Kailua, and the Vice-President is Ann James of Honolulu, with Sarah D. Barder from Kailua the Secretary-Treasurer.

Jeannie Bromley owns the Wilbro Beagles, one of whose dogs, Champion Pin Oaks Heavenly Heather, is the Number One 15″ Beagle in Hawaii, owned in partnership with Gayle C. Ah Nee. The Number One 13″ Beagle in Hawaii is her Champion Barder's Hi Lady Lovin.

Champion Bar Kohav, owned by Martha E. Crosby and bred by Karen M. Merrill, is the first male Beagle ever to have finished his championship in Hawaii. He was born and earned all his points there, defeated only once in point competition and that by his littermate.

Hoku Lele Pono, C.D., T.D., granddam of Mahina, dam of Ch. Bar Kohav, a noted "star" in obedience, bred and owned by Karen Merrill, Pearl City, Hawaii.

Ch. Pin Oaks Heavenly Heather, 15″ dog, by Plain and Fancy's Sir Baron ex Felty's Imogene, was sold by the Ralph Alderfers, Pin Oaks Beagles, to Jeannie Bromley and Gayle C. AhNee in Hawaii.

Chapter 6

Beagles in Australia

Beagles obviously are held in high esteem by Australian dog fanciers, and it is pleasing to hear the enthusiastic comments upon their return home from those who have journeyed there from the United States to judge assignments including the breed.

The biggest difference between the Australian standard for Beagles and the American standard is the fact that a larger hound is preferred in Australia. There, as in England, the standard states that size should be *over* thirteen inches and under *sixteen* inches, entirely eliminating the 13" Variety and permitting an extra inch of height more than Americans do on the largest "legal" members of the breed. There is no size disqualification for Beagles in Australia, and the measurements given are merely termed "desirable."

An event of major importance in the Australian Beagle world was the move to that country of Mrs. Thelma Gray, noted breeder, judge, and author, from England toward the close of the 1970's. Mrs. Gray's English and Australian Champion Rozavel Starlight, who accompanied her (among her other Beagles) in this move, was born in 1973, by Matchmaker of Rozavel from Rozavel Crystal Gift. In England Mrs. Gray had been one of the earliest fanciers to import Beagles from the United States. A 12½" Thornridge Wrinkles daughter, American Champion Rozavel Ritter's Sweet Sue, and her daughter by American Champion Johnson's Fancy King had been among her first purchases from America by Mrs. Gray. She also had brought over, in co-ownership with Mrs. Beck of Letton Kennels, American Champion Renoca's Showman after a successful career in the United States. Her

Am. and Can. Ch. Chardon Yankee Clipper, by Am. and Can. Ch. Chardon Magnific Marathoner ex Can. Ch. Chardon Kronion, is now owned by Bill Vaughan in Brisbane, Australia.

Miss Lesley Funnell, owner of Australia's noted Torbay Beagles, is pictured here with Edward, the son of Am. Ch. Rockaplenty's Wild Oats from a Page Mill bitch whom she imported in whelp to "Tuffy."

most outstanding importation to England from the United States had been English and American Champion Rozavel's Diamond Jerry, purchased from Mr. and Mrs. W. Stanley Elsy of the Pacific Coast. Unquestionably this superb Beagle would never have been permitted to leave our shores had it not been for the fact that, following a brilliant career here as a young dog, he kept right on growing and went oversize, making him exactly right for British standards. His influence on the breed in England was tremendous and we are sure that some of his descendants must have been among the dogs Mrs. Gray brought when she came to Australia.

Considering the length of time that is demanded in quarantine on bringing dogs from overseas to Australia, it is amazing the number who have been imported. To come from the United States, they must first spend six months in British quarantine (which is avoided in dogs going there from the United Kingdom), plus another nine months or so prior to release to their Australian owners. Despite this fact, a few breeders have imported Beagles and have been pleased with the results.

One such breeder is Miss Lesley Funnell, New South Wales, who brought over American Champion Page Mill Oscar, a son of American Champion Jana Nassau of Page Mill from American Champion Page Mill Fly By Night (a Trademark granddaughter) from the Page Mill

Kennels in California during the 1970's. Oscar's litter-sister, Page Mill Lady Luck, who was bred to American Champion Rockaplenty's Wild Oats prior to being shipped was also imported. Three handsome puppies were born in British quarantine; Edward, Charles, and Elizabeth. Charles went to Mrs. Joan Johnson as a stud dog. The other dog and the bitch remained with Miss Funnell. Representing the Champion Kings Creek Triple Threat line through Wild Oats (who also combines with the greatest of the early Page Mills), these brought some of America's most successful producing lines to their new homes.

Two of Australia's most influential and longest established Beagle kennels which have had tremendous impact on the breed there are Bali Hai and Serenata, and since they were so important in Beagle history in Australia, we would like to tell you a bit about them.

Bali Hai was founded by Mrs. Jill Kirk, who purchased her first Beagle in 1958, from the then very prominent Calumet Kennels. At ten months of age this dog, Calumet Scaramouche, became a K.C.C. champion; the title "Australian champion" at that time had not yet been inaugurated.

From the brood bitch Calumet Antoinette and a dog owned by Molly Wormaid, who owned both Beagles and Australian Terriers, came the noted Australian Champion Bali Hai Melody Maid and the

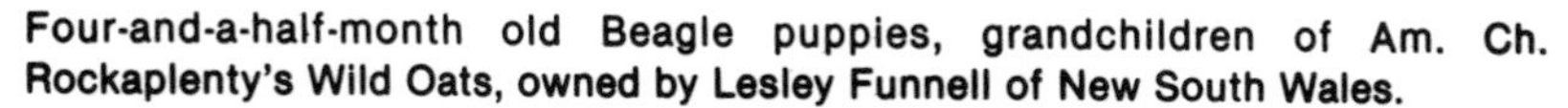

Four-and-a-half-month old Beagle puppies, grandchildren of Am. Ch. Rockaplenty's Wild Oats, owned by Lesley Funnell of New South Wales.

renowned Australian Champion Bali Hai Tiki. These two had Royal Challenge Certificates and Beagle Specialty honors; it is said that Tiki's show record may well still stand as one of the greatest ever attained by a member of the breed in Australia.

The famed American Champion Elsy's King of Diamonds came to Bali Hai in 1966, selected by Jill Kirk during a visit to the United States, when she selected him following his first Group win at six months of age and then personally campaigned him to both American and Canadian championships. On the same trip she also purchased a puppy, Lady Rum Lollypop, who was bred in quarantine to an import from the United Kingdom being held there who became Australian Champion Lees Pennon. The one puppy produced from this litter was future Australian Champion Bali Hai Bacardi Rum, who became an extremely influential sire with many important offspring to his credit.

Champion Elsy's King of Diamonds through his progeny, particularly his daughter, Australian Champion Renorey Miss Muffet, left many exciting and highly successful descendants who have made thrilling records in the show ring and as producers.

Serenata Kennels even preceded Bali Hai, having already been in existence when Bali Hai was founded. Jim and Jessie Wilmot were the owners, who started out by showing a Beagle for a friend. The first of their own was Benbruk Beeswing who gained many Challenge Certificates for them. Next came an imported dog, Champion Stanhurst Ringwood, a Best in Show winner his first time out for them and on frequent future occasions.

Mr. G. Hokin was selling out his imported stock (it was from him that Ringwood had been purchased), so the Wilmots decided to add Champion Truman of Oak Ridges (from the United Kingdom) and Guyzamce Pasty (also from the U.K.) to their rapidly growing Beagle family, along with the Australian-bred bitch, Australian Champion Shrubland Baymore, the latter subsequently giving them their first homebred puppies, sired by Beeswing.

Champion Belview Danny Boy was the Wilmots' especially outstanding dog, who won the Best Dog in Show on eight occasions and did much to gain the interest and admiration of the public for Beagles.

Champions Serenata Beeswing and Serenata Memory were two especially successful winners who followed Danny at this kennel, and Champion Derawawuda Bellmaid was imported from England's Fred Watson with memorable success both as a winner and through her progeny.

Chapter 7

Beagles in Canada

Right at the period when Joan Brearley and I (A.K.N.) were writing *The Wonderful World of Beagles and Beagling,* activity in the breed in Canada was at a low ebb; our inquiries for information of any then active kennels raising Beagles there brought nothing whatsoever in the way of response. This was after the great earlier kennels had become inactive and before many of the present ones had become truly involved. It has been quite different with this book, however, and we are pleased to bring you word of many fine Beagles and active owners from that area.

Briarpatch

Briarpatch Beagles, located at Headingway, Manitoba, a suburb of Winnipeg, are owned by Donna James, a lady who has had an interest in the canine circle for the better part of twenty years, since the mid-1960's.

Beagles especially attracted her attention, the result being that in 1969 she purchased her first two of the breed from the renowned Jacobi bloodlines.

Subsequently she acquired Penbroch Sir Galahad, also from Jacobi background. His show career spanned only a couple of years, but in that time frame he made an unforgettable impact on the breed in Canada.

In 1976, with limited Western Canadian showing, Champion Sir Galahad became Canada's Top Beagle, his wins including a Hound

Can. Ch. Briarpatch Quick As A Bunny, by Can. Ch. Briarpatch Justanuff Oats ex Flixton Carmen Jones, was Canada's No. 2 Beagle while still a puppy in 1982. Owned by Mrs. Donna James, Briarpatch Beagles.

Specialty with a large entry. He rarely lost the breed and had Group placements on 90% of the occasions he was shown. He directly produced over twenty champions, and his offspring produced numerous top Beagles in Canada under the Briarpatch prefix.

Mrs. James, in her breeding program, diversified from the Jacobi lines and sent some of her bitches to American Champion Rockaplenty's Wild Oats. The results from these breedings were very outstanding, among the consistent winners produced having been the dog Canadian Champion Briarpatch Justanuff Oats and the bitch Canadian Champion Briarpatch Miss Jedda James, both consistent win-

Can. Ch. Briarpatch Justanuff Oats, by Am. Ch. Rockaplenty's Wild Oats ex Flixton Briarpatch Brambles, is a consistent winner owned by Mrs. Donna James, Briarpatch Beagles. Mrs. James's daughter, Sue Rempel, is handling.

ners. At least eight additional Canadian champions, and several with titles in the United States, too, were bred by Mrs. James from her Briarpatch bitches and Wild Oats, a combination which did seem to work just right!

Mrs. James has continued very successfully with her breeding program over the years. One example of this is Canadian Champion Briarpatch Quick as a Bunny. As a puppy in 1982, this one became Canada's Number Two Beagle, losing out for the Number One spot by only 22 points.

Donna James's Beagles are proudly handled by her daughter and son-in-law, Jac and Sue Rempel.

Buttonwood

Buttonwood Beagles at Oil Springs, Ontario, are a highly successful kennel owned by Dorothy and Ray Hornbostel, who have been producing and winning with some very handsome dogs.

Although they had grown up with various mixtures of canines over the years, the first purebred owned by the Hornbostels was a Beagle, Brier Run Gentle Storm. Unknown to Dorothy, Ray had done some renovating and painting at Rudy Blanchard's kennels in Sarnia Township. At the time Rudy had five litters of newborn Beagles and offered Ray Hornbostel his pick of the five litters in payment for his work. This seemed like a good deal, and after very careful consideration, "Bonnie," as Gentle Storm was called, was selected. She had been born in May 1970 and was brought home the following September as a wedding anniversary gift. Rudy had shown some very good Beagles over the years, and "Bonnie" was strong in Wal-Dor and Jacobi breeding.

Having received some suggestions and pointers from Rudy Blanchard on how to make the most of a Beagle in the show ring, Ray Hornbostel entered Bonnie, at eight months of age, for the prestigious Sportsmens Dog Show in Toronto. Dorothy Hornbostel can still recall the excitement she felt when her husband and Bonnie returned with the news that Bonnie had been Winners Bitch and Best Puppy!

Bonnie was bred to The Whim's Hucklebuck, the first of the Beagles campaigned by David and Linda Hiltz, producing four puppies in January 1973. One of these was accidentally smothered when Bonnie sat on it, but the others all did very well. One became American and Canadian Champion Buttonwood's Beguiling Bandit, who became an American champion in four shows and a Canadian champion in five, won 30 Bests of Breed, sixteen Group placements, and a Canadian Best in Show, winding up the year second to the Top Beagle in Canada. Then there was American and Canadian Champion Buttonwood's Buckle's Buddy, also an American champion in four shows and a Canadian champion in five, who was Best Puppy in eight out of ten shows and, so far as the Hornbostels have been able to ascertain, was the only Canadian-bred Beagle ever to win the Chicago Beagle Club Specialty, which he did in 1974. The sister, American and Canadian Champion Buttonwood's Fancy Finish, did nearly as well, although her greatest claim to fame came through her sons, American and Canadian Champion Buttonwood's Bold Bomber, an all-breed Best in Show winner and litter-brother American and Cana-

Am. and Can. Ch. Meadow Crest's Top O'The Ninth, 15″ son of Ch. Hickorynuts Hangman ex Am. and Can. Ch. Starbuck's Meadow Song, bred by Annette M. Didier, owned and handled by Ray Hornbostel. "Topper" was ranked No. 3 Beagle in Canada for 1981.

Can. and Am. Ch. Buttonwood's Bold Bomber going Best in Show from the classes at thirteen months of age. Owned by Buttonwood's Beagles, Ray and Dorothy Hornbostel.

dian Champion Buttonwood's Carbon Copy; these two were whelped in June 1975 and sired by Champion The Whim's Buckeye.

Bonnie was bred only three times, but she was a Top Producer in 1975 and 1977, *Kennel Review* System. She was bred to Champion Starbuck's Hang 'Em High in 1975, adding Canadian and American Champion Buttonwood's November Morn, Canadian and American Champion Buttonwood's Domino, and American Champion Buttonwood's Banner High (deceased) to her offspring.

In August 1979 the Hornbostels purchased a male pup from Annette Didier, Meadow Crest's Top O'The Ninth, by Champion Hickorynuts Hangman ex American and Canadian Champion Starbuck's Meadow Song. He became an American and Canadian champion with several Group wins in Canada and is a flashy dog leaving his mark on his offspring. So far "Topper" has been used at stud only six times, yet he already has ten champions to his credit.

Densom

Dennis and Donna Somers, in Ontario, have been leaders of the breed during the 1970's. I shall never forget first seeing Dennis's magnificent dog Champion Wagon Wheels Wisecrack on one of my Canadian judging engagements. What a super Beagle! That he became Number One Beagle in Canada and a widely acclaimed Group and Best in Show dog is very easily understandable.

Breeding stock at Densom Kennels has been based largely on "Crackers" and his progeny (thus the Wagon Wheels line) and "children" of Champion Kings Creek Triple Threat and his son Champion Rockaplenty's Wild Oats. Included among them have been Champion Pixshire's Windfall (a Triple Threat son), Champion Pixshire's K.C. (a Triple Threat granddaughter), and Champion Foyscroft Little Trouble (a Triple Threat daughter), from whom the Somers have bred a whole series of top-flight champions. The Somers's bitches have produced several splendid champions by Wild Oats, and they have developed a very strong line of Beagles combining all of the above.

Two gorgeous Beagles owned by Dennis Somers, Densom Kennels. On the *left*, Mr. Somers with the 13″ bitch Ch. Pixshire's K.C. and on the *right*, Brian Taylor handling the famed Ch. Wagon Wheels Wisecrack, 15″ dog, also owned by Mr. Somers.

Yarra-Belle

Yarra-Belle Beagles, whose foundation sire was American and Canadian Champion The Whim's Sky Rocket, are owned by Gwen Marotte at Surrey, British Columbia.

Gwen being originally from Australia realized the high quality in Beagles to be found there, and so, soon after getting settled in Canada, she imported a bitch from Australia from breeder-judge Jill Wood, who was coming to Canada.

When Jill Wood returned to Australia, she had purchased a dog, the 15″ male from the Elsys, named Elsy's King of Diamonds. Jill Wood stayed in Vancouver for six months while King was campaigned to his American and Canadian championships. It took almost a year for King to reach his new home in Australia owing to the quarantine regulations, but when he did, a bitch was sent back to Gwen by him from Balihi Tamaki, the latter from Thelma Gray's Rozavel Kiwi, who had been originally Top Dog in New Zealand. The bitch which came to Gwen Marotte was not for show, having a broken tail, but she was a glorious brood bitch and together with Sky Rocket

Page Mill Yankee Clipper, by Ch. Rockaplenty's Wild Oats ex Page Mill Flying Night, owned by Gwen Marotte.

Ch. Yarra-Belle's Waltzing Matilda, by Am. and Can. Ch. The Whim's Sky-Rocket ex Bali Hai Brolga (Australian), owned and handled by Gwen Marotte.

produced some marvelous puppies. We understand the combination of the two improved considerably on Beagles on the West Coast of Canada.

Sky Rocket sired more than 25 champions and is to be found today behind most of the Beagles in the British Columbia area. Among his progeny, Yarra-Belle's Skys The Limit, owned by Jane Lloyd Edmonton, was Number One Beagle in 1980, 1981, and 1982.

Now Gwen has introduced Louise Merrill's Starcrest line into her breeding program. This has resulted in Dittrich Estralita Yarra-Belle, 14″, who has passed all of her owner's fondest expectations in the ring. Now she is retired and doing equally well as a brood bitch.

The latest acquisition at Yarra-Belle is a very outstanding dog, American and Canadian Champion Page Mill Yankee Clipper, who is a son of American Champion (and Canadian multiple Best in Show winner) Rockaplenty's Wild Oats. He is working in well with the Yarra-Belle breeding plan, and it is hoped that he will follow in the paw-prints of Sky Rocket, who lived to the splendid age of sixteen and a half and was a solid pleasure to his owner all the way.

Chapter 8

Beagles in South America

Our friends in South America are among the world's most enthusiastic dog fanciers, and Beagles are a breed to have come to particular attention and popularity there.

From the Brazilian area especially there are at least several very excellent breeders of Beagles, such as Mrs. Vera Lucia Costa, who has been actively involved with this breed since the late 1960's.

Mrs. Costa is owner of the Dreamland Beagles, at Sao Paulo. In the beginning she raised Beagles to be used for hunting, but then as she became better acquainted with the breed, she became interested in show Beagles. Her belief grew that a well-balanced Beagle should be a dog capable of working in the field, be a happy companion, and have the conformation of a show dog all within the same package, so to speak.

Today Mrs. Costa points with pride to more than fifty homebred champions produced at Dreamland, including Group winners, a Best in Show dog, and those who have won numerous other honors. Dogs bred in her kennel have gained championship not only in Brazil but also in Uruguay, Paraguay, and Chile, and there are some pointed dogs from there in Argentina.

At present Dreamland Kennels consists of about 30 beautiful and happy Beagles. These include some basic foundation dogs imported to enhance the breeding program, at which they have succeeded admirably. Among them are American and Brazilian Champion R.J.B. Sean, a sire of champions in five countries including the United States. Sean's influence in Brazil is easily noted since he is a Top Producer behind, we understand, some 40 champion progeny.

Mrs. Vera Lucia Costa of Dreamland Beagles in Brazil with her great producing bitch Ch. Lakeview Lois.

Am. and Braz. Ch. Busch's Flash Back of Eljons, multi-Group winner in Brazil with a Reserve Best in Show, Group winner in America is sire of champions in the U.S., Brazil and Chile. Owned by Dreamland Beagles.

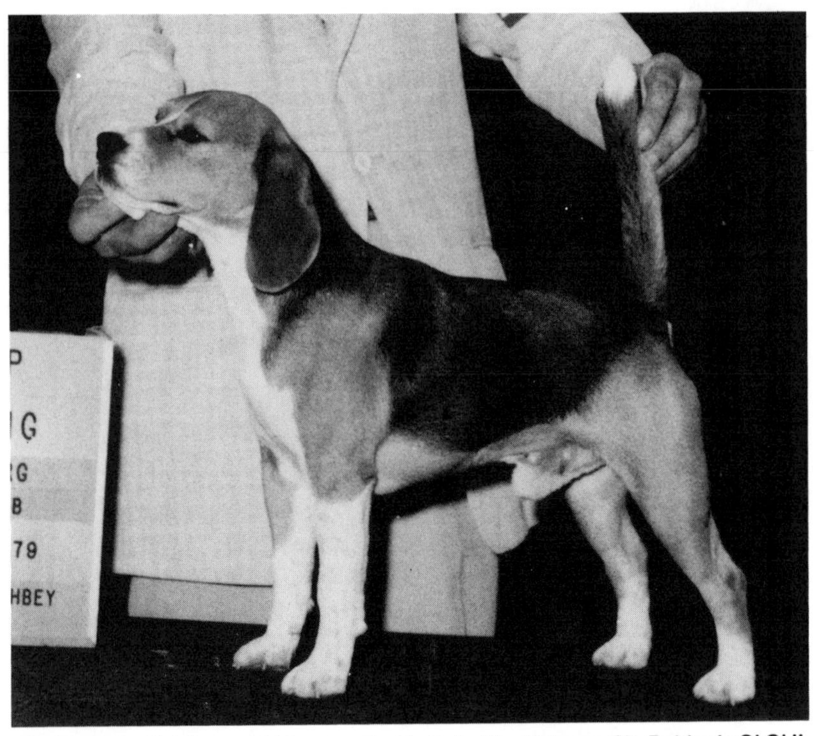

Ch. Pin Oaks Knicks and Chips, by Ch. Pin Oaks Mr. Chips ex Ch. Rubino's Gi Gi II. this 13″ dog, following an exciting career in the United States which included multiple Group placements, many Bests of Variety, and Best 13″ at a Southern New York Beagle Club Specialty was sold to Mr. Eduardo Quinterio in Brazil where "Nicky's" career has successfully continued.

Another of Mrs. Costa's importations is American and Brazilian Champion Pickadilly Wild Card, an especially important dog as he was largely responsible for introducing the bloodlines of his sire, American Champion Rockaplenty's Wild Oats, to Brazilian breeders. Also there is American and Brazilian Champion Busch's Flash Back of Eljon, a sire of, so far, more than twenty champions in three countries including the U.S.A.

American and Brazilian Ledgewood Gunslinger is a sire of great potential, with Group-placing offspring from his first litter with many others of show quality waiting to mature. He, too is a son of Champion Pin Oaks Mr. Chips from a Wild Oats daughter, and he had a good show career in the United States before his departure to Brazil.

The pride and joy at Dreamland Kennels is their ten-year-old bitch, American and Brazilian Champion Keystone Little Bit'Trip, the only daughter of the great Champion Kings Creek Triple Threat in Brazil.

"Bitsy" was from Trippe's last litter. After her purchase, Mrs. Costa sent her back to the United States to complete her championship in this country and to be bred to Trippe's son, Wild Oats. So pleased was Mrs. Costa with the results of this breeding that "Bitsy" returned again to the States to breed to Wild Oats a second time. Mrs. Costa also sent another beautiful bitch, American and Brazilian Champion Lakeview Lois, for breeding to Wild Oats. One of the results of the latter combination is Brazilian Champion Dreamland Wild Fire, 1981 top ranking Beagle, who is owned by Endless Summer Beagles.

Bangor Beagles, owned by Mr. Marcelo Tuck Schneider, is another kennel located at Sao Paulo, where it was started in 1977. With an average of two litters a year, and a bit over fourteen litters bred until early 1984, Bangor has gained national and international recognition as breeders of some of the top Beagles in Brazil.

The first acquisition from the United States was American and Brazilian Champion Pixshire's Come Fly With Me, sired by the Triple Threat son Champion Navan's Triple Trouble Rick. Fly is the

Ch. Chardon Arch Rival, by Am. and Can. Ch. Chardon Kentucky Derby ex Am. and Can. Ch. Chardon Match Point. Owned by Peter Nova, Dominican Republic.

Braz. Grand Ch. Bangor Flying High, by Am. Ch. Pixshire's Stockbroker ex Am. and Braz. Ch. Pixshire's Come Fly With Me, winning Best Puppy in Show, age three-and-a-half months. Bangor Beagles, owners. Sire of 20 Champions in Brazil and Argentina.

Am. and Braz. Ch. Bangor Sir Lancelot was owned by Bangor Beagles, Brazil, sired by Am. & Braz. Ch. The Whim's Cock'n Bull out of Am. and Braz. Ch. Pixshire's Come Fly With Me. He was bred in Brazil and was sent to America to finish. Sire of 15 Champions.

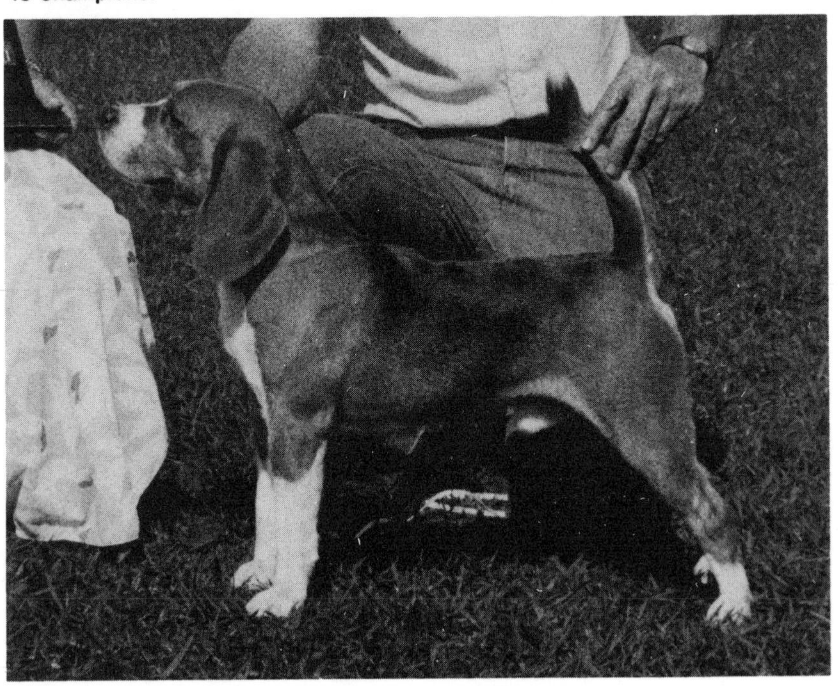

dam of about fifteen champions and a grand champion in Brazil, two champions in Argentina, and one champion each in Uruguay and the United States.

Next came two more bitches, Brazilian Grand Champion Thelson's Barney's Appeal, by American Champion Busch's Nuts To You of Brendon's, who has had a good show career and produced winning progeny; and American, Canadian, and Brazilian Grand Champion The Tavern's Alcoholics Anon, acquired from Mrs. Linda Forrest, who followed her good wins in the U.S. with Number One Beagle and Number Three Hound in Brazil for 1981.

Some other importations from the U.S. to Bangor Kennels include American and Brazilian Champion The Whim's Cock'n Bull, American, Canadian, and Brazilian Champion The Whim's Giant Killer, and the handsome red and white dog American and Brazilian Champion Pickadilly Doctor Sunshine.

Bangor Kennels have the honor to have bred the only Brazilian-bred Beagle to date that has won a championship in the United States: American and Brazilian Grand Champion Bangor Sir Lancelot. Bangor also bred Argentina and Brazilian Grand South American International Champion Bangor Sir Gawain, Top Male Beagle in Brazil 1980, Top Beagle in Argentina for 1980, 1981, and 1982, and Best Hound in 1982, and Brazilian Grand Champion Bangor Sir Galahad.

Dr. and Mrs. Eduardo Quinteiro, Alkahest Kennels, brought Champion Pickadilly Wild Card (now owned by Mrs. Costa) and American and Brazilian Champion Briarwood's Marcea (a Wild Oats daughter) to Brazil originally. Also they imported that marvelous little 13″ dog American Champion Pin Oaks Knicks and Chips who was an instant success in Brazil where he has made some excellent wins and produced well.

Dr. Jose Luiz Pinto Moreira visited American Beagle kennels a few years ago. He is the importer of still another Wild Oats son, American and Brazilian Champion Lockshire's Prime Minister.

Mr. Ramon Podesta, noted all-breed judge, is the owner of the American-bred Chilean, Brazilian, and American Champion Lokavi's Flash Back, by Wild Oats, who has won well in many countries.

Daniel Buckwald of Sao Paulo, whose mother is a famed Boxer breeder, has a special liking for Beagles and is the owner of American and Brazilian Champion Lanewae's Wildfire, a Wild Oats son whom he had the pleasure of personally finishing in the United States prior to taking the dog home with him in the early 1980's.

Chapter 9

Standards for the Beagle

The standard of the breed, to which one hears and reads such frequent reference, is the guide to those interested in breeding, showing, judging, or just becoming acquainted with a specific breed of dog. It outlines, in minute detail, each and every feature of that breed, both in physical characteristics and in temperament; it accurately describes the dog from whisker to tail, creating a clear impression of what is to be considered correct or incorrect, the features comprising "breed type" and the probable temperament and behavior patterns of typical members of that breed.

The standard is the guide for breeders endeavoring to produce dogs of quality for the show ring. It is the tool with which judges evaluate the dogs, enabling them to reach their decision in the show ring. It draws for new fanciers a word picture of what breeders and judges are seeking, of what the features of an ideal dog should be in accordance with the requirements of his breed. It tells what is beautiful, what adds up to correct type, and what makes this dog able to fulfill the purposes for which the breed was developed. It is the result of many patient hours spent in study and research and in dedicated work by fanciers with the best interests of this breed at heart.

Our present standards represent the best of the earlier ones, combined occasionally with modernization or clarification to make for better understanding. They are carefully thought-out tools for the protection of the breed, and our understanding of what they are telling us is essential for our own true appreciation of these dogs!

Birchwood Haretigger, by Ch. Briarpatch Birchwood Guy (Best in Show winning son of Wild Oats) ex Meado-Glo Birchwood's Windee, bred by Linda Lindberg, Cook, Minnesota, whelped in March 1981.

Ch. Plain and Fancy's Clover winning Best of Breed at the National Beagle Club Specialty in 1978. Owner-handled by Ray Scott.

American Standard

HEAD: The skull should be fairly long, slightly domed at occiput, with cranium broad and full. *Ears*—Ears set on moderately low, long, reaching when drawn out nearly, if not quite, to the end of the nose; fine in texture, fairly broad—with almost entire absence of erectile power—setting close to the head, with the forward edge slightly inturning to the cheek—rounded at tip. *Eyes*—Eyes large, set well apart—soft and houndlike—expression gentle and pleading; of a brown or hazel color. *Muzzle*—Muzzle of medium length—straight and square-cut—the stop moderately defined. *Jaws*—Level. Lips free from flews; nostrils large and open. *Defects*—A very flat skull, narrow across the top; excess of dome, eyes small, sharp and terrierlike, or prominent and protruding; muzzle long, snipy or cut away decidedly below the eyes, or very short. Roman-nosed, or upturned, giving a dish-face expression. Ears short, set on high or with a tendency to rise above the point of origin.

BODY: *Neck and Throat*—Neck rising free and light from the shoulders strong in substance yet not loaded, of medium length. The throat clean and free from folds of skin; a slight wrinkle below the angle of the jaw, however, may be allowable. *Defects*—A thick, short, cloddy neck carried on a line with the top of the shoulders. Throat showing dewlap and folds of skin to a degree termed "throatiness."

SHOULDERS AND CHEST: Shoulders sloping—clean, muscular, not heavy or loaded—conveying the idea of freedom of action with activity and strength. Chest deep and broad, but not broad enough to interfere with the free play of the shoulders. *Defects*—Straight, upright shoulders. Chest disproportionately wide or with lack of depth.

BACK, LOIN AND RIBS: Back short, muscular and strong. Loin broad and slightly arched, and the ribs well sprung, giving abundance of lung room. *Defects*—Very long or swayed or roached back. Flat, narrow loin. Flat ribs.

FORELEGS AND FEET: *Forelegs*—Straight, with plenty of bone in proportion to size of the hound. Pasterns short and straight. *Feet*—Close, round and firm. Pad full and hard. *Defects*—Out at elbows. Knees knuckled over forward, or bent backward. Forelegs crooked or Dachshundlike. Feet long, open or spreading.

HIPS, THIGHS, HIND LEGS AND FEET: Hips and thighs strong and well muscled, giving abundance of propelling power. Stifles strong and well let down. Hocks firm, symmetrical and moderately bent. Feet close and firm. *Defects*—Cowhocks, or straight hocks. Lack of muscle and propelling power. Open feet.

TAIL: Set moderately high; carried gaily, but not turned forward over the back; with slight curve; short as compared with the size of the hound; with brush. *Defects*—A long tail. Teapot curve or inclined forward from the root. Rat tail with absence of brush.

COAT: A close, hard, hound coat of medium length. *Defects*—A short, thin coat, or of a soft quality.

COLOR: Any true hound color.

GENERAL APPEARANCE: A miniature Foxhound, solid and big for his inches, with the wear-and-tear look of the hound that can last in the chase and follow his quarry to the death.

Ch. Teloca Lacoste Color Me Red, 15", by Ch. Navan's Triple Trouble Rick ex Ch. Teloca Brown Eyes Susan, C.D., winning High in Trial with score of 196 at the National Beagle Club Specialty in 1983. Judge Judy Brown. "Fred" handled and owned by Marie Shuart, Miami, Florida.

Ch. Foyscroft I'm Triple Tiger, son of Ch. Kings Creek Triple Threat ex Ch. Pixshire One and Only, winning 15″ Beagles at the Southern New York Beagle Specialty in conjunction with Westchester Kennel Club in 1979. Marcia Foy, breeder-owner-handler.

SCALE OF POINTS

HEAD			RUNNING GEAR		
Skull	5		Forelegs	10	
Ears	10		Hips, thighs and hind legs	10	
Eyes	5		Feet	10	30
Muzzle	5	25	Coat	5	
			Stern	5	10
BODY					
Neck	5				
Chest and shoulders	15				
Back, loin and ribs	15	35	TOTAL	100	

VARIETIES; There shall be two varieties:

Thirteen Inch—which shall be for hounds not exceeding 13 inches in height.

Fifteen Inch—which shall be for hounds over 13 but not exceeding 15 inches in height.

DISQUALIFICATION: Any hound measuring more than 15 inches shall be disqualified.

British Standard

CHARACTERISTICS: A merry hound whose essential function is to hunt, primarily hare, by following a scent. Bold with great activity, stamina and determination. Alert, intelligent and of even temperament.

GENERAL APPEARANCE: A sturdy and compactly-built hound, conveying the impression of quality without coarseness.

HEAD AND SKULL: Head fair length, powerful in the dog without being coarse, but finer in the bitch; free from frown and excessive wrinkle. Skull slightly domed, moderately wide, with indication of peak. Stop well defined and dividing length between occiput and top of nose as equally as possible. Muzzle not snipy, lips reasonably well flewed. Nose broad and nostrils well expanded; preferably black, but less pigmentation permissible in the lighter coloured hounds.

EYES: Dark brown or hazel, fairly large, not deep set or bulgy, set well apart and with a mild appealing expression.

EARS: Long with round tip, reaching nearly to end of nose when drawn out. Set on low, fine in texture and hanging gracefully close to cheek.

MOUTH: Teeth strongly developed. Upper incisors just overlapping and touching outer surface of lower incisors to form scissor bite.
NECK: Sufficiently long to enable hound to come down easily to scent, slightly arched and showing a little dewlap.
FOREQUARTERS: Shoulder clean and sloping. Forelegs straight and upright, well under the hound, of good substance, strong, hard and round in bone. Not tapering off to feet. Pasterns short. Elbows firm, turning neither in nor out. Height to elbow about half the hound's height to withers.
BODY: Topline straight and level. Chest well let down to below elbow. Ribs well sprung and extending well back. Short between the couplings. Loins powerful and supple, without excessive tuck-up.
HINDQUARTERS: Very muscular about the thighs. Stifles well bent. Hocks firm, well let down and parallel to each other.
FEET: Tight and firm. Well knuckled up and strongly padded. Not hare-footed. Nails short.
GAIT: Back level and no roll. Stride free, long-reaching and straight without high action. Hind legs showing drive. Should not move close behind or paddle or plait in front.
TAIL: Sturdy and moderate length. Set on high and carried gaily but not curled over back or inclined forward from the root. Well covered with hair, especially on underside.
COAT: Short, dense and weatherproof.
COLOUR: Any recognised hound colour other than liver. Tip of stern white.
WEIGHT AND SIZE: It is desirable that height from ground to withers should neither exceed 40cm (16″) nor fall below 33cm (13″).

Interpretation of the Standard

Elsewhere in this book we have described the Beagle's characteristics as the word is generally accepted by the layman. To the purebred dog enthusiast, however, this word takes on a far broader meaning; for, in "dog show talk" breed character is "type," the reference being to the composite of features which make a breed

Overleaf: →
Ch. Buglair The President, Best Opposite Sex to Best in Specialty at the National Beagle Club Specialty in conjunction with Santa Barbara under Lt. Col. Wallace Pede. This dog, then owned by the Garland Moores of Atwater, California, has since been exported to Denmark.

CENTRAL WYOMING
KENNEL CLUB
BEST IN SHOW

distinctive, setting it apart from all other breeds and making it easily recognizable as such. To be strong in breed character, or of "good type," a dog must adhere closely not only in personality and behavior but also in conformation and appearance to what is described in the standard as ideal.

The Beagle is a member of that group of dogs classified as scent hounds, *i.e.,* those who hunt with their noses rather than by sight. They were developed specifically for work in the fields trailing rabbits and perhaps other small game and for working with a huntsman on foot rather than on horseback. This type of work takes stamina, sturdiness, and good lasting power; and since the huntsman on foot wishes a dog with whom he can keep up, excessive speed is not desired. Thus a "typey" Beagle, or one strong in breed character, is a solidly built rugged little dog. To make him so, he needs all the bone possible as consistent with his size, powerful musculation (but never excessive, which would bring about exactly the opposite to the desired effect), and a strong, short-coupled well-ribbed body.

The Beagle must be equipped to travel considerable mileage in the course of a day in the field without fatigue (which will result if he is overdone or over muscled), and he should do so gaily with obvious pleasure as proven by his musical voice and gaily carried tail. Thus the conformation of forelegs and hindquarters comes in for great attention. Bones of the forelegs must be round and strong with firm pasterns and tight toughly padded feet. The shoulders should be nicely angulated, or sloping, enabling the dog to reach out well rather than move with short, choppy steps, since the latter is a fatiguing mode of travel. And the elbows should be carried close to the body and firm, providing no necessity for the dog to toe either in or out, the latter referred to as "paddling!"

The hindquarters provide the dog's propelling power and so, in the Beagle, must be broad at the hips, muscular, with good bend of stifle, hocks set low to the ground. In coordination with the correctly sloping shoulders, the hindquarters should angle nicely at stifle and hock, providing smooth-flexing and powerful drive from behind. A dog with

← **Overleaf:**
Am. and Can. Ch. Merry Song's Uppity Ms, by Am. and Can. Ch. Starbuck's Hang 'Em High ex Ch. Sun Valley's Honey Bear, in just four shows in 1982 won 2 Specialties: an all breed Best in Show and a Hound Group First. Owned by Drs. Nancy Bergstrom and Mara M. Baun, Elkhorn, Neb.

these requisites should hold up cheerfully through the longest hunting day!

The back for greatest efficiency should be short, firm, muscular, broad, and level, with the loin broad and slightly arched. A long, soft, sagging back or one that is "roached," denotes weakness, interferes with smoothness of action, and causes the dog to tire more readily. The ribs must be broad and deep, providing ample space for the well-developed lungs so essential in a Beagle.

The Beagle's neck should be long, strong, clean, and muscular, never short and thick, and it should be slightly arched on top. This length of neck brings the Beagle's nose easily to the ground for following the trail, while its strength must be equal to raising a hare from the ground. Scenting being his "stock in trade," the Beagle must have well-developed nasal equipment, with large open nostrils for freedom in breathing.

The Beagle's head, putting its stamp of special individuality upon the breed, is one of great beauty. It should be strong and fairly long, with the skull and foreface proportioned to each other. The skull is slightly domed at the occiput, with the cranium broad and full. The muzzle is square-cut, about equalling length of the skull, its strength carrying right to the tip which must never look sharply pointed or "snipey." The large, dark eyes are set well apart, with their soft and lovely expression, and the long, velvety, fairly low-set ears framing the face make the Beagle one of the most appealing and irresistible dogs to be found anywhere in the canine world. Bite should preferably be scissors.

The stern (tail) also comes in for its share of attention, putting the finishing touch on the little dog's appearance of strength and solidarity. Although the standard places emphasis on a correct tail being short, it should be remembered that this does not mean *excessively* so. A Beagle's tail should always end at a point higher than his head when the latter is carried at attention, and the importance of a good white tip on this tail should never be overlooked as this should be visible as the dog works his way through the field, permitting his master to keep track of him more readily. The tail should be thick in circumference, never scrawny or lacking fair substance. Set high, carried upright, it boasts a fair amount of brush all enhanced by the white "flag" tip.

There is no official color preference for Beagles. The majority of people seem to prefer the tricolor consisting of black saddle, tan head, and white markings. During the past ten years (early 1970's onward),

Busch's Razzle Dazzle (Ch. Busch's Ranch Hand ex Ch. Busch's Windyroc Libra) and Ch. Busch's Jigger of Gin (Ch. Busch's Gin Rickey ex Ch. Carter's Dymen Foxfyne). Bred and owned by Wm. and Cecile Busch, Cape Girardeau, Mo.

Opposite page: *(Top)* Ch. The Whim's Demon Rum, 13″ bitch going Best of Variety under judge Paula Hartinger. Owned by Michelle Sager and Tony Castellabo, bred by Judy Musladin. *(Bottom)* Navan's Kountry Sassie Cassie, 13″, going Best of Winners shown by breeder-owner Nancy Vanstrum. Ch. Teloca Patches Littl' Dickens going Best of Variety, owned by Wade S. Burns, handled by Marie Shuart. Dickens, a Group winner, was Best of Variety at Westminster 1984. Here with judge Barbara Heller at St. Petersburg, 1984.

BEST OF
VARIETY
SPRINGFIELD
KENNEL CLUB
1981
ASHBEY II

BEST OF BREED
OR VARIETY
ST PETERSBURG
DOG FANCIERS ASSN
JANUARY 1984
PHOTO BY Graham

A gorgeous head-study of Eng. Ch. Too Darn Hot for Tragband, owned by Andrew Brace, Uckfield, East Sussex. Daughter of Eng. and Am. Ch. Graadtre's Hot Pursuit of Rossut, she was Top Winning Beagle Bitch in England for 1983 and completed her title two days after reaching one year's age.

however, there has been a widespread general acceptance of the reds (called respectively "red and white," "golden," and "lemon") which has brought many lovely specimens of this color combination into the limelight. There are, in fact, several kennels at least trying to breed them in preference to tris, and they are seen now with impressive frequency in the winners circle at leading dog shows.

Also "blue tris" seem to be a new up-and-coming color. These dogs have a tri-pattern, some a very deep slate blue, tan, and white (with the tan and white having a bluish cast) and the slate color itself so dark that in some lights it appears more black than blue on the saddle . Some are a paler blue, a very obviously blue blanket on a tri, again with tan and white having bluish cast.

Also, but with less frequency, chocolate tris and chocolate and whites are now being seen.

On black tris and the red-yellow-golden colors, a dark eye is expected. On the blues and chocolates, however, it is almost genetically impossible to expect this, and a blue to gray eye in the blues and a yellowish cast in the chocolates is expected.

Black pigmentation in the black tris and reds or goldens is expected, except that allowance is made for "winter nose," a paling, or change in color, of the nose leather which sometimes occurs temporarily in winter months. In the blues, the pigmentation will most likely lean toward a slate coloring, while in the chocolates, brown will be seen.

Beagles come in two sizes: under 13″ and 13″ to 15″, those within each range being referred to respectively as "13″ Beagles" and "15″ Beagles," although the actual exact size of an individual dog may not be right on the line. The height of a Beagle is measured with a wicket made especially for this purpose, and the measurement is made with the wicket from the withers (highest point of the shoulder) to the ground, the dog standing in natural position. A height of over 15″ constitutes a disqualification. A height of over 13″ means that the dog must in the future be shown in the "under 15″ classification."

The British standard differs from the American standard in regard to height. According to the British standard, the "desirable" height of a Beagle is a minimum of 13″ tall at the withers but no taller than 16″. In Great Britain, Beagles are not regarded as having two varieties.

If you are evaluating a Beagle from the standpoint of a show dog, never overlook the importance of overall balance, for no matter how excellent in one or more individual features the dog may be, unless his general conformation presents a balanced picture, he will be seriously handicapped in bench competition. To be sure, there are some judges who may place the importance of certain individual features over the complete picture, but to the respected judges who are admired for their capability, it is the total dog that counts, and in order to make the grade under them, the overall quality, depicting breed character and type, must be there.

Although he is a capable working hound, the Beagle in no way lacks elegance and style. He travels gaily, reminding us constantly that he is, indeed, the "merry little Beagle." He is a dog of quality, intelligence, and charm. To a person appreciating the finest in canine beauty, a Beagle of good conformation and type is a striking dog indeed. And to the layman whose eye for purebred dogs may be entirely untrained, the Beagle also is a dog who attracts and excites admiration. A truly pretty dog, with his bright, attractive colorings. A no-nonsense dog, built for field work but still the perfect member of your home and family. An object of pride in ownership because of his good looks, his intelligence, his proficiency at his job, his ability in the obedience world, and his diversity. An adoring and adorable companion. And a dog to bring you pleasure in the show ring or at home. That, indeed, is the Beagle!

A proud moment for the progeny of Ch. Rockaplenty's Wild Oats was this one, at Westminster 1980, when his son, 15″ Ch. Bedlam Tiger Talk, bred and owned by Mandy Cronin and handled by Heck Rice; and his daughter, Ch. Hollyhox Pinky's Wild Laurel, 13″ bred by Mary Sease, co-owner with Eddie Dzuik who is handling her, gained *both* Bests of Variety at this prestigious show under judge Mrs. Potter Wear. Wild Oats is a son of Ch. Kings Creek Triple Threat ex Ch. Page Mill Call Girl.

BEST OF
BREED OR VARIETY
WESTMINSTER
KENNEL CLUB
1980
GILBERT PHOTO

Chapter 10

Versatility of the Beagle

To us it is amazing that so many people are of the opinion that the Beagle is only "a good rabbit dog," thinking of him as a purely outdoors creature who lives just to chase rabbit trails over the countryside! This could not possibly be further from the truth; although he is excellent for this type of work and has earned well the designation "rabbit dog," this is only one small side of his talents and personality. The actual truth is that the Beagle is as near as one can come to a perfect all-around dog who fits in beautifully to any situation.

The versatility of the Beagle seems almost endless when one has become thoroughly acquainted with the breed. Hardy dogs, they love and thrive on "Beagling," working with you through the longest day in the field, never losing their eagerness and excitement as they find and pursue each new scent, their happy voices confirming their exhilaration at its discovery. Beagles also enjoy accompanying you outdoors, and those of us not inclined toward hunting can also take pleasure in just hiking over the countryside and watching the joy with which a Beagle accompanies his master through the great outdoors.

The Beagle is an ideal dog for children, combining smallness of size with sturdiness. Even a very young child is entirely safe and in no danger of being accidentally hurt in the company of a Beagle, as these little dogs are not of a size to knock a youngster over in play or to be too rough with him. On the other side of the coin, the sturdiness of a Beagle makes him better able to cope with young children and the roughness with which they sometimes play, which is not quite true of many other breeds his size, with lighter build and finer bone, who can be and frequently are seriously injured by children's thoughtlessness. Understand, please, that children should be taught with a Beagle, as with any other pet, to treat their dog kindly and with gentleness; but should the child be rougher than is realized upon occasion, a Beagle is far better able to "take it" than many other breeds of small dog may be and is therefore less liable to suffer serious injury.

Am., Can., and Mex. Ch. The Whim's Rain On Your Parade, by Ch. The Whim's Cock of The Walk ex Ch. The Whim's Ten Ton Tessie, is enjoying a favorite toy. Bred by Mrs. A.C. Musladin and owned by Kitten Rodwell, Long Beach, California.

Overleaf: →
Our favorite "A.J." photo! Ch. Jo Mar's Repeat Performance persuading a ringsider that she really wants to share her sandwich with him. One of the nice things about Beagles is that seldom, if ever, are they picky feeders!

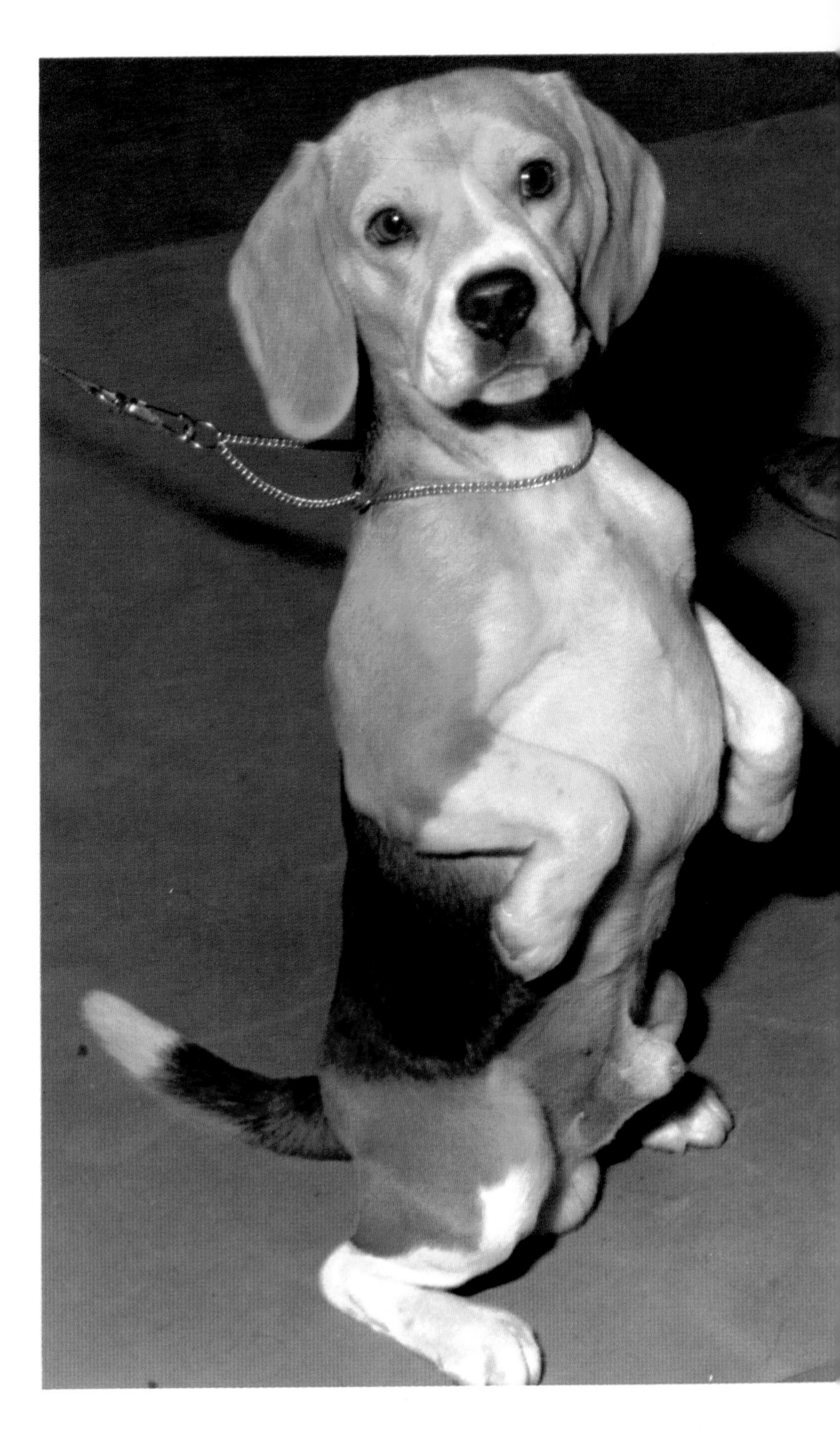

The Beagle's size combined with his hardiness and good appetite make him an easy dog to own, and he adapts well to any type of living conditions whether city, suburban, or country. He possesses all the true "dogginess" of the larger breeds, yet can fit in happily in the smallest apartment or on a farm or estate. He is amenable, good natured, loving and non-destructive once mature (puppies are puppies, and a young Beagle is no exception where youthful mischief is concerned, but he soon outgrows these tendencies as he matures). As for his appetite, it makes having him around a joy and his daily care a cinch as there is no necessity for plying him with "appetite teasers" which can be such a trial with many breeds. You will sigh with delight watching your Beagle's pleasure in his daily rations, the only problem being to resist the temptation to overfeed, as the amount of his food must be watched carefully to prevent his becoming overweight. If you have ever owned a "finicky" dog to feed, you will really appreciate the ease of satisfying a Beagle's taste! Should your Beagle lose interest in his food, run, don't walk, to the veterinarian, as this is a certain indication that something is seriously wrong.

Just as a Beagle enjoys his work in the field, so does he enjoy life as a household pet. Should your nature be more inclined toward inside activities than outdoor ones, your Beagle will be quite happy sharing your home, and you will find him a thoroughly satisfactory house dog basking in the comforts thus provided. It is a fallacy that Beagles must do endless daily mileage in order to keep fit. A Beagle will prosper with exactly the same amount of exercise as any other smallish dog; and free run of your house or apartment, plus the trips outdoors routine to all responsible dog owners, definitely are all that is required. Actually, in many cases this may add up to more regular mileage than the field Beagle averages, for let us not forget that when he is not running the trail, the hunting dog is largely kept in small pens or cages with little opportunity to more than barely stretch his legs. So if you have hesitated about owning a Beagle due to the thought that you could not provide field work for him, no longer allow that to deter you, as it really will not present a problem. If you can accommodate a dog at all, you can accommodate a Beagle; and you will find that his supervised exercise period on lead or in his fenced yard will provide

← **Overleaf:**
Head study of Ch. Brantwood's Desperado owned by Anita Tillman.

Tommy Lisano, Pasadena, Texas, with Cad-Mar's Luck Charm owned by his mother and dad, Rosalie and Jim Lisano, Cad-Mar Kennels.

him with fun for you to share, as even under those circumstances his sensitive nose finds much to excite and please him.

Never forget that it is the Beagle's nature to follow trails and that if you allow him to run free, there is a risk of his wandering away. Considering, however, that no dog should be permitted to roam the outdoors unprotected by either fence or lead or his master's presence, this is a problem that faces owners of *all* breeds. It is the height of irresponsibility not to protect one's pets from cars and dognappers, and people not planning to do so should refrain from dog ownership.

As a watchdog, the Beagle is alert, efficient, and forbidding, the latter due to his deep, throaty hound voice which would seem to indicate a far larger dog on guard.

Beagles make a splendid breed for people interested in showing dogs, for here is a breed that even an amateur can learn to condition, present, and handle well, with no need for the expenses of professional grooming or professional handling. For both conformation competition and for Junior Showmanship, a Beagle is easy to work with, making the showing of Beagles a rewarding family hobby. Beagles excel at obedience and tracking, too, if those facets of competition interest you. In fact, whatever it may be that you require of a dog, you will find the Beagle ready, willing, and able to provide for you admirably.

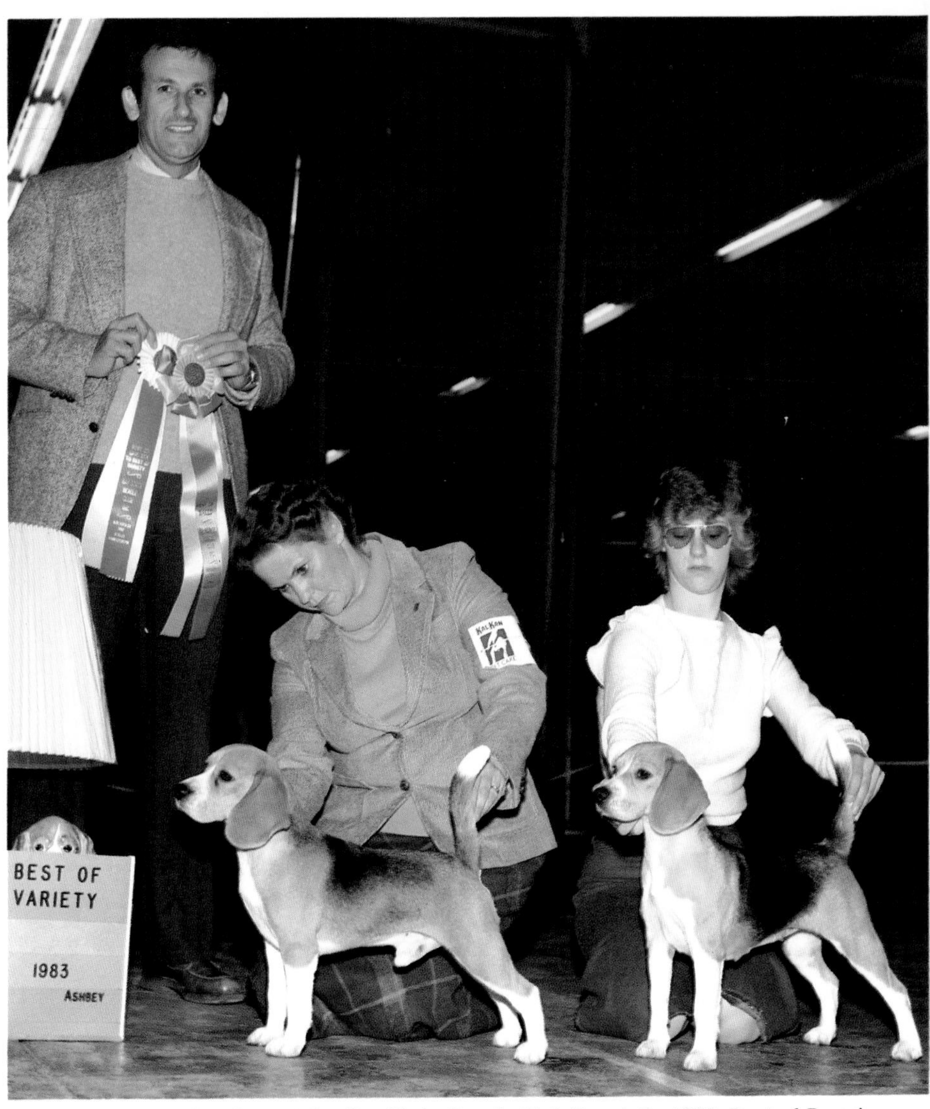

Father and daughter at the Bay State Beagle Club Specialty 1983. Best of Breed, Ch. Chrisette's Macho Man, owned by Anthony Attalla, handled by Phyllis Wright, bred by Sandy Robichaud. Best 15″ Variety and Best of Opposite Sex to Best of Breed, Ch. Junior's Tess of Chrisette, by Macho Man ex Ch. Junior's Fun Machine, owned by Chrisette Beagles and handled by Nannette Robichaud. The judge, Dr. Robert Indeglia.

Opposite page: *(Top)* John D. White, Jr., owner-handling his famous 13″ bitch, Ch. Colegren Sonnet of Briarwood, to a Group First under judge Anna Katherine Nicholas on the way to Best in Show at Lancaster K. C. Bred by Mrs. William Coleman of Colegren, "Mouse" is a multiple Group and Best in Show winner. *(Bottom)* Ralph Alderfer with Ch. Pin Oaks Mello Maverick, son of Ch. Rockaplenty's Wild Oats ex Ch. Herthside Lovely Talisman, winning Group Second under Mrs. Augustus Riggs at Catonsville, 1982. Pin Oaks Kennels, J. Ralph and Helga Alderfer, Souderton, Pa.

HOUND
GROUP
GROUP
PLACING
CATONSVILLE
KENNEL CLUB
1982

Chapter 11

The Purchase of Your Beagle

Careful consideration should be given to what breed of dog you wish to own prior to your purchase of one. If several breeds are attractive to you, and you are undecided which you prefer, learn all you can about the characteristics of each before making your decision. As you do so, you are thus preparing yourself to make an intelligent choice; and this is very important when buying a dog who will be, with reasonable luck, a member of your household for at least a dozen years or more. Obviously since you are reading this book, you have decided on the breed—so now all that remains is to make a good choice.

It is never wise to just rush out and buy the first cute puppy who catches your eye. Whether you wish a dog to show, one with whom to compete in obedience, or one as a family dog purely for his (or her) companionship, the more time and thought you invest as you plan the purchase, the more likely you are to meet with complete satisfaction. The background and early care behind your pet will reflect in the dog's future health and temperament. Even if you are planning the purchase purely as a pet, with no thoughts of showing or breeding in the dog's or puppy's future, it is essential that if the dog is to enjoy a trouble-free future you assure yourself of a healthy, properly raised puppy or adult from sturdy, well-bred stock.

Throughout the pages of this book you will find the names and locations of many well-known and well-established kennels in various areas. Another source of information is the American Kennel Club (51 Madison Avenue, New York, NY 10010) from whom you can obtain a

Greg Eaton with a friend. Son of Nadine Eaton, Waldorf, Maryland, with a Daisyrun puppy.

list of recognized breeders in the vicinity of your home. If you plan to have your dog campaigned by a professional handler, by all means let the handler help you locate and select a good dog. Through their numerous clients, handlers have access to a variety of interesting show prospects; and the usual arrangement is that the handler re-sells the dog to you for what his cost has been, with the agreement that the dog be campaigned for you by him throughout the dog's career. We most strongly recommend that prospective purchasers follow these suggestions, as you thus will be better able to locate and select a satisfactory puppy or dog.

Your first step in searching for your puppy is to make appointments at kennels specializing in the chosen breed, where you can visit and inspect the dogs, both those available for sale and the kennel's basic breeding stock. You are looking for an active, sturdy puppy with bright eyes and intelligent expression and who is friendly and alert; avoid puppies who are hyperactive, dull, or listless. The coat should be clean and thick, with no sign of parasites. The premises on which he was raised should look (and smell) clean and be tidy, making it ob-

Ray Scott owner-handling Ch. Kamelot's Queen Bee to Best in Show. A 13″ daughter of Ch. Rockaplenty's Wild Oats ex Ch. Kamelot's Bumble Bee, ''Polly'' was No. 1 among 13″ Beagles in the U.S. for 1982.

Ch. Holmehill's Maximum, by Ch. Pin Oaks Ruffles N Ridges ex Pin Oaks Dolly, has been a consistent Eastern winner during the early 1980's for Dr. George Roedell and his son Jeff Roedell who is handling.

vious that the puppies and their surroundings are in capable hands. Should the kennels featuring the breed you intend owning be sparse in your area or not have what you consider attractive, do not hesitate to contact others at a distance and purchase from them if they seem better able to supply a puppy or dog who will please you *so long as it is a recognized breeding kennel of that breed.* Shipping dogs is a regular practice nowadays, with comparatively few problems when one considers the number of dogs shipped each year. A reputable, well-known breeder wants the customer to be satisfied; thus he will represent the puppy fairly. Should you not be pleased with the puppy upon arrival, a breeder such as we have described will almost certainly permit its return. A conscientious breeder takes real interest and concern in the welfare of the dogs he or she causes to be brought into the world. Such a breeder also is proud of a reputation for integrity. Thus on two counts, for the sake of the dog's future and the breeder's reputation, to such a person a *satisfied* customer takes precedence over a sale at any cost.

If your puppy is to be a pet or "family dog," we feel the earlier the age at which it joins your household the better. Puppies are weaned and ready to start out on their own, under the care of a sensible new owner, at about six weeks old; and if you take a young one, it is often easier to train it to the routine of your household and your requirements of it than is the case with an older dog which, even though still a puppy technically, may have already started habits you will find difficult to change. The younger puppy is usually less costly, too, as it stands to reason the breeder will not have as much expense invested in it. Obviously, a puppy that has been raised to five or six months old represents more in care and cash expenditure on the breeder's part than one sold earlier and therefore should be and generally is priced accordingly.

There is an enormous amount of truth in the statement that "bargain" puppies seldom turn out to be that. A "cheap" puppy, cheaply raised purely for sale and profit, can and often does lead to great heartbreak including problems and veterinarian's bills which can add up to many times the initial cost of a properly reared dog. On the other hand, just because a puppy is expensive does not assure one that is healthy and well reared. We know of numerous cases where unscrupulous dealers have sold for several hundred dollars puppies that were sickly, in poor condition, and such poor specimens that the breed of which they were supposedly members was barely recognizable. So one cannot always judge a puppy by price alone. Common sense must guide a prospective purchaser, plus the selection of a *reliable,* well-

Nylabone® is available in various sizes suitable to different ages and breeds of dogs. Your Beagle will enjoy either meat- or chocolate-flavored Nylabone.

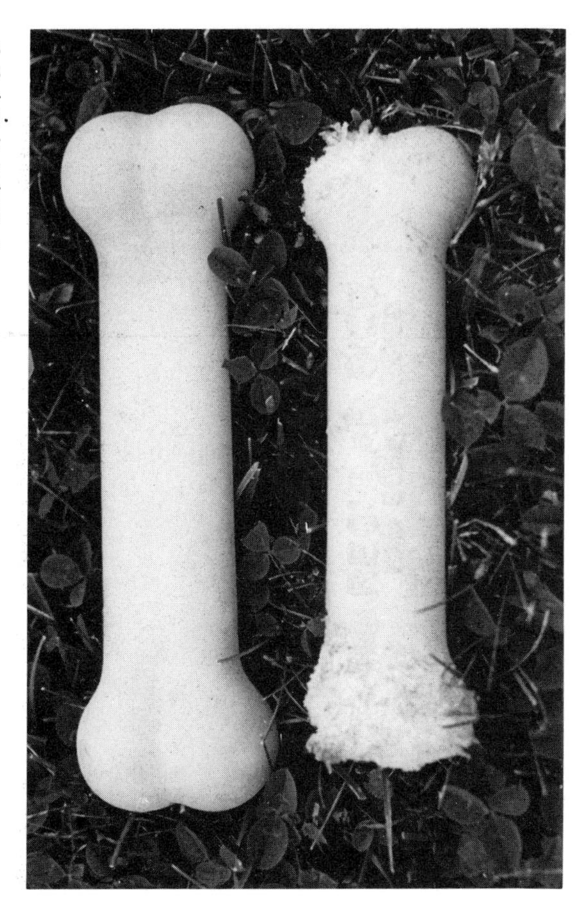

recommended dealer whom you know to have well-satisfied customers or, best of all, a specialized breeder. You will probably find the fairest pricing at the kennel of a breeder. Such a person, experienced with the breed in general and with his or her own stock in particular, through extensive association with these dogs has watched enough of them mature to have obviously learned to assess quite accurately each puppy's potential—something impossible where such background is non-existent.

One more word on the subject of pets. Bitches make a fine choice for this purpose as they are usually quieter and more gentle than the

Overleaf: →
Ch. The Whim's Cock of the Walk, 13″ dog by Ch. The Whim's Buckeye ex Ch. The Whim's Chatterbox. Top 13″ Beagle in 1976, he is a Specialty and all-breed Best in Show winner; a multiple Group winner, and a Top Producer. Handled by Marvin Cates for breeder-owner Mrs. A. C. Musladin, Los Gatos, California.

A future Lightninridge "star"! One of the puppies at Vic Lopez's kennel, Katonah, New York.

males, easier to house train, more affectionate, and less inclined to roam. If you do select a bitch and have no intention of breeding or showing her, by all means have her spayed, for your sake and for hers. The advantages to the owner of a spayed bitch include avoiding the nuisance of "in season" periods which normally occur twice yearly, with the accompanying eager canine swains haunting your premises in an effort to get close to your female, plus the unavoidable messiness and spotting of furniture and rugs at this time, which can be annoying if she is a household companion in the habit of sharing your sofa or bed. As for the spayed bitch, she benefits as she grows older because this simple operation almost entirely eliminates the possibility of breast cancer ever occurring. We personally believe that all bitches should eventually be spayed—even those used for show or breeding when their careers are ended—in order that they may enjoy a happier, healthier old age. Please take note, however, that a bitch who has been spayed (or an altered dog) *cannot be shown at American Kennel Club Dog shows once this operation has been performed.* Be certain that you are *not* interested in showing her before taking this step.

Also in selecting a pet, never underestimate the advantages of an older dog, perhaps a retired show dog or a bitch no longer needed for breeding, who may be available quite reasonably priced by a breeder anxious to place such a dog in a loving home. These dogs are settled and can be a delight to own, as they make wonderful companions, especially in a household of adults where raising a puppy can sometimes be a trial.

Everything we have said about careful selection of your pet puppy and its place of purchase applies, but with many further considerations, when you plan to buy a show dog or foundation stock for a future breeding program. Now is the time for an in-depth study of the breed, starting with every word and every illustration in this book and all others you can find written on the subject. The standard of the breed now has become your guide, and you must learn not only the words but also how to interpret them and how they are applicable in actual dogs before you are ready to make an intelligent selection of a show dog.

If you are thinking in terms of a dog to show, obviously you must have learned about dog shows and must be in the habit of attending them. This is fine, but now your activity in this direction should be increased, with your attending every single dog show within a reasonable distance from your home. Much can be learned about a breed at ringside at these events. Talk with the breeders who are exhibiting. Study the dogs they are showing. Watch the judging with concentration, noting each decision made and attempt to follow the reasoning by which the judge has reached it. Note carefully the attributes of the dogs who win and, for your later use, the manner in which each is presented. Close your ears to the ringside know-it-alls, usually novice owners of only a dog or two and very new to the fancy, who have only derogatory remarks to make about all that is taking place unless they happen to win. This is the type of exhibitor who "comes and goes" through the fancy and whose interest is usually of very short duration owing to lack of knowledge and dissatisfaction caused by the failure to recognize the need to learn. You, as a fancier who we hope will last and enjoy our sport over many future years, should develop independent thinking at this stage; you should learn to draw your own conclusions about the merits, or lack of them, seen before you in the ring and thus, sharpen your own judgment in preparation for choosing wisely and well.

Note carefully which breeders campaign winning dogs, not just an occasional isolated good one but consistent, homebred winners. It is from one of these people that you should select your own future "star."

If you are located in an area where dog shows take place only occasionally or where there are long travel distances involved, you will need to find another testing ground for your ability to select a worthy show dog. Possibly, there are some representative kennels raising this breed within a reasonable distance. If so, by all means ask permission of the owners to visit the kennels and do so when permission is granted. You may not necessarily buy then and there, as they may not have available what you are seeking that very day, but you will be able to see the type of dog being raised there and to discuss the dogs with the breeder. Every time you do this, you add to your knowledge. Should one of these kennels have dogs which especially appeal to you, perhaps you could reserve a show-prospect puppy from a coming litter. This is frequently done, and it is often worth waiting for a puppy, unless you have seen a dog with which you are truly greatly impressed and which is immediately available.

We have already discussed the purchase of a pet puppy. Obviously this same approach applies in a far greater degree when the purchase involved is a future show dog. The only place at which to purchase a show prospect is from a breeder who raises show-type stock; otherwise, you are almost certainly doomed to disappointment as the puppy

An informal snapshot of the beautiful Eng. Ch. Too Darn Hot for Tragband. This daughter of Eng. and Am. Ch. Graadtree's Hot Pursuit of Rossut is owned by Andrew Brace, Uckfield, East Sussex.

Opposite page: *(Top)* Bedlam Beagles' 5-couple pack at Bryn Mawr Hound Show. Mandy Cronin, M.B., Monroe, Virginia. *(Bottom)* Eng. and Am. Ch. Graadtrees Hot Pursuit of Rossut is Top Winning Beagle in England and 2nd Top Winning Dog All Breeds for 1983! 24 Challenge Certificates, 22 Bests of Breed, 3 Bests in Show, a Reserve Best in Show, and 10 Groups. Owned by Mrs. Catherine Sutton, Rossut Kennels, College Town, Camberley.

Puppies by Gozell Luque ex Mistylaw Lydia (daughter of Mistylaw Helter Skelter), several of which will soon be shown by Mr. and Mrs. J.U. Whyte, Howwood, Renfrewshire, England.

matures. Show and breeding kennels obviously cannot keep all of their fine young stock. An active breeder-exhibitor is, therefore, happy to place promising youngsters in the hands of people also interested in showing and winning with them, doing so at a fair price according to the quality and prospects of the dog involved. Here again, if no kennel in your immediate area has what you are seeking, do not hesitate to contact top breeders in other areas and to buy at long distance. Ask for pictures, pedigrees, and a complete description. Heed the breeder's advice and recommendations, after truthfully telling exactly what your expectations are for the dog you purchase. Do you want something with which to win just a few ribbons now and then? Do you want a dog who can complete his championship? Are you thinking of the real "big time" (*i.e.,* seriously campaigning with Best of Breed, Group wins, and possibly even Best in Show as your eventual goal)? Consider it all carefully in advance; then honestly discuss your plans with the breeder. You will be better satisfied with the results if you do this, as the breeder is then in the best position to help you choose the dog who is most likely to come through for you. A breeder selling a show dog is just as anxious as the buyer for the dog to succeed, and the breeder will represent the dog to you with truth and honesty. Also, this type of breeder does not lose interest the moment the sale has been made but when necessary will be right there ready to assist you with beneficial advice and suggestions based on years of experience.

As you make inquiries of at least several kennels, keep in mind that show-prospect puppies are less expensive than mature show dogs, the latter often costing close to four figures, and sometimes more. The reason for this is that, with a puppy, there is always an element of chance, the possibility of its developing unexpected faults as it matures or failing to develop the excellence and quality that earlier had seemed probable. There definitely is a risk factor in buying a show-prospect puppy. Sometimes all goes well, but occasionally the swan becomes an ugly duckling. Reflect on this as you consider available puppies and young adults. It just might be a good idea to go with a more mature, though more costly, dog if one you like is available.

When you buy a mature show dog, "what you see is what you get"; and it is not likely to change beyond coat and condition which are dependent on your care. Also advantageous for a novice owner is the fact that a mature dog of show quality almost certainly will have received show ring training and probably match show experience, which will make your earliest handling ventures far easier.

Frequently it is possible to purchase a beautiful dog who has completed championship but who, owing to similarity in bloodlines, is not needed for the breeder's future program. Here you have the opportunity of owning a champion, usually in the two- to five-year-old range, which you can enjoy campaigning as a "special" (for Best of Breed competition) and which will be a settled, handsome dog for you and your family to enjoy with pride.

If you are planning foundation for a future kennel, concentrate on acquiring one or two really superior bitches. These need not necessari-

Overleaf: →

Ch. Starbuck's Fair Warning, by Ch. Meadow Crest Grand Slam ex Ch. Starbuck's Carry Nation. A two-time Best in Show winner, this 15" bitch was No. 2 (15") Beagle in 1982 and No. 1 Beagle *both varieties* in 1983. Breeders, David and Linda Hiltz. Owner-handler, Mrs. Robin Zieske, Cambridge, Minn. Co-owner David Hiltz.

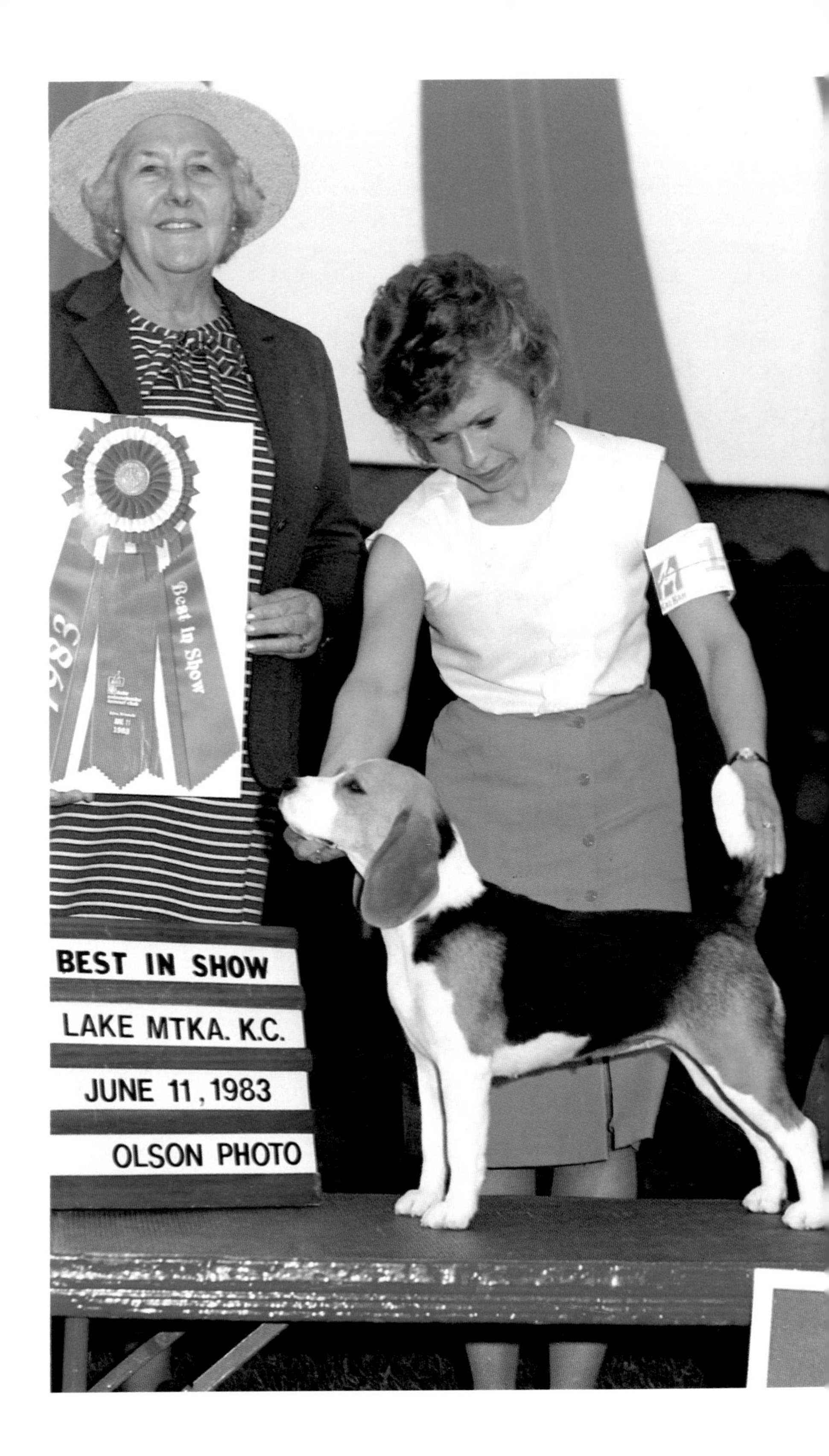
1983
Best In Show
BEST IN SHOW
LAKE MTKA. K.C.
JUNE 11, 1983
OLSON PHOTO

DEL MONTE
KENNEL CLUB INC

ly be top show-quality, but they should represent your breed's finest producing bloodlines from a strain noted for producing quality, generation after generation. A proven matron who is already the dam of show-type puppies is, of course, the ideal selection; but these are usually difficult to obtain, no one being anxious to part with so valuable an asset. You just might strike it lucky, though, in which case you are off to a flying start. If you cannot find such a matron available,

Ch. Junior's Foyscroft Wild Kid taking a Group placement. Kid is a son of Ch. Rockaplenty's Wild Oats ex Ch. Bonnie V of Beagle Chase. Owner-handled by Marcia Foy.

← **Overleaf:**
Ch. Page Mill On The Road Again, the current Special from Page Mill Kennels, is having a highly successful career for owner Carroll G. Diaz, Page Mill Kennels, Los Gatos, California.

select a young bitch of finest background from top producing lines who is herself of decent type, free of obvious faults, and of good quality.

Great attention should be paid to the pedigree of the bitch from whom you intend to breed. If not already known to you, try to see the sire and dam. It is generally agreed that someone starting with a breed should concentrate on a fine collection of top-flight bitches and raise a few litters from these before considering keeping one's own stud dog. The practice of buying a stud and then breeding everything you own or acquire to that dog does not always work out well. It is better to take advantage of the many noted sires who are available to be used at stud, who represent all of the leading strains, and in each case carefully to select the one who in type and pedigree seems most compatible to each of your bitches, at least for your first several litters.

To summarize, if you want a "family dog" as a companion, it is best to buy it young and raise it to the habits of your household. If you are buying a show dog, the more mature it is, the more certain you can be of its future beauty. If you are buying foundation stock for a kennel, then bitches are better, but they must be from the finest *producing* bloodlines.

When you buy a pure-bred dog that you are told is eligible for registration with the American Kennel Club, you are entitled to receive from the seller an application form which will enable you to register your dog. If the seller cannot give you the application form you should demand and receive an identification of your dog consisting of the name of the breed, the registered names and numbers of the sire and dam, the name of the breeder, and your dog's date of birth. If the litter of which your dog is a part is already recorded with the American Kennel Club, then the litter number is sufficient identification.

Do not be misled by promises of papers at some later date. Demand a registration application form or proper identification as described above. If neither is supplied, do not buy the dog. So warns the American Kennel Club, and this is especially important in the purchase of show or breeding stock.

Overleaf: →

Ch. The Whim's Tooth Fairy, 13″ dog by Ch. The Whim's Buckeye ex Ch. The Whim's Priscilla Mullins, bred and owned by Mrs. A. C. Musladin. The Nation's Top 13″ Beagle 1979 and 1980. Handled by Jeri Cates.

Chapter 12

The Care of Your Beagle Puppy

Preparing for Your Puppy's Arrival

The moment you decide to be the new owner of a puppy is not one second too soon to start planning for the puppy's arrival in your home. Both the new family member and you will find the transition period easier if your home is geared in advance for the arrival.

The first things to be prepared are a bed for the puppy and a place where you can pen him up for rest periods. We are firm believers that every dog should have a crate of its own from the very beginning, so that he will come to know and love it as his special place where he is safe and happy. It is an ideal arrangement, for when you want him to be free, the crate stays open. At other times you can securely latch it and know that the pup is safely out of mischief. If you travel with him, his crate comes along in the car; and, of course, in travelling by plane there is no alternative but to have a carrier for the dog. If you show your dog, you will want him upon occasion to be in a crate a good deal of the day. So from every consideration, a crate is a very sensible and sound investment in your puppy's future safety and happiness and for your own peace of mind.

The crates we recommend are the wooden ones with removable side panels, which are ideal for cold weather (with the panels in place to keep out drafts) and in hot weather (with the panels removed to allow

← **Overleaf:**
The great Canadian winner, Ch. Wagon Wheels Wisecrack, top Beagle in Canada of all time. Brian Taylor handling for Densom Beagles, Dennis Somers, Ontario.

better air circulation). Wire crates are all right in the summer, but they give no protection from cold or drafts. We intensely dislike aluminum crates due to the manner in which aluminum reflects surrounding temperatures. If it is cold, so is the metal of the crate; if it is hot, the crate becomes burning hot. For this reason I consider aluminum crates neither comfortable nor safe.

When you choose the puppy's crate, be certain that it is roomy enough not to become outgrown. The crate should have sufficient height so the dog can stand up in it as a mature dog and sufficient area so that he can stretch out full length when relaxed. When the puppy is young, first give him shredded newspaper as a bed; the papers can be replaced with a mat or turkish towels when the dog is older. Carpet remnants are great for the bottom of the crate, as they are inexpensive and in case of accidents can be quite easily replaced. As the dog matures and is past the chewing age, a pillow or blanket in the crate is an appreciated comfort.

Sharing importance with the crate is a safe area in which the puppy can exercise and play. If you are an apartment dweller, a baby's play-pen for a toy dog or a young puppy works out well; for a larger breed or older puppy use a portable exercise pen which you can then use later when traveling with your dog or for dog shows. If you have a yard, an area where he can be outside in safety should be fenced in prior to the dog's arrival at your home. This area does not need to be huge, but it does need to be made safe and secure. If you are in a suburban area where there are close neighbors, stockade fencing works out best as then the neighbors are less aware of the dog and the dog cannot see and bark at everything passing by. If you are out in the country where no problems with neighbors are likely to occur, then regular chain-link fencing is fine. For added precaution in both cases, use a row of concrete blocks or railroad ties inside against the entire bottom of the fence; this precludes or at least considerably lessens the chances of your dog digging his way out.

Be advised that if yours is a single dog, it is very unlikely that it will get sufficient exercise just sitting in the fenced area, which is what

Overleaf: →

Best of Breed at the National Beagle Club Specialty in 1983. Ch. Alpha Centauri's Crackerjack, by Ch. Johjean Popcorn (Ch. Johjean Jubilation T Cornball ex Ch. Colegren's Billy) from Gradam's Good Time Girl (Ch. Alpha Centauri's Lil Abner ex Ch. Alpha Centauri's Lariat), 15″ dog bred and owned by Robert and Judy Goodfellow, Mason, Illinois. Handled by Bob Goodfellow.

NATIONAL BEAGLE CLUB
1887

This promising puppy grew up to become Braz. Ch. Dreamland's I'm Triple Wild and was bred and owned by Mrs. Vera Lucia Costa, Dreamland Kennels. Four months old here, "Mutt" is a son of Am. Ch. Rockaplenty's Wild Oats ex Am. & Braz. Ch. Keystone Little Bit O'Trip, a Triple Threat daughter.

most of them do when they are there alone. Two or more dogs will play and move themselves around, but from my own experience, one by itself does little more than make a leisurely tour once around the area to check things over and then lie down. You must include a daily walk or two in your plans if your puppy is to be rugged and well. Exercise is extremely important to a puppy's muscular development and to keep a mature dog fit and trim. So make sure that those exercise periods, or walks, a game of ball, and other such activities, are part of your daily program as a dog owner.

If your fenced area has an outside gate, provide a padlock and key and a strong fastening for it, and use them, so that the gate can not be opened by others and the dog taken or turned free. The ultimate convenience in this regard is, of course, a door (unused for other purposes) from the house around which the fenced area can be enclosed, so that all you have to do is open the door and out into his area he goes. This arrangement is safest of all, as then you need not be using a gate, and it is easier in bad weather since then you can send the dog out without taking him and becoming soaked yourself at the same time. This is not always possible to manage, but if your house is arranged so that you could do it this way, we are sure you would never regret it due to the convenience and added safety thus provided. Fencing in the entire yard, with gates to be opened and closed whenever a caller, deliveryman, postman, or some other person comes on your property, really is not safe at all because people not used to gates and their importance are frequently careless about closing and latching gates *securely*. We know of many heartbreaking incidents brought about by someone carelessly only half closing a gate which the owner had thought to be firmly latched and the dog wandering out. For greatest security a fenced *area* definitely takes precedence over a fenced *yard*.

The puppy will need a collar (one that fits now, not one to be grown into) and lead from the moment you bring him home. Both should be an appropriate weight and type for his size. Also needed are a feeding dish and a water dish, both made preferably of unbreakable material. Your pet supply shop should have an interesting assortment of these and other accessories from which you can choose. Then you will need grooming tools of the type the breeder recommends and some toys. One of the best toys is a beef bone, either rib, leg, or knuckle (the latter the type you can purchase to make soup), cut to an appropriate size for your puppy dog. These are absolutely safe and are great exercise for the teething period, helping to get the baby teeth quickly out of the

Ch. Rockaplenty's Wild Oats winning the Veterans Class at the Southern New York Beagle Club Specialty in 1981, owner-handled by Anna Katherine Nicholas.

Opposite page: Ch. Incewood Buttercup, an English-bred Beagle brought to the U.S. by Penny Morrise-Smith, Houston, Texas, has completed her title in the U.S. "Princess" created much interest here due to her coloring which is rarely seen in the American show ring. She is the dam of a champion daughter from her only litter.

14

way with no problems. Equally satisfactory is Nylabone® a nylon bone that does not chip or splinter and that "frizzles" as the puppy chews, providing healthful gum massage. Rawhide chews are safe, too, *IF made in the United States.* There was a problem a few years back owing to the chemicals with which some foreign rawhide toys had been treated, since which time we have carefully avoided giving them to our own dogs. Also avoid plastics and any sort of rubber toys, *particularly* those with squeakers which the puppy may remove and swallow. If you want a ball for the puppy to use when playing with him, select one of very hard construction made for this purpose and do not leave it alone with him because he may chew off and swallow bits of the rubber. Take the ball with you when the game is over. This also applies to some of those "tug of war" type rubber toys which are fun when used with the two of you for that purpose but again should *not* be left behind for the dog to work on with his teeth. Bits of swallowed rubber, squeakers, and other such foreign articles can wreak great havoc in the intestinal tract—do all you can to guard against them.

Too many changes all at once can be difficult for a puppy. For at least the first few days he is with you, keep him on the food and feeding schedule to which he is accustomed. Find out ahead of time from the breeder what he feeds his puppies, how frequently, and at what times of the day. Also find out what, if any, food supplements the breeder has been using and recommends. Then be prepared by getting in a supply of the same food so that you will have it there when you bring the puppy home. Once the puppy is accustomed to his new surroundings, then you can switch the type of food and schedule to fit your convenience, but for the first several days do it as the puppy expects.

Your selection of a veterinarian also should be attended to before the puppy comes home, because you should stop at the vet's office for the puppy to be checked over as soon as you leave the breeder's premises. If the breeder is from your area, ask him for recommendations. Ask your dog-owning friends for their opinions of the local veterinarians, and see what their experiences with those available have been. Choose someone whom several of your friends recommend highly, then contact him about your puppy, perhaps making an appointment to stop in at his office. If the premises are clean, modern, and well equipped, and if you like the veterinarian, make an appointment to bring the puppy in on the day of purchase. Be sure to obtain the puppy's health record from the breeder, including information on such things as shots and worming that the puppy has had.

Joining the Family

Remember that, exciting and happy an occasion as it is for you, the puppy's move from his place of birth to your home can be, for him, a traumatic experience. His mother and littermates will be missed. He quite likely will be awed or frightened by the change of surroundings. The person on whom he depended will be gone. Everything should be planned to make his arrival at your home pleasant—to give him confidence and to help him realize that yours is a pretty nice place to be after all.

Never bring a puppy home on a holiday. There just is too much going on with people and gifts and excitement. If he is in honor of an "occasion," work it out so that his arrival will be a few days earlier or, perhaps even better, a few days later than the "occasion." Then your home will be back to its normal routine and the puppy can enjoy your undivided attention. Try not to bring the puppy home in the evening. Early morning is the ideal time, as then he has the opportunity of getting acquainted and the initial strangeness should wear off before bedtime. You will find it a more peaceful night that way, we are sure. Allow the puppy to investigate as he likes, under your watchful eye. If you already have a pet in the household, keep a careful watch that the relationship between the two gets off to a friendly start or you may quickly find yourself with a lasting problem. Much of the future attitude of each toward the other will depend on what takes place that first day, so keep your mind on what they are doing and let your other activities slide for the moment. Be careful not to let your older pet become jealous by paying more attention to the puppy than to him, as that will start a bad situation immediately.

If you have a child, here again it it important that the relationship start out well. Before the puppy is brought home, you should have a talk with the youngster about puppies, so that it will be clearly understood that puppies are fragile and can easily be injured; therefore, they should not be teased, hurt, mauled, or overly rough-housed. A puppy is not an inanimate toy; it is a living thing with a right to be loved and handled respectfully, treatment which will reflect in the dog's attitude toward your child as both mature together. Never permit your children's playmates to mishandle a puppy, as we have seen happen. tormenting the puppy until it turns on the children in self-defense. Children often do not realize how rough is too rough. You, as a responsible adult, are obligated to assure that your puppy's relationship with children is a pleasant one.

Ch. Linvens Super Star, Group winning 13″ Beagle by Ch. Rockaplenty's Wild Oats ex Ch. Birchwood Linvens Betsy Ross, is a consistent winner in breed and Group competitions. Owned by N. N. Goodman, Jr., Cleveland, Ohio. Handled by Jerry and Elaine Rigden.

Opposite page: *(Top)* Ch. Busch's Xanadu, by Ch. Busch's Nuts to You of Brendons ex Ch. Busch's Dynamint, is a Top 10 13″ Beagle in 1982 and 1983; owned and bred by Wm. and Cecile Busch, Cape Girardeau, Mo. *(Bottom)* Ch. Junior's Foyscroft Wild Kid, by Ch. Rockaplenty's Wild Oats ex Ch. Bonnie V of Beagle Chase, outstanding 15″ Group winning dog, was a consistent winner of the mid-1970's. Bred by Dick Johnson and owned by Marcia Foy.

Do not start out by spoiling your puppy. A puppy is usually pretty smart and can be quite demanding. What you had considered to be "just for tonight" may be accepted by the puppy as "for keeps." Be firm with him, strike a routine, and stick to it. The puppy will learn more quickly this way, and everyone will be happier at the result. A radio playing softly or a dim night light are often comforting to a puppy as it gets accustomed to new surroundings and should be provided in preference to bringing the puppy to bed with you—unless, of course, you intend him to share the bed as a permanent arrangement.

Socializing and Training Your New Puppy

Socialization and training of your puppy should start the very day of his arrival in your home. Never address him without calling him by name. A short, simple name is the easiest to teach as it catches the dog's attention quickly, so avoid elaborate call names. Always address the dog by the same name, not a whole series of pet names; the latter will only confuse the puppy.

Using his name clearly, call the puppy over to you when you see him awake and wandering about. When he comes, make a big fuss over him for being such a good dog. He thus will quickly associate the sound of his name with coming to you and a pleasant happening.

Several hours after the puppy's arrival is not too soon to start accustoming him to the feel of a light collar. He may hardly notice it; or he may struggle, roll over, and try to rub it off his neck with his paws. Divert his attention when this occurs by offering a tasty snack or a toy (starting a game with him) or by petting him. Before long he will have accepted the strange feeling around his neck and no longer appear aware of it. Next comes the lead. Attach it and then immediately take the puppy outside or otherwise try to divert his attention with things to see and sniff. He may struggle against the lead at first, biting at it and trying to free himself. Do not pull him with it at this point; just hold the end loosely and try to follow him if he starts off in any direction. Normally his attention will soon turn to investigating his surroundings if he is outside or you have taken him into an unfamiliar room in your house; curiosity will take over and he will become interested in sniffing around the surroundings. Just follow him with the lead slackly held until he seems to have completely forgotten about it; then try with gentle urging to get him to follow you. Don't be rough or jerk at him; just tug gently on the lead in short quick motions (steady pulling can become a battle of wills), repeating his name or trying to get him to follow your hand which is holding a bit of food or an interesting toy. If you have an older lead-trained dog, then it should be a cinch to get the puppy to follow along after *him*. In any event, the average puppy learns quite quickly and will soon be trotting along nicely on the lead. Once that point has been reached, the next step is to teach him to follow on your left side, or heel. Of course this will not likely be accomplished all in one day but should be done with short training periods over the course of several days until you are satisfied with the result.

During the course of house training your puppy, you will need to take him out frequently and at regular intervals: first thing in the morning directly from the crate, immediately after meals, after the puppy has been napping, or when you notice that the puppy is looking for a spot. Choose more or less the same place to take the puppy each time so that a pattern will be established. If he does not go immediately, do not return him to the house as he will probably relieve himself the moment he is inside. Stay out with him until he has finished; then be lavish with your praise for his good behavior. If you catch the puppy having an accident indoors, grab him firmly and rush him outside, sharply saying "No!" as you pick him up. If you do not see the accident occur, there is little point in doing anything except cleaning it up, as once it has happened and been forgotten, the puppy will most likely not even realize why you are scolding him.

Especially if you live in a big city or are away many hours at a time, having a dog that is trained to go on paper has some very definite advantages. To do this, one proceeds pretty much the same way as taking the puppy outdoors, except now you place the puppy on the newspaper at the proper time. The paper should always be kept in the same spot. An easy way to paper train a puppy if you have a playpen for it or an exercise pen is to line the area with newspapers; then gradually, every day or so, remove a section of newspaper until you are down to just one or two. The puppy acquires the habit of using the paper; and as the prepared area grows smaller, in the majority of cases the dog will continue to use whatever paper is still available. My own

Overleaf:
Ch. Plain and Fancy's Clover, by Ch. Mitey Cute Just Like Daddy ex Plain and Fancy's Miss Muffet, owner-handled by Ray Scott winning Best in Show at James River Kennel Club, 1979. Clover's record includes the National Specialty and a list of Specialty awards with Best of Variety under Desmond Murphy at Southern New York Beagle Club Specialty, 1982.

PHOTO

BEST OF VARIETY
MN. RIVER VALLEY K.C.
APRIL 11, 1981
OLSON PHOTO

experience, with dogs is that this works out well. It is pleasant, if the dog is alone for an excessive length of time, to be able to feel that if he needs it the paper is there and will be used.

The puppy should form the habit of spending a certain amount of time in his crate, even when you are home. Sometimes the puppy will do this voluntarily, but if not it should be taught to do so, which is accomplished by leading the puppy over by his collar, gently pushing him inside, and saying firmly "Down" or "Stay." Whatever expression you use to give a command, stick to the very same one each time for each act. Repetition is the big thing in training—and so is association with what the dog is expected to do. When you mean "Sit" always say exactly that. "Stay" should mean *only* that the dog should remain where he receives the command. "Down" means something else again. Do not confuse the dog by shuffling the commands, as this will create training problems for you.

As soon as he has had his immunization shots, take your puppy with you whenever and wherever possible. There is nothing that will build a self-confident, stable dog like socialization, and it is extremely important that you plan and give the time and energy necessary for this whether your dog is to be a show dog or a pleasant, well-adjusted family member. Take your puppy in the car so that he will learn to enjoy riding and not become carsick as dogs may do if they are infrequent travelers. Take him anywhere you are going where you are certain he will be welcome: visiting friends and relatives (if they do not have housepets who may resent the visit), busy shopping centers (keeping him always on lead), or just walking around the streets of your town. If someone admires him (as always seems to happen when we are out with puppies), encourage the stranger to pet and talk with him. Socialization of this type brings out the best in your puppy and helps

← **Overleaf:**
(Top) Ch. Briarwood Travelin' Man, son of Ch. Jo-Mar's Repeat Performance, with owner Linda Lindberg in 1981. *(Bottom)* Marcia Foy awards Best of Variety, 15", to Ch. Jo-hill Lee's Red Jason and Best of Winners-Best of Opposite Sex to Jason's half sister Ch. Lee's Red Queen of Hearts, 15". Jason finished at seven months and has more than 100 Bests of Variety and many Hound Group placements. He was Best of Breed at Bay State Beagle Club Specialty 1981. Queenie finished at seven months and has been Best Opposite to Jason on many occasions. She was Best of Winners and Best Opposite Sex at Bay State Specialty in 1982, and is now with E. Kim Beck, D.V.M., New Brunswick, Canada.

him to grow up with a friendly outlook, liking the world and its inhabitants. The worst thing that can be done to a puppy's personality is to overly shelter him. By keeping him always at home away from things and people unfamiliar to him you may be creating a personality problem for the mature dog that will be a cross for you to bear later on.

Feeding Your Dog

Time was when providing nourishing food for our dogs involved a far more complicated procedure than people now feel is necessary. The old school of thought was that the daily ration must consist of fresh beef, vegetables, cereal, egg yolks, and cottage cheese as basics with such additions as brewer's yeast and vitamin tablets on a daily basis.

During recent years, however, many minds have changed regarding this procedure. We still give eggs, cottage cheese, and supplements to the diet, but the basic method of feeding dogs has changed; and the change has been, in the opinion of many authorities, definitely for the better. The school of thought now is that you are doing your dogs a favor when you feed them some of the fine commercially prepared dog foods in preference to your own home-cooked concoctions.

The reason behind this new outlook is easily understandable. The dog food industry has grown to be a major one, participated in by some of the best known and most respected names in the American way of life. These trusted firms, it is agreed, turn out excellent products, so people are feeding their dog food preparations with confidence and the dogs are thriving, living longer, happier, and healthier lives than ever before. What more could we want?

There are at least half a dozen absolutely top-grade dry foods to be mixed with broth or water and served to your dog according to directions. There are all sorts of canned meats, and there are several kinds of "convenience foods," those in a packet which you open and dump out into the dog's dish. It is just that simple. The "convenience" foods are neat and easy to use when you are away from home, but generally speaking we prefer a dry food mixed with hot water or soup and meat. We also feel that the canned meat, with its added fortifiers, is more beneficial to the dogs than the fresh meat. However, the two can be alternated or, if you prefer and your dog does well on it, by all means use fresh ground beef. A dog enjoys changes in the meat part of his diet, which is easy with the canned food since all sorts of beef are available (chunk, ground, stewed, and so on), plus lamb, chicken, and

Ch. Navan's Triple Trouble Rick *(left)*, owned by Nancy Vanstrum and Virginia Flowers, won the National, 1975 and 1976. Ch. Garber's Cupcake, owned by Marcia Foy and Virginia Flowers, won the National, 1979. These two together produced consistent winners Ch. Pixshire's Fortune Cookie and Ch. Pixshire's K.C.

even such concoctions as liver and egg, just plain liver flavor, and a blend of five meats.

There also is prepared food geared to every age bracket of your dog's life, from puppyhood on through old age, with special additions or modifications to make it particularly nourishing and beneficial. Our grandparents, and even our parents, never had it so good where the canine dinner is concerned, because these commercially prepared foods are tasty and geared to meeting the dog's gastronomic approval.

Additionally, contents and nutrients are clearly listed on the labels, as are careful instructions for feeding just the right amount for the size, weight, and age of each dog.

With these foods we do not feel the addition of extra vitamins is necessary, but if you do there are several kinds of those, too, that serve as taste treats as well as being beneficial. Your pet supplier has a full array of them.

Of course there is no reason not to cook up something for your dog if you would feel happier doing so. But it seems to us unnecessary when such truly satisfactory rations are available with so much less trouble and expense.

How often you feed your dog is a matter of how it works out best for you. Many owners prefer to do it once a day. We personally think that two meals, each of smaller quantity, are better for the digestion and more satisfying to the dog, particularly if yours is a household member who stands around and watches preparations for the family meals. Do not overfeed. That is the shortest route to all sorts of problems. Follow directions and note carefully how your dog is looking. If your dog is overweight, cut back the quantity of food a bit. If the dog looks thin, then increase the amount. Each dog is an individual and the food intake should be adjusted to his requirements to keep him feeling and looking trim and in top condition.

From the time puppies are fully weaned until they are about twelve weeks old, they should be fed four times daily. From three months to six months of age, three meals should suffice. At six months of age the puppies can be fed two meals, and the twice daily feedings can be continued until the puppies are close to one year old, at which time feeding can be changed to once daily if desired.

If you do feed just once a day, do so by early afternoon at the latest and give the dog a snack, or biscuit or two, at bedtime.

Remember that plenty of fresh water should always be available to your puppy or dog for drinking. This is of utmost importance to his health.

Chapter 13

The Making of a Show Dog

If you have decided to become a show dog exhibitor, you have accepted a very real and very exciting challenge. The groundwork has been accomplished with the selection of your future show prospect. If you have purchased a puppy, we assume that you have gone through all the proper preliminaries concerning good care, which should be the same if the puppy is a pet or future show dog with a few added precautions for the latter.

General Considerations

Remember the importance of keeping your future winner in trim, top condition. Since you want him neither too fat nor too thin, his appetite for his proper diet should be guarded, and children and guests should not be permitted to constantly be feeding him "goodies." The best treat of all is a small wad of raw ground beef or a packaged dog treat. To be avoided are ice cream, cake, cookies, potato chips, and other fattening items which will cause the dog to put on weight and may additionally spoil his appetite for the proper, nourishing, well-balanced diet so essential to good health and condition.

The importance of temperament and showmanship cannot possibly be overestimated. They have put many a mediocre dog across while lack of them can ruin the career of an otherwise outstanding specimen. From the day your dog joins your family, socialize him. Keep him accustomed to being with people and to being handled by people. Encourage your friends and relatives to "go over" him as the judges will in the ring so this will not seem a strange and upsetting experience.

Ch. Pin Oak's Fire N'Ice at the age of ten weeks. Bred by Helga Alderfer and owned by Louise E. Prince. This smashing red and white puppy bitch is a daughter of Ch. Rockaplenty's Wild Oats from one of the Alderfer's excellent producing dams. Note how beautifully she "stacks" even at this youthful age.

Practice showing his "bite" (the manner in which his teeth meet) quickly and deftly. It is quite simple to slip the lips apart with your fingers, and the puppy should be willing to accept this from you or the judge without struggle. This is also true of further mouth examination when necessary. Where the standard demands examination of the roof of the mouth and the tongue, accustom the dog to having his jaws opened wide in order for the judge to make this required examination. When missing teeth must be noted, again, teach the dog to permit his jaws to be opened wide and his side lips separated as judges will need to check them one or both of these ways.

Some judges prefer that the exhibitors display the dog's bite and other mouth features themselves. These are the considerate ones, who do not wish to chance the spreading of possible infection from dog to dog with their hands on each one's mouth—a courtesy particularly appreciated in these days of virus epidemics. But the old-fashioned judges still persist in doing it themselves, so the dog should be ready for either possibility.

Take your future show dog with you in the car, thus accustoming him to riding so that he will not become carsick on the day of a dog show. He should associate pleasure and attention with going in the car, or van or motor home. Take him where it is crowded: downtown, to the shops, everywhere you go that dogs are permitted. Make the expeditions fun for him by frequent petting and words of praise; do not just ignore him as you go about your errands.

Do not overly shelter your future show dog. Instinctively you may want to keep him at home where he is safe from germs or danger. This can be foolish on two counts. The first reason is that a puppy kept away from other dogs builds up no natural immunity against all the things with which he will come in contact at dog shows, so it is wiser actually to keep him well up to date on all protective shots and then let him become accustomed to being among dogs and dog owners. Also, a dog who never is among strange people, in strange places, or among strange dogs, may grow up with a shyness or timidity of spirit that will cause you real problems as his show career draws near.

Grooming the Beagle

For a pet Beagle living in your home, a good brushing once a week and a run through with a fine comb will help keep the shedding to a minimum. The nails should be clipped off at least once a month to keep them short and to avoid snagging. Be sure to not cut into the quick which will cause them to bleed. Should you accidentally do so, immediately apply a styptic powder to stop the bleeding.

Beagles living in a home situation seldom require bathing as their type coat does not hold dirt. Dogs running in the field may upon occasion need to be bathed, although usually a good rub-down with a turkish towel if the dog becomes wet will suffice. Should your Beagle run afoul of a skunk, soak the coat in tomato juice and then bathe.

A show Beagle requires more trimming than one might imagine to appear at his best. However, it should be done in such a way as to never appear obvious.

For equipment you will need: a rubber-topped grooming table with arm, electric clippers (#15 or #10 blade), curved regular shears, thinning shears, combs (both fine-toothed and regular), a hound glove, and nail clippers or an electric grinder.

You should begin well in advance of the show date, as trimming must be done at least several times before beginning to blend in and

Sylvia Lopez showing Ch. Lightninridge Short N Sweet, nicely "stacked" on the table, as the judge checks the "bite."

look correct. I would suggest at first practicing on a dog you do not show before actually undertaking your star, so that you can accustom yourself to the "feel" of the clippers and the amount of pressure required to do it exactly right.

For a dog being campaigned you will be able to trim just prior to showing once the coat has been worked into a proper blend. The more times it is done, the better it will look.

If possible you should trim in front of a mirror, so that you can see all sides as you work.

Beginning with the front of the neck, use your clippers with the grain (or as the hair lies). Start just under the chin and clip down to just below the point of chest. Take down the neck to the end of the white on either side; then blend in with the thinning shears. *Never press down hard.* It is better to keep going over lightly. Thin; then comb out over each area as you clip, until the frill is blended into the clipped neck. Try to avoid clipping into the colored hair, the underneath of which is lighter and which will cause a color change if you do so in that area.

Turn the dog on his back and clip the hair off the penis and the area around it. There is a natural line where the heavy hair of the chest stops, all below which should be clipped. Also lightly clip the inside of the thighs.

Stand the dog up and with the clippers lightly trim the rear to remove the straggly hairs from just below the anus. Then blend in with the thinning shears. With the curved shears tidy up the rough hair on the back of both hind legs.

The tip of the tail should be rounded with the curved shears. It normally is not necessary to trim elsewhere on the tail unless there is really excess scraggly hair. Remember, you want a nice, full brush on the tail.

Again lay the dog down and trim the hair from between the toes and round off any excess scraggly hair from the foot. Trim the pastern to give a clean look. If necessary, trim any excess frill from the back of the front legs.

With the dog standing up, clip the insides of both ears with the electric clippers, which permits the ears to lie flatter. You can also do the whiskers with the electric clippers, or you can use your curved shears to do this. Usually there is a tuft of hair behind each ear which should be rounded off with the curved shears. Don't forget the whiskers on either side of the muzzle and on the upper cheeks.

I do not believe in using a stripping knife on a Beagle. I open the thinning shears and rake the coat with it. This pulls out the undercoat but does not break the outer coat. This should be done more often in the spring to get all the winter coat out of the way. The coat may then be brushed with a hound glove to bring up the shine.

Once you are finished, look the dog over carefully, checking to be certain that no stray hairs have been missed.

Avoid bathing your show Beagle as it will take time for the coat to lie properly again. The white may be bathed with a special product which is rubbed in but not rinsed out. While the white coat is still slightly damp, you can brush in loose chalk; then when the coat is totally dry, carefully brush it out. The white will then be sparkling.

NOTE: Marcia Foy, who wrote this grooming section, was honored one year when her great Beagle, Champion Kings Creek Triple Threat won the award for Best Groomed Hound.

Ch. Magic Noire Wilma, Danish import, pictured with junior handler Carol Moore winning first in Junior Showmanship at the Blossom Valley Beagle Club Specialty. Carol is the daughter of Garland and Karen Moore, Atwater, California.

15″ Ch. Busch's All That Jazz and Stacy Busch, by Ch. Busch's Nuts to You of Brendons ex Ch. Busch's Dynamite. Breeders-owners are Wm. and Cecile Busch, Cape Girardeau, MO.

Danish and U.S. Ch. Buglair Sun Flare finishing American championship at Rio Hondo K.C. under judge Tom Stevenson. Buglair Kennels, owners, Garland, Karen and Carol Moore.

Assuming that you will be handling the dog yourself, or even if he will be professionally handled, a few moments each day of dog show routine is important. Practice setting him up as you have seen the exhibitors do at the shows you've attended, and teach him to hold this position once you have him stacked to your satisfaction. Make the learning period pleasant by being firm but lavish in your praise when he responds correctly. Teach him to gait at your side at a moderate rate on a loose lead. When you have mastered the basic essentials at home, then hunt out and join a training class for future work. Training classes are sponsored by show-giving clubs in many areas, and their popularity is steadily increasing. If you have no other way of locating one, perhaps your veterinarian would know of one through some of his other clients; but if you are sufficiently aware of the dog show world to want a show dog, you will probably be personally acquainted with other people who will share information of this type with you.

Accustom your show dog to being in a crate (which you should be doing with a pet dog as well). He should relax in his crate at the shows "between times" for his own well being and safety.

A show dog's teeth must be kept clean and free of tartar. Hard dog-biscuits can help toward this, but if tartar accumulates, see that it is removed promptly by your veterinarian. Bones are not suitable for show dogs as they tend to damage and wear down the tooth enamel.

Match Shows

Your show dog's initial experience in the ring should be in match show competition for several reasons. First, this type of event is intended as a learning experience for both the dog and the exhibitor. You will not feel embarrassed or out of place no matter how poorly your puppy may behave or how inept your attempts at handling may be, as you will find others there with the same type of problems. The important thing is that you get the puppy out and into a show ring where the two of you can practice together and learn the ropes.

Only on rare occasions is it necessary to make match show entries in advance, and even those with a pre-entry policy will usually accept entries at the door as well. Thus you need not plan several weeks ahead, as is the case with point shows, but can go when the mood strikes you. Also there is a vast difference in the cost, as match show entries only cost a few dollars while entry fees for the point shows may be over ten dollars, an

Best 15" Beagle at Westminster 1983, Ch. Hollypines Daisy Run Sun with his handler Mary Ann Alston stepping smartly around the Group ring. Mrs. George Eaton, owner, Waldorf, MD.

amount none of us needs to waste until we have some idea of how the puppy will behave or how much more pre-show training is needed.

Match shows very frequently are judged by professional handlers who, in addition to making the awards, are happy to help new exhibitors with comments and advice on their puppies and their presentation of them. Avail yourself of all these opportunities before heading out to the sophisticated world of the point shows.

Point Shows

As previously mentioned, entries for American Kennel Club point shows must be made in advance. This must be done on an official entry blank of the show-giving club. The entry must then be filed either personally or by mail with the show superintendent or the show secretary (if the event is being run by the club members alone and a superintendent has not been hired, this information will appear on the premium list) in time to reach its destination prior to the published closing date or filling of the quota. These entries must be made carefully, must be signed by the owner of the dog or the owner's agent (your professional handler), and must be accompanied by the entry fee; otherwise they will not be accepted. Remember that it is not when the entry leaves your hands that counts but the date of arrival at its destination. If you are relying on the mails, which are not always dependable, get the entry off well before the deadline to avoid disappointment.

A dog must be entered at a dog show in the name of the actual owner at the time of the entry closing date of that specific show. If a registered dog has been acquired by a new owner, it must be entered in the name of the new owner in any show for which entries close after the date of acquirement, regardless of whether the new owner has or has not actually received the registration certificate indicating that the dog is recorded in his name. State on the entry form whether or not transfer application has been mailed to the American Kennel Club, and it goes without saying that the latter should be attended to promptly when you purchase a registered dog.

In filling out your entry blank, type, print, or write clearly, paying particular attention to the spelling of names, correct registration numbers, and so on.

The Puppy Class is for dogs or bitches who are six months of age and under twelve months, were whelped in the United States, and are not champions. The age of a dog shall be calculated up to and inclusive of the first day of a show. For example, the first day a dog whelped on January 1st is eligible to compete in a Puppy Class at a show is July 1st of the same year; and he may continue to compete in Puppy Classes up to and including a show on December 31st of the same year, but he is *not* eligible to compete in a Puppy Class at a show held on or after January 1st of the following year.

The Puppy Class is the first one in which you should enter your puppy. In it a certain allowance will be made for the fact that they *are* puppies, thus an immature dog or one displaying less than perfect showmanship will be less severely penalized than, for instance, would be the case in Open. It is also quite likely that others in the class will be suffering from these problems, too. When you enter a puppy, be sure to check the classification with care, as some shows divide their Puppy Class into a 6-9 months old section and a 9-12 months old section.

The Novice Class is for dogs six months of age and over, whelped in the United States or Canada, who *prior to the official closing date for entires* have *not* won three first prizes in the Novice Class, any first prize at all in the Bred-by-Exhibitor, American-bred, or Open Classes, or one or more points toward championship. The provisions for this class are confusing to many people, which is probably the reason exhibitors do not enter in it more frequently. A dog may win any number of first prizes in the Puppy Class and still retain his eligibility for Novice. He may place second, third or fourth not only in Novice on an unlimited number of occasions but also in Bred-by-Exhibitor, American-bred and Open and still remain eligible for Novice. But he may no longer be shown in Novice when he has won three blue ribbons in that class, when he has won even one blue ribbon in either Bred-by-Exhibitor, American-bred, or Open, or when he has won a single championship point.

In determining whether or not a dog is eligible for the Novice Class, keep in mind the fact that previous wins are calculated according to the official published date for closing of entries, not by the date on which you may actually have made the entry. So if in the interim, between the time you made the entry and the official closing date, your dog makes a win causing him to become ineligible for Novice, change your class *immediately* to another for which he will be eligible, preferably such as either Bred-by-Exhibitor or American-bred. To do this, you must contact the show's superintendent or secretary, at first by telephone to save time and at the same time confirm it in writing. The Novice Class always seems to have the fewest entries of any class, and therefore it is a splendid "practice ground" for you and your young dog while you are getting the "feel" of being in the ring.

Bred-by-Exhibitor Class is for dogs whelped in the United States or, if individually registered in the American Kennel Club Stud Book, for dogs whelped in Canada who are six months of age or older, are not champions, and are owned wholly or in part by the person or by the spouse of the person who was the breeder or one of the breeders of record. Dogs entered in this class must be handled in the class by an owner or by a member of the immediate family of the owner. Members of an immediate family for this purpose are husband, wife,

Ch. Alpha Centauri's Sandpiper, 15″ dog, Best of Winners from the puppy class, National Beagle Club 1973. Bred and owned by Robert E. and Judy Goodfellow, Mason, IL.

The last of the champions bred by Isabella Hoopes at her renowned Saddlerock Kennels, Ch. Saddlerock Sandman, II, a son of Ch. Kings Creek Triple Threat. "Sandy" now belongs to Trudi Reveira and Mary Powell in California.

Ch. Chrisette's Timothy Oates, C.D., a son of Ch. Rockaplenty's Wild Oats, was bred by Sandra Robichaud. Owned, trained, and handled for both show and obedience by Cathy Czachorowski of Torrington, CT.

Famed "Mr. Dog," Ch. Navan's Triple Trouble, C.D. One of the Best in Show sons of Ch. Kings Creek Triple Threat. Owned by Lori Takacs.

father, mother, son, daughter, brother or sister. This is the class which is really the "breeders' showcase," and the one which breeders should enter with particular pride to show off their achievements.

The American-bred Class is for all dogs excepting champions, six months of age or older, who were whelped in the United States by reason of a mating which took place in the United States.

The Open Class is for any dog six months of age or older (this is the only restriction for this class). Dogs with championship points compete in it, dogs who are already champions are eligible to do so, dogs who are imported can be entered, and, of course, American-bred dogs compete in it. This class is, for some strange reason, the favorite of exhibitors who are "out to win." They rush to enter their pointed dogs in it, under the false impression that by doing so they assure themselves of greater attention from the judges. This really is not so, and in my opinion to enter in one of the less competitive classes, with a better chance of winning it and thus earning a second opportunity of gaining the judge's approval by returning to the ring in the Winners Class, can often be a more effective strategy.

One does not enter for the Winners Class. One earns the right to compete in it by winning first prize in Puppy, Novice, Bred-by-Exhibitor, American-bred, or Open. No dog who has been defeated on the same day in one of these classes is eligible to compete for Winners, and every dog who has been a blue-ribbon winner in one of them and not defeated in another, should he have been entered in more than one class, (as occasionally happens) *must* do so. Following the selection of the Winners Dog or the Winners Bitch, the dog or bitch receiving that award leaves the ring. Then the dog or bitch who placed second in that class, unless previously beaten by another dog or bitch in another class at the same show, re-enters the ring to compete against the remaining first-prize winners for Reserve. The latter award indicates that the dog or bitch selected for it is standing "in reserve" should the one who received Winners be disqualified or declared ineligible through any technicality when the awards are checked at the American Kennel Club. In that case, the one who placed Reserve is moved up to Winners, at the same time receiving the appropriate championship points.

Winners Dog and Winners Bitch are the awards which carry points toward championship with them. The points are based on the number of dogs or bitches actually in competition, and the points are scaled one through five, the latter being the greatest number available to any one dog or bitch at any one show. Three-, four-, or five-point wins are considered majors. In order to become a champion, a dog or bitch must have won two majors under two different judges, plus at least one point from a third judge, and the additional points necessary to bring the total to fifteen. When your dog has gained fifteen points as described above, a championship certificate will be issued to you, and your dog's name will be published in the champions of record list in the *Pure-Bred Dogs/American Kennel Gazette,* the official publication of the American Kennel Club.

The scale of championship points for each breed is worked out by the American Kennel Club and reviewed annually, at which time the number required in competition may be either changed (raised or lowered) or remain the same. The scale of championship points for all breeds is published annually in the May issue of the *Gazette,* and the current ratings for each breed within that area are published in every show catalog.

When a dog or bitch is adjudged Best of Winners, its championship points are, for that show, compiled on the basis of which sex had the greater number of points. If there are two points in dogs and four in bitches and the dog goes Best of Winners, then *both* the dog and the bitch are awarded an equal number of points, in this case four. Should the Winners Dog or the Winners Bitch go on to win Best of Breed or Best of Variety, additional points are accorded for the additional dogs and bitches defeated by so doing, provided, of course, that there were entries specifically for Best of Breed Competition or Specials, as these specific entries are generally called.

If your dog or bitch takes Best of Opposite Sex after going Winners, points are credited according to the number of the same sex defeated in both the regular classes and Specials competition. If Best of Winners is also won, then whatever additional points for each of these awards are available will be credited. Many a one- or two-point win has grown into a major in this manner.

Moving further along, should your dog win its Variety Group from the classes (in other words, if it has taken either Winners Dog or Winners Bitch), you then receive points based on the greatest number of points awarded to any member of any breed included within that Group during that show's competition. Should the day's winning also include Best in Show, the same rule of thumb applies, and your dog or bitch receives the highest number of points awarded to any other dog of any breed at that event.

Best of Breed competition consists of the Winners Dog and the Win-

One of the world's most titled Beagles, Am. Ch. Lokavi's Flash Back holds championship honors in several South American countries where he has been a consistent winner for Ramon Podesta. A son of Ch. Rockaplenty's Wild Oats ex a Lokavi bitch, bred by Lori Norman Takacs here taking Winners Dog, at Southern New York Beagle Club Specialty in 1982.

Am. and Can. Ch. Ledgewood's Precious Duncan, by Ch. Pin Oaks Mr. Chips ex Ch. Pickadilly Prima Donna, bred by Edward Nelson, handled by Terry Childs, owned by Susan Beecher Tartaglia; started by going Best of Variety, completed Canadian Championship in one week at the Sportsmans, gathering Bests of Breed and Group placements, seven times Best Puppy in Breed, was Reserve Winners at Westminster 1979. Sadly, Duncan was stolen just prior to starting as a Special.

Braemoor's Wild Child wins the Puppy Group at his first Match show. An exciting young son of Champion Junior's Foyscroft Wild Kid ex Topono's Brenda Braemoor, owned by Wilma, Sue and Keaton Plaiss, Braemoor Kennels, Kenosha, Wisconsin.

Cad-Mar's Lucky Charm winning Best Brood Bitch at the San Jacinto Beagle Club Specialty, handled by Tommy Lisano. Owners, Rosalie and Jim Lisano, Pasadena, Texas.

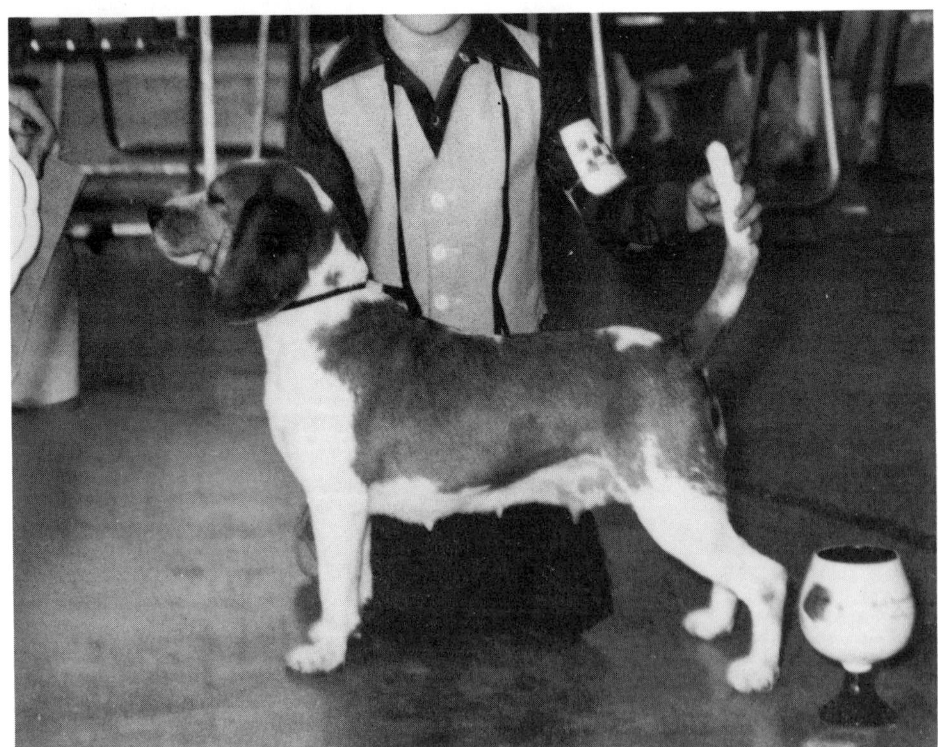

ners Bitch, who automatically compete on the strength of those awards, in addition to whatever dogs and bitches have been entered specifically for this class for which champions of record are eligible. Since July 1980, dogs who, according to their owner's records, have completed the requirements for a championship after the closing of entries for the show, but whose championships are unconfirmed, may be transferred from one of the regular classes to the Best of Breed competition, provided this transfer is made by the show superintendent or show secretary *prior to the start of any judging at the show.*

This has proved an extremely popular new rule, as under it a dog can finish on Saturday and then be transferred and compete as a Special on Sunday. It must be emphasized that the change *must* be made *prior* to the start of *any* part of the day's judging, not for just your individual breed.

In the United States, Best of Breed winners are entitled to compete in the Variety Group which includes them. This is not mandatory, it is a privilege which exhibitors value. (In Canada, Best of Breed winners *must* compete in the Variety Group, or they lose any points already won.) The dogs winning *first* in each of the seven Variety Groups *must* compete for Best in Show. Missing the opportunity of taking your dog in for competition in its Group is foolish as it is there where the general public is most likely to notice your breed and become interested in learning about it.

Non-regular classes are sometimes included at the all-breed shows, and they are almost invariably included at Specialty Shows. These include Stud Dog Class and Brood Bitch Class, which are judged on the basis of the quality of the two offspring accompanying the sire or dam. The quality of the latter two is beside the point and should not be considered by the judge; it is the youngsters who count, and the quality of *both* are to be averaged to decide which sire or dam is the best and most consistent producer. Then there is the Brace Class (which, at all-breed shows, moves up to Best Brace in each Variety Group and then Best Brace in Show), which is judged on the similarity and evenness of appearance of the two members of the brace. In other words, the two dogs should look like identical twins in size, color, and conformation and should move together almost as a single dog, one person handling with precision and ease. The same applies to the Team Class competition, except that four dogs are involved and, if necessary, two handlers.

The Veterans Class is for the older dogs, the minimum age of whom is seven years. This class is judged on the quality of the dogs, as the winner competes in Best of Breed competition and has, on a respectable number of occasions, been known to take that top award. So the point is *not* to pick out the oldest dog, as some judges seem to believe, but the best specimen of the breed, exactly as in the regular classes.

Then there are Sweepstakes and Futurity Stakes sponsored by many Specialty clubs, sometimes as part of their regular Specialty Shows and sometimes as separate events on an entirely different occasion. The difference between the two stakes is that Sweepstakes entries usually include dogs from six to eighteen months age with entries made at the same time as the others for the show while for a Futurity the entries are bitches nominated when bred and the individual puppies entered at or shortly following their birth.

If you already show your dog, if you plan on being an exhibitor in the future, or if you simply enjoy attending dog shows, there is a book, written by me, which you will find to be an invaluable source of detailed information about all aspects of show dog competition. This book is *Successful Dog Show Exhibiting* (T.F.H. Publications, Inc.) and is available wherever the one you are reading was purchased.

Junior Showmanship Competition

If there is a youngster in your family between the ages of ten and sixteen, I can suggest no better or more rewarding hobby than becoming an active participant in Junior Showmanship. This is a marvelous activity for young people. It teaches responsibility, good sportsmanship, the fun of competition where one's own skills are the deciding factor of success, proper care of a pet, and how to socialize with other young folks. Any youngster may experience the thrill of emerging from the ring a winner and the satisfaction of a good job well done.

Entry in Junior Showmanship Classes is open to any boy or girl who is at least ten years old and under seventeen years old on the day of the show. The Novice Junior Showmanship Class is open to youngsters who have not already won, at the time the entries close, three firsts in this class. Youngsters who have won three firsts in Novice may compete in the Open Junior Showmanship Class. Any junior handler who wins his third first-place award in Novice may participate in the Open Class at the same show, provided that the Open Class has at least one other junior handler entered and competing in it that day. The Novice and Open Classes may be divided into Junior and Senior Classes. Youngsters between the ages of ten and twelve, inclusively, are eligible

Patty Keenan, Barbara Keenan's daughter, here is winning Best Junior Handler at North Shore Kennel Club with her 13" bitch, Ch. Laurhel's Lil Tuffer-n-Luv, a daughter of Ch. Englandale's Fawnglen Ruffian ex Ch. Laurhel's Buttercup. Patty has this nice young bitch within a point of her title as we go to press, and is winning consistently in Junior Showmanship as well.

Ch. Jana Ace in the Hole, 13″, by Ch. Jana Tommyhawk, C.D. ex Jana Queen of Sheba, has proven an outstanding sire, with seven champions including a Group winner to his credit since coming East.

Ch. Brantwood Lee's Daisy Be Red, by Ch. Rockaplenty's Wild Oats, is a consistent winner in Specials here in the East. Pictured on the day she became a champion, handled by Vic Capone.

for the Junior division; and youngsters between thirteen and seventeen, inclusively, are eligible for the Senior division.

Any of the foregoing classes may be separated into individual classes for boys and for girls. If such a division is made, it must be so indicated on the premium list. The premium list also indicates the prize for Best Junior Handler, if such a prize is being offered at the show. Any youngster who wins a first in any of the regular classes may enter the competition for this prize, provided the youngster has been undefeated in any other Junior Showmanship Class at that show.

Junior Showmanship Classes, unlike regular conformation classes in which the quality of the dog is judged, are judged solely on the skill and ability of the junior handling the dog. Which dog is best is not the point—it is which youngster does the best job with the dog that is under consideration. Eligibility requirements for the dog being shown in Junior Showmanship, and other detailed information, can be found in *Regulations for Junior Showmanship,* available from the American Kennel Club.

A junior who has a dog that he or she can enter in both Junior Showmanship and conformation classes has twice the opportunity for success and twice the opportunity to get into the ring and work with the dog, a combination which can lead to not only awards for expert handling but also, if the dog is of sufficient quality, for making a conformation champion.

Pre-Show Preparations for Your Dog and You

Preparation of the items you will need as a dog show exhibitor should not be left until the last moment. They should be planned and arranged for at least several days in advance of the show in order for you to remain calm and relaxed as the countdown starts.

The importance of the crate has already been mentioned, and we hope it is already part of your equipment. Of equal importance is the grooming table, which very likely you have also already acquired for use at home. You should take it along with you to the shows, as your dog will need last minute touches before entering the ring. Should you have not yet made this purchase, folding tables with rubber tops are made specifically for this purpose and can be purchased at most dog shows, where concession booths with marvelous assortments of "doggy" necessities are to be found, or at your pet supplier. You will also need a sturdy tack box (also available at the dog show concessions) in which to carry your grooming tools and equipment. The latter

Jean Refieuna with the great winning bitch Ch. Socum Tammy and judge Anna Katherine Nicholas *(left)* in 1961. Owned by Edward B. Jenner.

should include brushes, comb, scissors, nail clippers, whatever you use for last minute clean-up jobs, cotton swabs, first-aid equipment, and anything you are in the habit of using on the dog, including a leash or two of the type you prefer, some well-cooked and dried-out liver or any of the small packaged "dog treats" for use as bait in the ring, an atomizer in case you wish to dampen your dog's coat when you are preparing him for the ring, and so on. A large turkish towel to spread under the dog on the grooming table is also useful.

Take a large thermos or cooler of ice, the biggest one you can accommodate in your vehicle, for use by "man and beast." Take a jug of water (there are lightweight, inexpensive ones available at all sporting goods shops) and a water dish. If you plan to feed the dog at the show, or if you and the dog will be away from home more than one day, bring food for him from home so that he will have the type to which he is accustomed.

You may or may not have an exercise pen. Personally we think one a *must*, even if you only have one dog. While the shows do provide areas for the exercise of the dogs, these are among the most likely places to have your dog come in contact with any illnesses which may be going around, and we feel that having a pen of your own for your dog's use is excellent protection. Such a pen can be used in other ways, too, such as a place other than the crate in which to put the dog to relax (that is roomier than the crate) and a place in which the dog can exercise at motels and rest areas. These, too, are available at the show concession stands and come in a variety of heights and sizes. A set of "pooper scoopers" should also be part of your equipment, along with a package of plastic bags for cleaning up after your dog.

Bring along folding chairs for the members of your party, unless all of you are fond of standing, as these are almost never provided any-more by the clubs. Have your name stamped on the chairs so that there will be no doubt as to whom the chairs belong. Bring whatever you and your family enjoy for drinks or snacks in a picnic basket or cooler, as show food, in general, is expensive and usually not great. You should always have a pair of boots, a raincoat, and a rain hat with you (they should remain permanently in your vehicle if you plan to at-tend shows regularly), as well as a sweater, a warm coat, and a change of shoes. A smock or big cover-up apron will assure that you remain tidy as you prepare the dog for the ring. Your overnight case should include a small sewing kit for emergency repairs, bandaids, headache and indigestion remedies, and any personal products or medications you normally use.

In your car you should always carry maps of the area where you are headed and an assortment of motel directories. Generally speaking, we have found Holiday Inns to be the nicest about taking dogs. Ramadas and Howard Johnsons generally do as cheerfully (with a few excep-tions). Best Western generally frowns on pets (not always, but often enough to make it necessary to find out which do). Some of the smaller chains welcome pets. The majority of privately owned motels do not.

Have everything prepared the night before the show to expedite your departure. Be sure that the dog's identification and your judging program and other show information are in your purse or briefcase. If you are taking sandwiches, have them ready. Anything that goes into the car the night before the show will be one thing less to remember in

The blue-tri Beagle Ch. Touchstone's Smokey Bear, C.D., by Ch. Starbuck's Hang 'Em High ex Ch. Plain and Fancy's June Bug, at the Sweepstakes at National Beagle Club Specialty 1977. Owned by Kathleen Carling, Echo Run Beagles.

One of the breed's great bitches, Ch. Foyscroft Triple Lina Wor-Lo winning the Hound Group, owner-handled by Marcia Foy at Albany Kennel Club in 1972. By Ch. Kings Creek Triple Threat ex Ch. Lawndale's Wind Storm, Lina was bred by Judy Colan. A multiple Group winner, she is the dam of Ch. Foyscroft Red Barn, and of Ch. Foyscroft Wild Flower, both by Ch. Rockaplenty's Wild Oats.

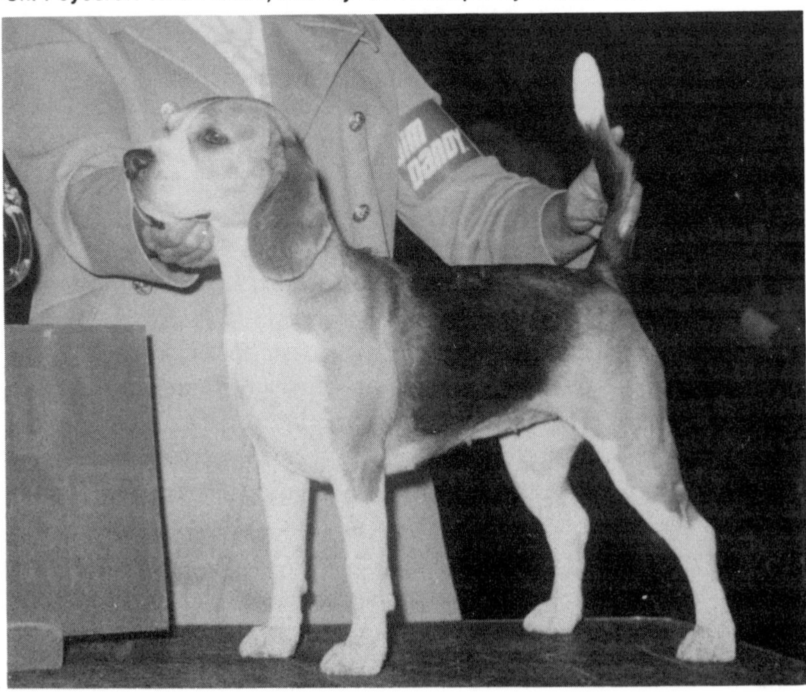

the morning. Decide upon what you will wear and have it out and ready. If there is any question in your mind about what to wear, try on the possibilities before the day of the show; don't risk feeling you may want to change when you see yourself dressed a few moments prior to departure time!

In planning your outfit, make it something simple that will not detract from your dog. Remember that a dark dog silhouettes attractively against a light background and vice-versa. Sport clothes always seem to look best at dog shows, preferably conservative in type and not overly "loud" as you do not want to detract from your dog, who should be the focus of interest at this point. What you wear on your feet is important. Many types of flooring can be hazardously slippery, as can wet grass. Make it a habit to wear rubber soles and low or flat heels in the ring for your own safety, especially if you are showing a dog that likes to move out smartly.

Your final step in pre-show preparation is to leave yourself plenty of time to reach the show that morning. Traffic can get amazingly heavy as one nears the immediate area of the show, finding a parking place can be difficult, and other delays may occur. You'll be in better humor to enjoy the day if your trip to the show is not fraught with panic over fear of not arriving in time!

Enjoying the Dog Show

From the moment of your arrival at the show until after your dog has been judged, keep foremost in your mind the fact the he is your reason for being there and that he should therefore be the center of your attention. Arrive early enough to have time for those last-minute touches that can make such a great difference when he enters the ring. Be sure that he has ample time to exercise and that he attends to personal matters. A dog arriving in the ring and immediately using it as an exercise pen hardly makes a favorable impression on the judge.

When you reach ringside, ask the steward for your arm-card and anchor it firmly into place on your arm. Make sure that you are where you should be when your class is called. The fact that you have picked up your arm-card does not guarantee, as some seem to think, that the judge will wait for you. The judge has a full schedule which he wishes to complete on time. Even though you may be nervous, assume an air of calm self-confidence. Remember that this is a hobby to be enjoyed, so approach it in that state of mind. The dog will do better, too, as he will be quick to reflect your attitude.

Always show your dog with an air of pride. If you make mistakes in presenting him, don't worry about it. Next time you will do better. Do not permit the presence of more experienced exhibitors to intimidate you. After all, they, too, once were newcomers.

The judging routine usually starts when the judge asks that the dogs be gaited in a circle around the ring. During this period the judge is watching each dog as it moves, noting style, topline, reach and drive, head and tail carriage, and general balance. Keep your mind and your eye on your dog, moving him at his most becoming gait and keeping your place in line without coming too close to the exhibitor ahead of you. Always keep your dog on the inside of the circle, between yourself and the judge, so that the judge's view of the dog is unobstructed.

Calmly pose the dog when requested to set up for examination. If you are at the head of the line and many dogs are in the class, go all the way to the end of the ring before starting to stack the dog, leaving sufficient space for those behind you to line theirs up as well as requested by the judge. If you are not at the head of the line but between other exhibitors, leave sufficient space ahead of your dog for the judge to examine him. The dogs should be spaced so that the judge is able to move among them to see them from all angles. In practicing to "set up" or "stack" your dog for the judge's examination, bear in mind the importance of doing so quickly and with dexterity. The judge has a schedule to meet and only a few moments in which to evaluate each dog. You will immeasurably help yours to make a favorable impression if you are able to "get it all together" in a minimum amount of time. Practice at home before a mirror can be a great help toward bringing this about, facing the dog so that you see him from the same side that the judge will and working to make him look right in the shortest length of time.

Listen carefully as the judge describes the manner in which the dog is to be gaited, whether it is straight down and straight back; down the ring, across, and back; or in a triangle. The latter has become the most popular pattern with the majority of judges. "In a triangle" means the dog should move down the outer side of the ring to the first corner, across that end of the ring to the second corner, and then back to the judge from the second corner, using the center of the ring in a diagonal line. Please learn to do this pattern without breaking at each corner to twirl the dog around you, a senseless maneuver we sometimes have noted. Judges like to see the dog in an uninterrupted triangle, as they are thus able to get a better idea of the dog's gait.

Ch. Garber's Cupcake, co-owned by the Foys and Virginia Flowers, winning a Hound Group. Dam of numerous noted Beagles. Marcia Foy made her a champion within a 36-hour period. She also was the first bitch to win Best of Breed at the National Specialty.

It is impossible to overemphasize that the gait at which you move your dog is tremendously important, and considerable study and thought should be given to the matter. At home, have someone move the dog for you at different speeds so that you can tell which shows him off to best advantage. The most becoming action almost invariably is seen at a moderate gait, head up and topline holding. Do not gallop your dog around the ring or hurry him into a speed atypical of his breed. Nothing being rushed appears at its best; give your dog a chance to move along at his (and the breed's) natural gait. For a dog's action to be judged accurately, that dog should move with strength and power but not excessive speed, holding a straight line as he goes to and from the judge.

As you bring the dog back to the judge, stop him a few feet away and be sure that he is standing in a becoming position. Bait him to show the judge an alert expression, using whatever tasty morsel he has been trained to expect for this purpose or, if that works better for you, use a small squeak-toy in your hand. A reminder, please, to those using liver or treats. Take them with you when you leave the ring. Do not just drop them on the ground where they will be found by another dog.

When the awards have been made, accept yours graciously, no matter how you actually may feel about it. What's done is done, and arguing with a judge or stomping out of the ring is useless and a reflection on your sportsmanship. Be courteous, congratulate the winner if your dog was defeated, and try not to show your disappointment. By the same token, please be a gracious winner; this, surprisingly, sometimes seems to be still more difficult.

Chapter 14

Your Beagle and Obedience

For its own protection and safety, every dog should be taught, at the very least, to recognize and obey the commands "Come," "Heel," "Down," "Sit," and "Stay." Doing so at some time might save the dog's life and in less extreme circumstances will certainly make him a better behaved, more pleasant member of society. If you are patient and enjoy working with your dog, study some of the excellent books available on the subject of obedience and then teach your canine friend these basic manners. If you need the stimulus of working with a group, find out where obedience training classes are held (usually your veterinarian, your dog's breeder, or a dog-owning friend can tell you) and you and your dog can join up. Alternatively, you could let someone else do the training by sending the dog to class, but this is not very rewarding because you lose the opportunity of working with your dog and the pleasure of the rapport thus established.

If you are going to do it yourself, there are some basic rules which you should follow. You must remain calm and confident in attitude. Never lose your temper and frighten or punish your dog unjustly. Be quick and lavish with praise each time a command is correctly followed. Make it fun for the dog and he will be eager to please you by responding correctly. Repetition is the keynote, but it should not be continued without recess to the point of tedium. Limit the training sessions to ten- or fifteen-minute periods at a time.

Formal obedience training can be followed, and very frequently is, by entering the dog in obedience competition to work toward an obedience degree, or several of them, depending on the dog's aptitude and your own enjoyment. Obedience trials are held in conjunction with

Roth's Henry of Harnett, C.D., 15″ tri, bred by John Potter, handled and owned by Richard H. Roth, Wilmington, N.C. Finishing his C.D. here at the Greater Columbia Obedience Trial Club in May 1982, earning Highest Scoring Beagle in Trial, Highest Scoring Dog in Hound Group, and 3rd place in Novice A Class, score of 193½. Henry again went High Hound in Trial the next day in Charleston. He was ranked No. 13 obedience Beagle in fall 1982, then moved up to No. 6 that winter.

the majority of all-breed conformation dog shows, with Specialty shows, and frequently as separate Specialty events. If you are working alone with your dog, a list of trial dates might be obtained from your dog's veterinarian, your dog breeder, or a dog-owning friend; the A.K.C. *Gazette* lists shows and trials to be scheduled in the coming months; and if you are a member of a training class, you will find the information readily available.

The goals for which one works in the formal A.K.C. Member or Licensed Trials are the following titles: Companion Dog (C.D.), Companion Dog Excellent (C.D.X.), and Utility Dog (U.D.). These degrees are earned by receiving three "legs," or qualifying scores, at each level of competition. The degrees must be earned in order, with

Sure Luv's Mist-er Beau Jangles, C.D., 15″ tri, by Ch. Sure Luv's Syd A Dream Maker Too ex Ch. Sure Luv's Heather Mist, completing C.D. at the Raleigh K.C. in March 1983. Bred by Helen Daley, owned by Ann H. Roth, Wilmington, N.C. Ranked No. 5 Obedience Beagle in the U.S., *Show Beagle Reporter.*

one completed prior to starting work on the next. For example, a dog must have earned C.D. prior to starting work on C.D.X.; then C.D.X. must be completed before U.D. work begins. The ultimate title attainable in obedience work is Obedience Trial Champion (O.T.Ch.).

When you see the letters "C.D." following a dog's name, you will know that this dog has satisfactorily completed the following exercises: heel on leash, heel free, stand for examination, recall, long sit and long stay. "C.D.X." means that tests have been passed on all of those just mentioned plus heel free, drop on recall, retrieve over high jump, broad jump, long sit, and long down. "U.D." indicates that the dog has additionally passed tests in scent discrimination (leather article), scent discrimination (metal article), signal exercises, directed retrieve, directed jumping, and group stand for examination. The letters "O.T.Ch." are the abbreviation for the only obedience title which precedes rather than follows a dog's name. To gain an obedience trial championship, a dog who already holds a Utility Dog degree must win

Magoo's Happy Valentine, Am. and Can. C.D.X., by Woodlands Sam-I-Am ex Woodlands Gal Cleo, winning second place in Open A at Thunder Bay Kennel and Training Club with a score of 191 in 1979. This was 1979's No. 1 Obedience Beagle and No. 2 Obedience Hound in Canada, competing in Open. Owned by Linda Lindberg, Birchwood Beagles, Cook, Minn.

a total of one hundred points and must win three firsts, under three different judges, in Utility and Open B Classes.

There is also a Tracking Dog title (T.D.) which can be earned at tracking trials. In order to pass the tracking tests the dog must follow the trail of a stranger along a path on which the trail was laid between thirty minutes and two hours previously. Along this track there must be more than two right-angle turns, at least two of which are well out in the open where no fences or other boundaries exist for the guidance of the dog or the handler. The dog wears a harness and is connected to the handler by a lead twenty to forty feet in length. Inconspicuously dropped at the end of the track is an article to be retrieved, usually a glove or wallet, which the dog is expected to locate and the handler to pick up. The letters "T.D.X." are the abbreviation for Tracking Dog Excellent, a more difficult version of the Tracking Dog test with a longer track and more turns to be worked through.

Chapter 15

Hound Shows and National Beagle Club Recognized Packs

Hound shows are competitions regarded with particular esteem by sportsmen and sportswomen who admire the working Beagle. Enthusiasm for them has always been high (just think of the many references to Peterborough one finds on reading early literature dealing with Beagles, Foxhounds, Bassets, and Harriers), and sharing honors with Peterborough as prestigious events are those of the Clonmel in Ireland and Bryn Mawr in the United States.

These hound shows are events quite separate from any held under the jurisdiction of such groups as the Kennel Club in England or the American Kennel Club in the United States which control bench show activities. Rather, they come under the suspices of the Association of Masters of Harriers and Beagles in England (Peterborough), the Association of Irish Masters in Ireland (Clonmel), and the National Beagle Club (Bryn Mawr). These groups maintain their own Stud Books, handling registration of the recognized packs, and it is they who govern the hound shows in their respective countries.

When Joan Brearley and I (A.K.N.) wrote our *The Wonderful World of Beagles and Beagling* back in the early 1970's some twenty packs were recognized and registered by the National Beagle Club. Now we find, in March 1984, that the number has grown by a half dozen or so and that enthusiasm has never been so keen. The masters of these packs

First 8 Couple in the Field, Fall 1983. Nantucket-Treweryn Pack. David B. Sharp, M.B., Middleburg, Virginia.

are most happy to assist newcomers wishing to form their own packs by providing suitable hounds and helpful advice to those contacting them.

To Pearl N. Baker, editor and general manager of the excellent publication, *Better Beagling,* we are indebted for the following explanation:

> For a pack to be recognized and registered with the National Beagle Club, a formal process must be followed. This is done in two steps and usually takes at least a year. The first step is to be registered with the National Beagle Club as an organized hunt. This requires a minimum of four couple of hounds, a recorded country where the hunts are to be held with permission of the landowners and any other recognized hunt, and an acceptable livery. In order to be recognized the pack must have five couple of hounds, acceptable kennel facilities, a formal hunt card and be regularly hunting their country. Each new pack is formally inspected by a committee appointed by the National Beagle Club. The N.B.C. actively encourages the formation of new packs, and helps existing packs when problems arise. The N.B.C. also publishes an annual Stud Book recording all hounds owned by the various packs.
>
> Although the National Beagle Club has an American Kennel Club delegate (currently, Mandy Cronin), individual hounds in the packs are not required to be registered. Although almost all of the newer packs do register their hounds with the American Kennel Club, some of the older packs no longer do so.

PACKS OF BEAGLES
SCORE OF POINTS FOR JUDGING

Hounds—General levelness of pack		40%
Individual merit of hounds	30%	70%
Manners		20%
Appointments		10%
Total		100%

Waldingfield Beagles, Arie M. Rijke and Forbes R. Reback, Joint Masters, pictured at the Fall 1983 Pack Trials at Aldie. Photo courtesy of William Bobbitt, Jr.

LEVELNESS OF PACK: The first thing in a pack to be considered is that they present a unified appearance. The hounds must be as near to the same height, weight, conformation and color as possible.
INDIVIDUAL MERIT OF THE HOUNDS: Is the individual bench-show quality of the hounds. A very level and sporty pack can be gotten together and not a single hound be a good Beagle. This is to be avoided.
MANNERS: The hounds must all work gaily and cheerfully, with flags up—obeying all commands cheerfully. They should be broken to heel up, kennel up, follow promptly and stand. Cringing, sulking, lying down to be avoided. Also, a pack must not work as though in terror of master and whips. In Beagle packs it is recommended that the whip be used as little as possible.
APPOINTMENTS: Master and whips should be dressed alike, the master of huntsman to carry horn—the whips and master to carry light thong whips. One whip should carry extra couplings on shoulder strap.

The Winners! Fox Valley 5 Couple Pack, William R. King, M.B. taking first place in the competition for the 13" Pack Class at the prestigious Bryn Mawr Hound Show. Fox Valley Beagles are from Bedford, Virginia. Leslie King, Whip.

RECOMMENDATIONS FOR SHOW LIVERY

Black velvet cap, white stock, green coat, white breeches or knickerbockers, green or black stockings, white spats, black or dark brown shoes. Vest and gloves optional. Ladies should turn out exactly the same except for a white skirt instead of white breeches.

The preceding is the Standard for Packs of Beagles and Score of Points for judging them.

The National Beagle Club is the parent club of the Beagle world, and it is the governing body of masters of not only Beagle Packs but also of Bassets and Harriers. It was founded in 1888, and it maintains its own magnificent grounds at Aldie, Virginia.

National Beagle Club Pack Trials are open to all. Usually, however, the majority of entries come from registered packs belonging to the members. All hounds competing at the National pack trials must belong to an individual or to a hunt organization. Classification includes two, four or eight couple packs, plus individual stakes which resemble the hare trials, with the qualification that competing hounds must previously have run in one of the pack classes.

There are two pack type classifications: private packs, owned or financially maintained by an individual, and subscription packs, supported by contributions from members and subscribers. Packs hunt, customarily, at least on Sunday afternoons and holidays, March through October.

The oldest still active of the Beagle packs remains Sir Sister, established in 1897 and registered in 1903. Sir Sister is very deservedly renowned for quality, both of the pack and of the individual hounds. The pack, referred to in its earliest days as "Smith's Beagles," was formally registered with the National by Chetwood Smith, who became a respected and knowledgeable authority whose services were greatly in demand as a judge at leading dog shows. The name "Sir Sister" was chosen for the pack, the story goes, as the result of Mr. Smith's receiving considerable chiding from his peers for his calling it "Smith's Beagles." When Mr. Smith decided to change the name, he felt "Sir Sister" would be appropriate because all the dogs' names were preceded by "Sir" and the bitches by "Sister." Chetwood Smith followed his brother Harry Worcester Smith as Master of the Sir Sister Hounds in 1903, remaining such until 1952. Then it was that Mr. and Mrs. Henri Prunaret became Joint Masters, maintaining their interest and involvement right up until the present time. The Prunarets live at Natick, Massachusetts.

It was Mrs. Prunaret's very good idea that red and white Beagles would be more easily visible than the tricolors against the New England terrain, and it was at her suggestion that the pack consist of this color, which is very attractive.

Although they do not maintain a show kennel, the Prunarets do show their Beagles upon occasion, usually at the Bay State and National Specialty Shows and at Bryn Mawr, which they seem to enjoy.

The second longest-established pack when *Beagles and Beagling* was written was Wolver, owned by C. Oliver Iselin, dating back to 1913. Since then Mr. Iselin has passed away; but we are happy to report that Wolver continues to carry on with Frederick Stone of Middleburg, Virginia, as Master.

America's third longest established pack is Treweryn which has merged with the fourth oldest, Nantucket, to form the Nantucket-Treweryns. Treweryn was founded in 1924, Nantucket two years later. They merged in 1964, with Mr. and Mrs. David B. Sharp, Jr., as Joint Masters. The Sharps are noted for the beauty and performance of their dogs, and they have won a great many honors with them at the trials and at the only hound show they attend, Bryn Mawr.

Waddingfield Beagles had been originally established in 1885, but the pack was disbanded and inactive over a lengthy period of time. Reorganization took place in 1972 and the pack is now again a busy one with Arie M. Rijkte, M.D., and Forbes R. Reback its Joint Masters at Charlottesville, Virginia.

The Sandonona Hare Hounds, long associated with the late Morgan Wing, since his death has been taken over by Mr. Oakley B. Thorne and Mrs. J.M. Park as Joint Masters at Millbrook, New York.

Fox Valley Beagles, William R. King, Master, is an active and successful pack, consisting of both field and show breeding. We note with pride that Fox Valley's Briarwood Junior Barnes, 13″ son of Champion Rockaplenty's Wild Oats and Champion Hollyhox Lady T. of Briarwood, won the Treweryn Bugler Bowl as Champion 13″ Beagles, Fox Valley going on to take the third Vernon Somerset Cup for the best five couple of Beagles, either sex, any age, any size not to exceed fifteen inches. Fox Valley is at Bedford, Virginia.

A unique pack is Bedlam, owned by Mrs. Mandy Cronin at Monroe, Virginia, of which she is M.B.—"unique" as this highly successful pack consists of field-bred dogs and some very excellent show-bred dogs. Champion Bedlam Tiger Talk is a multiple Group winner in bench show competition and is, we understand, alert and expert on the trail. Several other of Mrs. Cronin's pack members are also definitely dual-purpose dogs, excelling in the field while at the same time bringing home many a prestigious win from such events as Westminster along with those from Bryn Mawr.

Other National Beagle Club Member Packs include:

Androssan, St. David's, PA—Robert M. Scott, Master; L. Stockton Illoway, Huntsman.

Bare Cove, Frenchtown, NJ—Richard Roth, Master.

Chillybrook, Sweetbriar, VA—Paul B. Cronin, Master.

Fairfield County, CT—Hon. T.F. Gilroy Daly and Nicholas Niles, Jr., Masters.

Far Cry, Phoenixville, PA—Mr. and Mrs. M.C. Barton Higham, Joint Masters.

Fincastle, Jeffersonville, KY—Mrs. J.S. Rhodes and Hon. McAuley Smith, Joint Masters.

Fox Hill, Richmond, VA—Virginia Hayard, Master.

Glenbarr, Waynesboro, VA—Mr. and Mrs. W.F. Bobbitt, Jr., Joint Masters.

M.O.C. Beagles, The Plains, VA—Mrs. Paul Font, Master; Henry Wooman, Huntsman. (Hunts on horseback.)

Middletown Valley, Middletown, MD—James P. Farber, Warren Browning, and Mrs. R.P. Moran, Joint Masters.

Mountain Road, The Plains, VA—Capt. R.P. Foreman, Master.

New Covert, Whitehall, MD—Mrs. W. Perry Arnold, Master.

Octorora,—Lawrence Bright, Master; J. Clayton Bright, Huntsman.

Old Chatham Foot Beagles, Kinderhook, NY—Thomas G. Kelly, Master.

Widge Woode, Durham, NC—Dr. C.C. Pilkington, Master.

Rocky Fork, Columbus, OH—David O. Edwards and Ernest H. Clarke, Masters.

Rollington Foot Beagles, PeWee Valley, KY—Mr. and Mrs. W.P. Wiseman, Joint Masters.

Woodfield, Miccosukee, FL—Mrs. G.W. Humphrey and G. Watt Humphrey, Jr., Joint Masters.

Chapter 16

Field Trials

By Pearl N. Baker

The National Beagle Club, located in Aldie, Virginia, is the parent club of beagling in this country. They held the very first field trial in Hyannis, Massachusetts, in 1890. Since that time field trials have grown in popularity and there are now well over four hundred Beagle Clubs holding an A.K.C. (American Kennel Club) licensed trial each year. Even so, the primary use of the Beagle continues to be for hunting, mainly hare and/or cottontail. In some states they are also used to hunt fox, deer and occasionally other game ranging from wild boar to pheasants.

Thousands of Beagles used strictly for hunting are not registered and have no pedigree record, but they have been kept purebred. The disadvantage of not registering is that there is no record of hound families (bloodlines) when planning a breeding program. The American Kennel Club is the primary registry for dogs, including the Beagle, in this country. In 1983, 39,992 individual Beagles were registered putting them in 7th place of the 128 breeds registered with the A.K.C. A large percentage of these Beagles are bred primarily for show competition (conformation to the A.K.C. standard). The title of "Champion" is awarded to individual hounds that meet all requirements.

Only a very small number of show Beagles are also hunted or used for any type of field work. In many, the natural hunting instincts have been virtually bred out of them. However, careful study and knowledgeable breeding may help the beagler who wants to improve

Field Ch. Duffy Moon of Sugar River, with owner Gilbert "Butch" Keene, earned his championship in both Large Pack and Small Pack competition, 13″ dog. Photo courtesy of *Better Beagling Magazine.*

Measuring hounds for Winners Pack at Pine Hill's licensed trial 1983. Pine Hill Beagle Club is located in Guilderland, New York. Photo courtesy of ***Better Beagling Magazine.***

the conformation of his hunting stock. This should not be attempted by any but the experienced breeders as a litter of pups of little use for show or field work could result.

The American Kennel Club has four different types of field trials, set up to test the field work (hunting abilty) of the Beagle. As stated, there are now over four hundred Beagle clubs throughout the country approved by the A.K.C. to hold licensed field trials at which wins and points may be earned toward a "Field Champion" (Fd. Ch.) title. A hound must earn three wins and 120 points in one or more of the four types of field trials to earn his title.

A booklet, *Beagle Field Trial Rules and Standard Procedures,* which explains the rules for all four types of trials in detail, is available from the American Kennel Club, 51 Madison Avenue, New York, 10010 (single copies free, 25 cents each in quantities). Basically the four types of trials are: 1) BRACE On Rabbit or Hare—Two hounds compete at one time until the entire class is completed and a top winner, as well as second, third and fourth places, determined. 2) SMALL PACK On Rabbit or Hare—The total number of starters is broken down into packs of four to seven and first, second and sometimes third series are run. A "Winners Pack" of five to nine hounds good enough to still be in competition after first and second series is then run to determine the winning hound and second, third and fourth place. 3) SMALL PACK OPTION On Rabbit or Hare—This is the newest type of field trial, first recognized by the American Kennel Club in April of 1980. This trial is much like Small Pack but is designed to better determine a hound's hunting ability by a test for gunshyness, by firing a blank cartridge over the pack while in pursuit of a rabbit/hare. All hounds showing fear of the gunfire are eliminated from further competition. 4) LARGE PACK On Hare—All hounds in the class are usually run at one time, in one large pack, averaging in size from twenty to thirty hounds. This number of Beagles, excited and anxious to hunt, makes an impression on those seeing it for the first time. In spite of the large number of hounds, the hare is seldom in any real danger.

It is not uncommon in Large Pack trials to have a class of fifty or more. If a class numbers twenty-five or more the individual club's Field Trial Committee has the option of splitting it into two or more divisions. However, this is seldom done.

All four types of A.K.C.-licensed field trials are divided into four classes: 1(13″ BITCH—for females measuring under thirteen inches. 2) 13″ DOG—for males measuring under thirteen inches. 3) 15″

BITCH—for females measuring over 13 inches but not more than 15 inches. 4) 15″ DOG—for males measuring over 13 inches but not more than 15 inches. Any hound measuring over 15″ is not eligible to run in A.K.C. Beagle Field Trial competition.

All four types give points for desirable field qualities as listed in the Rule Book but determined by the judges. This interpretation of the rules has caused considerable controversy in recent years and resulted in very different types or "styles" of hounds being placed in the various trials. A hound may be demerited for faulty action or, if serious enough to warrant, eliminated from further competition in that trial.

In addition to first through fourth place, an NBQ (next best qualified) award is usually given in each class at all four types of trials.

Each class has two or more judges who may judge on foot or horseback.

Of the more than four hundred A.K.C.-licensed trials held each year, approximately forty are Large Pack On Hare, thirty are Small Pack Option, forty are Small Pack and the remainder are Brace.

Unfortunately for those interested in a Hunting Beagle, the Brace and Small Pack trials (as is the case of field trials for so many hunting breeds) no longer offer a true test for a Beagle of any use to the average "rabbit hunter." The searching and running ability has been bred out of most of them in the name of "style." They make what should be an easy line to follow look difficult and actually accomplish very little. Many refer to them as "Walkie-Talkies" because they trail the rabbit at a slow walk, spending considerable time barking in each track. Since the average gun hunter must have a hound capable of moving the game at a much faster pace, the present-day Brace Trial hound is of little use for any other purpose. The majority of the Small Pack hounds are little better than Brace for hunting purposes, but Small Pack Option and Large Pack on Hare are different stories.

Since Large Pack trials are run on hare, these clubs are limited to areas within the range of the snowshoe hare. Although currently three clubs are holding Large Pack trials on the large swamp rabbits of Louisiana and Texas, the remainder of these clubs are in Michigan, New York, Vermont, New Hampshire, Massachusetts and Maine. Beaglers entering their hounds in these trials are for the most part hunters as well and enter the same hound in a trial as they take on an actual hunt. A person in search of a "rabbit dog" could feel quite safe in checking out this source for a puppy or running hound. Any

Closecall Checkmate Charlie, good worker in the field, owned by Bayberry Beagles, Andy and Carolyn Hayduck.

reputable breeder should be willing to answer questions and tell the buyer whether or not he feels his stock could meet his requirements.

Hounds in Large Pack competition are the fastest of all field trial hounds due to the game they run, but the good ones adjust their speed to game and scenting conditions and many are capable of running cottontail just as well as they do hare.

Most Large Pack trials are judged on foot because of the rough terrain and thick woods where hare are found. Due to the speed of the hounds few judges are able to keep up with the pack for more than short distances. They should be "woods wise" enough to know where the hare is apt to circle in order to be in position to see "marked lines" (the hare going through an opening or area) and get to a "check" (temporary loss of scent by the pack) on time. These judges must be in good physical condition because the pack must run for at least three hours and frequently will run for four to five hours or more.

As previously stated, the Small Pack Option trial is the newest type of A.K.C. field trial. In the mid-1970's a small group of hunters in the South and Deep South grew tired of the difficulty in finding suitable registered replacement stock for their personal packs. Since they considered Brace and Small Pack to no longer be a test for a hunting Beagle, they also wanted a trial in which they could compete. Most were too far from Large Pack areas to make that type of trial practical; besides they hunted cottontail, not hare. Thus they set about writing their own rules and holding small local "fun trials." They referred to themselves as the "Gundog Movement" and it caught on, growing by leaps and bounds. It soon covered such a wide area, resulting in so many varied and sometimes conflicting ideas, that it broke up into two major federations: the Deep South Beagle Gundog Federation (D.S.B.G.F.) and the United Beagle Gundog Federation (U.B.G.F.) While membership in both federations is open to clubs from any state, the D.S.B.G.F. is centered mainly in the Deep South and the U.B.G.F. in the Midwest and East. There are also two smaller groups, The Southern New York Gundog Affiliation and the Mid-West Gundog Association, in the Ohio area.

After several years of hard work and compromise, they were accepted by the American Kennel Club and written into the field trial rules as Small Pack Option. The first A.K.C.-licensed Small Pack Option trial held by a newly organized "Gundog Club" was held by Acadiana Beagle Club, Eunice, Louisiana, on February 28 and March 1, 1981. They had 173 starting hounds in the four classes. In 1983, twenty-seven clubs in fifteen states held A.K.C.-licensed Small Pack Option trials, with more scheduled for 1984. The location of these trials ranges from Vermont to Texas.

Due to the wide geographical area covered, varied terrain and conditions, local preferences in Hunting Beagles, and so on, the running style of Beagles seen at the Small Pack Option trials may differ considerably from one area to another. However, all are hunting Beagles and, as long as they continue to judge their trials with a Hunting Beagle in mind, this could also be a good source to find a useful "rabbit dog." Again, the buyer should ask questions to determine if the hound offered for sale will meet his needs.

The United Beagle Gundog Federation, comprising twenty-three clubs, has a Certified Hunting Beagle (C.H.B.) program. Under this program a hound may earn a C.H.B. title and go on to earn the title of Gundog Champion (Gd. Ch.). Only hounds owned by members of member clubs are eligible for these titles and they are only recognized by the United Beagle Gundog Federation. They have no connection with the field champion title given by the American Kennel Club, even though some of the clubs do hold A.K.C.-licensed trials as well as their own CHB trials. The C.H.B. and Gd. Ch. titles are earned by getting the required score in both field and show competition at U.B.G.F. events.

Chapter 17

Training Hounds

by Ray Libby

We are very pleased to bring you this chapter on training hounds for the field, which was written by the well-known Beagler, Ray Libby, and is used with permission of *Better Beagling* magazine.

A.K.N.

There is no secret to training a Beagle to run a rabbit or a hare. All it takes is a little common sense and a few precautions. This holds true with young hounds especially. A *properly bred* Beagle has all the inborn instincts of wanting to hunt and run. All he requires is the opportunity to do so.

A good time to start this training is around eight months old. This is plenty early enough. By this time he is slightly more settled than at an earlier age. If starting youngsters with an older experienced hound, make sure it is a clean one, honest in its work. If it is on the slow side, so much the better. However, once you get the hounds started, run them by themselves. When they gain the experience to follow the line

Field Ch. North Bend Billy Grimshaw, owned by Joe Hanlon, earned his championship with wins in both Large Pack and Small Pack Option Competition. 15″ Dog. Photo courtesy of *Better Beagling Magazine.*

accurately and show ability to find their own checks without any trouble, then you can think about letting them do some running with older experienced *honest* hounds. Don't try to push them however. Young hounds are sometimes like young boys—subject to making mistakes if over-competed. If these mistakes are made often then they must be considered faults.

To you young beaglers (and older experienced ones as well), how fortunate you are if you live where you have cottontail as well as hare to train your hounds on. There is nothing better to start your young hound on than cottontail, so don't be afraid to give your pup a lot of training on them. They will be better hounds for it. The cottontail is an ideal game to train young hounds on because normally he is a "ducker" and a "dodger" that many times lays a twisting and turning trail. This makes him unbeatable for giving hounds experience in the art of learning to find checks.

Keep in mind the easiest part of a hound's work is following the line. The harder and more important part of his work is finding those checks.

Some beaglers run their derbies against older experienced hounds in the field trials. While it has been done with success and without doing any damage to some of these young hounds, I was always very careful about this. It is only my opinion, but I have always felt it was better to wait until they were at least two years old before running them in field trials. This still gives young hounds plenty of time to compete in trials. Since they are older they will be more mature and, if properly bred, less excitable. Probably I am more cautious than some, and it is not my purpose to tell any beagler at what age he should enter his hounds in trials, but I have seen several good prospects damaged by running too much in packs continually that contained faulty hounds. Although the old adage is "you can't spoil a good hound," I wonder if we should apply that theory to younger hounds. While it definitely can apply to an older experienced and confident hound, when we show a careless attitude by exposing our young hounds on a more or less continual basis, we may give them the kind of competition they are not ready for. This especially holds true of the youngster that needs a little more time and experience to adjust to the faster, more experienced, harder driving hound. And we should be even more concerned about exposing impressive youngsters to the over-competitive, faulty hounds, a few of which are found in most every pack trial. I cannot emphasize this too strongly.

Any hound, young or old, is under a certain amount of pressure when running in a pack. You see this continually in packs where hounds overrun badly, gamble, and reach. These faults are a combination of a lack of brains and an over-competitive, aggressive spirit. Beagles properly bred are less susceptible to these faults, but they can acquire them if exposed to them too often. This holds true in young hounds especially.

I for one was never enthusiastic about running my hounds at the Beagle Club during times when the area was being used by other beaglers running hounds of all descriptions. I always tried to get over there when everyone else had gone home. However, a great deal of my training was done in an open area right here behind my home. Although occasionally I used to like to run with the other boys, I never made a practice of it.

Young hounds also should be gunned over and have game shot ahead of them. I think it has a tendency to make them want to hunt and run more. Years ago when I was a very young beagler I had an experience I will never forget. I had bought a pup of Uncle Sam breeding close up. Being young and anxious to get this youngster running when he was around five months old and because I wanted to get him started before snow covered the ground (it was November) I began giving him sight chases on cottontail I had forced out of stone walls with another hound. Now anyone familiar with Uncle Sam breeding and pups by him out of aggressive bitches is perfectly aware those youngsters had to be handled differently. Many of these youngsters had to be given more time to settle down, but once they began you had the makings of a real good gun dog. They were just full of hunting desire and anxious to drive their game hard.

After giving him all those sight chases on those cottontail, and he was big enough and had speed enough to catch them in a forty acre cow pasture, I began taking him out to the woods and starting him on hare. As I mentioned above, it was in latter November, the ground was bare, and all the foliage off the trees. If nothing else at the time he was a hard fast searcher and there were plenty of hare—all white. He would jump those hare, give them a sight chase, and never stop to look for the line of scent after they got out of his sight. He would just keep on going looking for another sight chase on others. After spending a little more time with him trying to straighten him out, I disposed of him. It was a lesson I learned and fortunately learned early. I never practiced that particular brand of training again. From that time on I let nature take its course. Incidentally, I owned several other youngsters whose breeding contained a lot of Uncle Sam and you had to use better patience with them and a lot of common sense.

Every beagler has his own ideas about training. The most important factor: when you think he is ready for his first lessons get him on game so he will have plenty of opportunity to develop his potential talents.

Chapter 18

Gundog Trials

By Kathleen Carling

The following information was obtained from Dan Bush, Past President and Past Field Secretary of the Rainbow Beagle Club. The Rainbow Club (a member of the United Beagle Gundog Federation) was established around 1959 and was founded as a Brace club. They later combined functions as a Gundog club also in 1976. The A.K.C. has sanctioned the trials but has not yet recognized the certificate awarded, Certified Hunting Beagle (C.H.B.). The trials are run under the Small Pack Option and there are between four and seven dogs in the packs. They are also judged that day on their conformation. This is one of the first group of clubs to combine conformation with field work. It surely demonstrates an interest in the dual-purpose Beagle.

The main differences between the existing Brace trials and the Gundog trials would be that the Brace trials run just two dogs together rather than four to seven in a pack; the gundogs are cast as a group to find game, and the gundogs are shot over with a 32 caliber blank pistol. This last item I find very important because any dog used in the field should be accustomed to the sound of shotgun fire and show no evidence of gun-shyness. The dogs arrive early the day of the trial and the numbers are picked for the packs randomly. The judges are selected weeks before by the Field Trial Committee.

The first running of the dogs is the First Series. This is a general observation of the packs and the weeding out of any undesirables. It is

State of Michigan Small Pack Gundog Champion 1982 "Irish Jake" 15" male. *(Left to right)* judge Tony Chillofto, hound owner Mike Johnson, judge Kurt Visniski, hound handler Bob Johnson, judge Mario Santoro, and judge Steve Fulks.

Four 1st place hounds run as one pack in Michigan State Gundog Championship Trial. *(Left to right)* "Suzy's Pete Driver," Jim Cleaver owner; "Alder Creek Windstorm," Tony Chillofto, owner; "Vineyard's M's Sally," Walt Fulks, owner; "Irish Jake," Bob Johnson, handler. Background: judges Kurt Visniski, Steve Fulks, and Mario Santoro.

Michigan State Gundog Championship Trial October 1982 15″ Male Class. *(Left to right)* "Irish Jake," Bob Johnson, handler; "Lake Country Henry," Tim Cleaver, handler; "Morgan Mac Rae," Larry Freeman, owner, "Deerfield Boomer," John Ciesielski, owner; "Pirman's Ko-Ko Smokey," Ruth Pirman, handler. Background: Tony Chillofto, George Pirman, field marshal, and Kurt Visniski, judge.

optional to shoot over and measure the First Series, for it can also be done over Winners Pack. Second Series is optional. It is at the judges' discretion depending on the number of hounds entered that day. It may be necessary to run a Second Series if there are a great number entered because the maximum for Winners Pack is nine hounds. Winners Pack is run last and the cream of the crop that day is judged here. From this group of not more than nine is picked the one through fourth placements and the N.B.Q. (Next Best Qualifier).

Usually in the afternoon the conformation judging begins. As in field judging, the 13″ and 15″ are judged separately, but if the entry is low that day the sexes may be combined. The field work has 1 to 100 points available as does the show competition. Sixty points or more are required to qualify in either. In order for a hound to receive his C.H.B. Certificate he must place in the field one through four or N.B.Q. and have received at least 60 or more points in conformation that day. This must be done on the same day. A dog cannot win in the field and not the show, and then take his field points to a future trial. In order to enter the National Run-Off, a dog must have his C.H.B. or have qualified for one.

In regard to field judging, after the hounds are cast, the judge is looking for the following qualities: 1) searching ability, 2) eagerness to search and aptitude to find good cover, 3) pursuing ability, 4) keeping control of the trail and making the best possible progress, 5) accuracy in trailing, 6) proper use of voice, 7) proclaiming all finds, 8) noting all forward progress by giving tongue, 9) keeping silent while not making progress, and 10) endurance. Some of the faults the field judges look for are: 1) quitting, 2) backtracking, 3) ghost trailing, and 4) pottering (lack of effort or desire to make forward progress on the line). The hound with the highest combined score of field and show together that day is the Grand Final Winner and the hound with the second highest combined score is Grand Final Runner-Up.

The conformation judging is done much like our shows. Most of the field handlers haven't learned the use of the show lead and other aspects of showing, but they have come a long way in the past few years. A little show training, table work and patience will bring out the best in their hounds. It can be difficult to judge a nice class when the best hounds, structure wise, are completely untrained to walk on lead. I hope to see this change in the future, because it's a shame when the best dog can't win just because he is not trained. Even with the limited judging I've done, there are some excellent hounds out there. I've seen beautiful heads and angulation and basically good rears. As a general observation most of the fronts need to be improved. It is hard to judge feet quality because most of these dogs are kept on wire runs. This tends to spread the toes and encourages very long nails. This may not seem important, but the foot of the hunting hound is very essential. It is that part of his body that comes in contact with the ground and takes the most punishment. Therefore it should be cared for carefully.

Most of the dogs carry good pigment and coats. I've seen a few light eyes but not many. In a recent fun trial I witnessed a few very nice 13″ dogs, their movement being smooth and free with excellent fronts. They were true 13″, not just very short-legged 15″.

I truly enjoy this new sport. I would like to see in the future more show people using their dogs in the field. It is an excellent test for movement. A well-built, correctly angulated animal can run almost effortlessly all day, poor structure showing up in fatigue and lack of grace. The gundog people are on the right track. Breeding and training for a beautiful hound that can also hunt will insure the future of our breed. I hope the A.K.C. some day will recognize this effort.

Chapter 19

Breeding Your Beagle

The Beagle Brood Bitch

We have in an earlier chapter discussed selection of a bitch you plan to use for breeding. In making this important purchase, you will be choosing a bitch who you hope will become the foundation of your kennel. Thus she must be of the finest producing bloodlines, excellent in temperament, of good type, and free of major faults or unsoundness. If you are offered a "bargain" brood bitch, be wary, as for this purchase you should not settle for less than the best and the price will be in accordance with the quality.

Conscientious breeders feel quite strongly that the only possible reason for producing puppies is the ambition to improve and uphold quality and temperament within the breed—definitely *not* because one hopes to make a quick cash profit on a mediocre litter, which never seems to work out that way in the long run and which accomplishes little beyond perhaps adding to the nation's heartbreaking number of unwanted canines. The only reason ever for breeding a litter is, with conscientious people, a desire to improve the quality of dogs in their own kennel or, as pet owners, because they wish to add to the number of dogs they themselves own with a puppy or two from their present favorites. In either case breeding should not take place unless one has definitely prospective owners for as many puppies as the litter may contain, lest you find yourself with several fast-growing young dogs and no homes in which to place them.

Bitches should not be mated earlier than their second season, by which time they should be from fifteen to eighteen months old. Many breeders prefer to wait and first finish the championships of their show bitches before breeding them, as pregnancy can be a disaster to a

Ch. Teloca Red's Middle Child, C.D., 13" red female, by Ch. King's Creek Triple Threat ex Ch. Robin's Red of Honey Hill, C.D., with litter of tri-colored puppies. Middle Child is owned by Susan Wade. Puppies are Ch. Teloca Me and My CB, Ch. Teloca Bunnyrun Baby Love, Ch. Teloca Hippity Hoppins, and Ch. Teloca Faux Paw. Sired by Ch. The Whim's Cock Of The Walk.

show coat and getting the bitch back in shape again takes time. When you have decided what will be the proper time, start watching at least several months ahead for what you feel would be the perfect mate to best complement your bitch's quality and bloodlines. Subscribe to the magazines which feature your breed exclusively and to some which cover all breeds in order to familiarize yourself with outstanding stud dogs in areas other than your own for there is no necessity nowadays to limit your choice to a nearby dog unless you truly like him and feel that he is the most suitable. It is quite usual to ship a bitch to a stud dog a distance away, and this generally works out with no ill effects. The important thing is that you need a stud dog strong in those features where your bitch is weak or lacking and of bloodlines compatible to hers. Compare the background of both your bitch and the stud dog under consideration, paying particular attention to the quality of the puppies from bitches with backgrounds similar to your bitch's. If the puppies have been of the type and quality you admire, then this dog would seem a sensible choice for yours, too.

Stud fees may be a few hundred dollars, sometimes even more under special situations for a particularly successful sire. It is money well spent, however. Do *not* ever breed to a dog because he is less expensive than the others unless you honestly believe that he can sire the kind of puppies who will be a credit to your kennel and your breed.

Contacting the owners of the stud dogs you find interesting will bring you pedigrees and pictures which you can then study in relation to your bitch's pedigree and conformation. Discuss your plans with other breeders who are knowledgeable (including the one who bred your own bitch). You may not always receive an entirely unbiased opinion (particularly if the person giving it also has an available stud dog), but one learns by discussion so listen to what they say, consider their opinions, and then you may be better qualified to form your own opinion.

As soon as you have made a choice, phone the owner of the stud dog you wish to use to find out if this will be agreeable. You will be asked about the bitch's health, soundness, temperament, and freedom from serious faults. A copy of her pedigree may be requested, as might a picture of her. A discussion of her background over the telephone may be sufficient to assure the stud's owner that she is suitable for the stud dog and of type, breeding, and quality herself to produce puppies of the quality for which the dog is noted. The owner of a top-quality stud is often extremely selective in the bitches permitted to be bred to his dog, in an effort to keep the standard of his puppies high. The owner of a

Ch. Daisyrun's Pooh Bear taking Winners Bitch at the National Specialty in 1978. Breeder-owner-handler Nadine Eaton.

Am. and Can. Ch. Birchwood India Ink, Best of Breed. Ch. Birchwood Bogie Blue, Best of Opposite Sex. Judge Melbourne Downing. These are blue-tri littermates, bred by Linda Lindberg, Birchwood Beagles, Cook, Minn. by Ch. Linvens Super Star ex Am. and Can. Ch. Meado-Glo Birchwoods Holly. India Ink owner-handled by Linda Lindberg. Bogie handled by Nancy Spaeth for owner Linda Robertson.

stud dog may require that the bitch be tested for brucellosis, which should be attended to not more than a month previous to the breeding.

Check out which airport will be most convenient for the person meeting and returning the bitch if she is to be shipped and also what airlines use that airport. You will find that the airlines are also apt to have special requirements concerning acceptance of animals for shipping. These include weather limitations and types of crates which are acceptable. The weather limits have to do with extreme heat and extreme cold at the point of destination, as some airlines will not fly dogs into temperatures above or below certain levels, fearing for their safety. The crate problem is a simple one, since if your own crate is not suitable, most of the airlines have specially designed crates available for purchase at a fair and moderate price. It is a good plan to purchase one of these if you intend to be shipping dogs with any sort of frequency. They are made of fiberglass and are the safest type to use for shipping.

Normally you must notify the airline several days in advance to make a reservation, as they are able to accommodate only a certain number of dogs on each flight. Plan on shipping the bitch on about her eighth or ninth day of season, but be careful to avoid shipping her on a weekend, when schedules often vary and freight offices are apt to be closed. Whenever you can, ship your bitch on a direct flight. Changing planes always carries a certain amount of risk of a dog being overlooked or wrongly routed at the middle stop, so avoid this danger if at all possible. The bitch must be accompanied by a health certificate which you must obtain from your veterinarian before taking her to the airport. Usually it will be necessary to have the bitch at the airport about two hours prior to flight time. Before finalizing arrangements, find out from the stud's owner at what time of day it will be most convenient to have the bitch picked up promptly upon arrival.

It is simpler if you can plan to bring the bitch to the stud dog. Some people feel that the trauma of the flight may cause the bitch to not conceive; and, of course, undeniably there is a slight risk in shipping which can be avoided if you are able to drive the bitch to her destination. Be sure to leave yourself sufficient time to assure your arrival at the right time for her for breeding (normally the tenth to fourteenth day following the first signs of color); and remember that if you want the bitch bred twice, you should allow a day to elapse between the two matings. Do not expect the stud's owner to house you while you are there. Locate a nearby motel that takes dogs and make that your headquarters.

Just prior to the time your bitch is due in season, you should take her

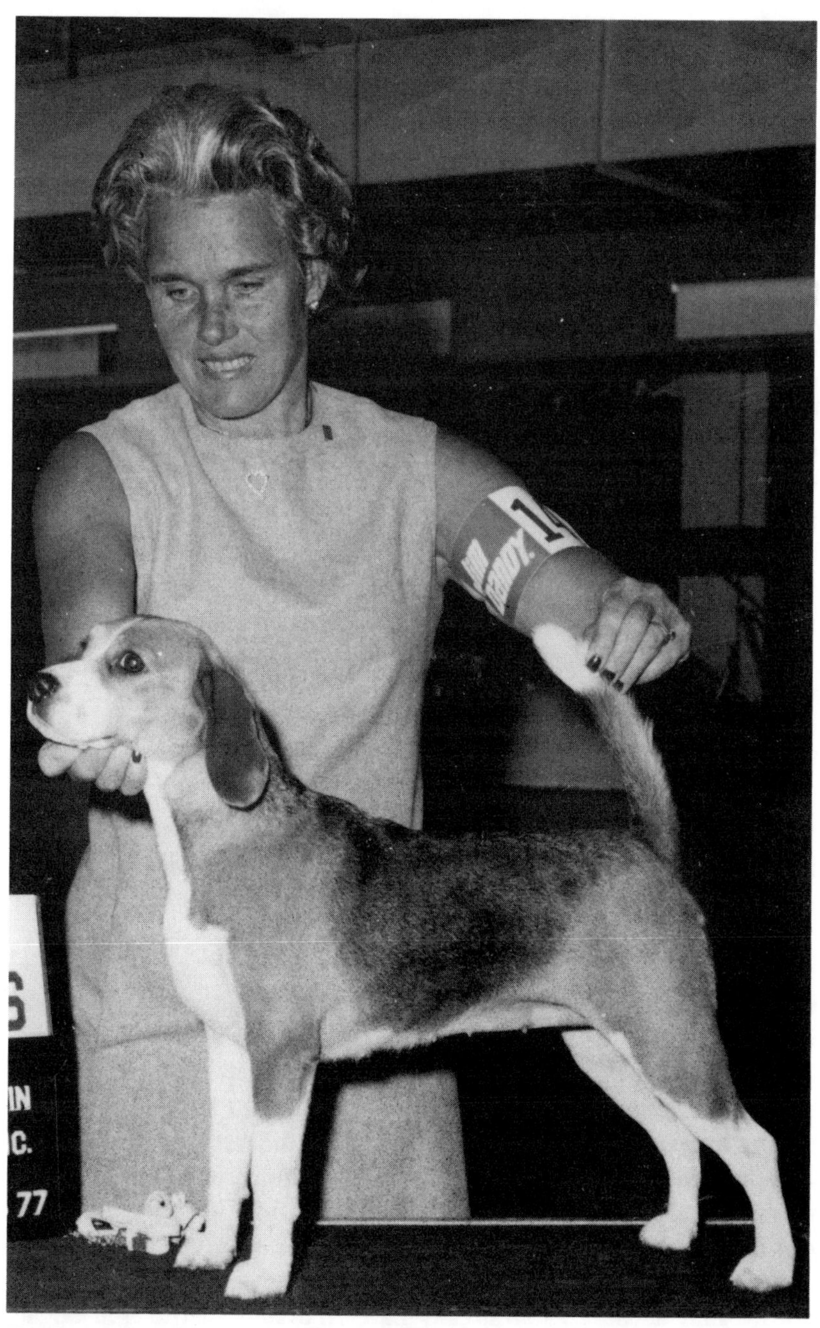

The foundation bitch for Brantwood's Beagles, Ch. Lokavi's Double Trouble, by Ch. Beaujangles of Beagle Chase ex Ch. Foyscroft Triple Trollop, handled by Jane Forsyth for owner Anita Tillman.

to visit your veterinarian. She should be checked for worms and should receive all the booster shots for which she is due plus one for parvo virus, unless she has had the latter shot fairly recently. The brucellosis test can also be done then, and the health certificate can be obtained for shipping if she is to travel by air. Should the bitch be at all overweight, now is the time to get the surplus off. She should be in good condition, neither underweight nor overweight, at the time of breeding.

The moment you notice the swelling of the vulva, for which you should be checking daily as the time for her season approaches, and the appearance of color, immediately contact the stud's owner and settle on the day for shipping or make the appointment for your arrival with the bitch for breeding. If you are shipping the bitch, the stud fee check should be mailed immediately, leaving ample time for it to have been received when the bitch arrives and the mating takes place. Be sure to call the airline making her reservation at that time, too.

Do not feed the bitch within a few hours before shipping her. Be certain that she has had a drink of water and been well exercised before closing her in the crate. Several layers of newspapers, topped with some shredded newspaper, make a good bed and can be discarded when she arrives at her destination; these can be replaced with fresh newspapers for her return home. Remember that the bitch should be brought to the airport about two hours before flight time as sometimes the airlines refuse to accept late arrivals.

If you are taking your bitch by car, be certain that you will arrive at a reasonable time of day. Do not appear late in the evening. If your arrival in town is not until late, get a good night's sleep at your motel and contact the stud's owner first thing in the morning. If possible, leave children and relatives at home, as they will only be in the way and perhaps unwelcome by the stud's owner. Most stud dog owners prefer not to have any unnecessary people on hand during the actual mating.

After the breeding has taken place, if you wish to sit and visit for awhile and the stud's owner has the time, return the bitch to her crate in your car (first ascertaining, of course, that the temperature is comfortable for her and that there is proper ventilation). She should not be permitted to urinate for at least one hour following the breeding. This is the time when you get the business part of the transaction attended to. Pay the stud fee, upon which you should receive your breeding certificate and, if you do not already have it, a copy of the stud dog's pedigree. The owner of the stud dog does not sign or furnish a litter registration application until the puppies have been born.

This is Ch. Page Mill Call Girl, dam of Ch. Rockaplenty's Wild Oats, handled by Bobby Barlow to a Best of Variety under Edith Hellerman in 1970. Owned by Paul H. Miller and Carroll Gordon, who is now Carroll Diaz.

Upon your return home, you can settle down and plan in happy anticipation a wonderful litter of puppies. A word of caution! Remember that although she has been bred, your bitch is still an interesting target for all male dogs, so guard her carefully for the next week or until you are absolutely certain that her season has entirely ended. This would be no time to have any unfortunate incident with another dog.

The Beagle Stud Dog

Choosing the best stud dog to complement your bitch is often very difficult. The two principal factors to be considered should be the stud's conformation and his pedigree. Conformation is fairly obvious; you want a dog that is typical of the breed in the words of the standard of perfection. Understanding pedigrees is a bit more subtle since the pedigree lists the ancestry of the dog and involves individuals and bloodlines with which you may not be entirely familiar.

To a novice in the breed, then, the correct interpretation of a pedigree may at first be difficult to grasp. Study the pictures and text of this book and you will find many names of important bloodlines and members of the breed. Also make an effort to discuss the various dogs behind the proposed stud with some of the more experienced breeders,

The foundation dog at Chrisette Beagles: Ch. Foyscroft Red Barn, by Ch. Rockaplenty's Wild Oats ex Ch. Foyscroft Triple Lina Wor Lo. This was Sandy Robichaud's first Beagle, and he was quite a trail blazer for the red and white color which was a decade ago only rarely seen in the show ring.

starting with the breeder of your own bitch. Frequently these folks will be personally familiar with many of the dogs in question, can offer opinions of them, and may have access to additional pictures which you would benefit by seeing.

It is very important that the stud's pedigree should be harmonious with that of the bitch you plan on breeding to him. Do not rush out and breed to the latest winner with no thought of whether or not he can produce true quality. By no means are all great show dogs great producers. It is the producing record of the dog in question and the dogs and bitches from which he has come which should be the basis on which you make your choice.

Breeding dogs is never a money-making operation. By the time you pay a stud fee, care for the bitch during pregnancy, whelp the litter, and rear the puppies through their early shots, worming, and so on, you will be fortunate to break even financially once the puppies have been sold. Your chances of doing this are greater if you are breeding for a show-quality litter which will bring you higher prices as the pups are sold as show prospects. Therefore, your wisest investment is to use the best dog available for your bitch regardless of the cost; then you should wind up with more valuable puppies. Remember that it is equally costly to raise mediocre puppies as top ones, and your chances of financial return are better on the latter. To breed to the most excellent, most suitable stud dog you can find is the only sensible thing to do, and it is poor economy to quibble over the amount you are paying in stud fee.

It will be your decision which course you decide to follow when you breed your bitch, as there are three options: line-breeding, inbreeding, and outcrossing. Each of these methods has its supporters and its detractors! Line-breeding is breeding a bitch to a dog belonging originally to the same canine family, being descended from the same ancestors, such as half-brother to half-sister, grandsire to granddaughters, niece to uncle (and vice-versa) or cousin to cousin. Inbreeding is breeding father to daughter, mother to son, or full brother to sister. Outcross breeding is breeding a dog and a bitch with no or only a few mutual ancestors.

Line-breeding is probably the safest course, and the one most likely to bring results, for the novice breeder. The more sophisticated inbreeding should be left to the experienced, long-time breeders who thoroughly know and understand the risks and the possibilities involved with a particular line. It is usually done in an effort to intensify some ideal feature in that strain. Outcrossing is the reverse of inbreeding, an effort to introduce improvement in a specific feature needing correction, such as a shorter back, better movement, more correct head or coat, and so on.

It is the serious breeder's ambition to develop a strain or bloodline of their own, one strong in qualities for which their dogs will become distinguished. However, it must be realized that this will involve time, patience, and at least several generations before the achievement can be claimed. The safest way to embark on this plan, as we have mentioned, is by the selection and breeding of one or two bitches, the best you can buy and from top-producing kennels. In the beginning you do *not* really have to own a stud dog. In the long run it is less expensive and sounder judgment to pay a stud fee when you are ready to breed a bitch than to purchase a stud dog and feed him all year; a stud dog does not win any popularity contests with owners of bitches to be bred until he becomes a champion, has been successfully Specialed for awhile, and has been at least moderately advertised, all of which adds up to a quite healthy expenditure.

The wisest course for the inexperienced breeder just starting out in dogs is as we have outlined above. Keep the best bitch puppy from the first several litters. After that you may wish to consider keeping your own stud dog if there has been a particularly handsome male in one of your litters that you feel has great potential or if you know where there is one available that you are interested in, with the feeling that he would work in nicely with the breeding program on which you have embarked. By this time, with several litters already born, your eye should have developed to a point enabling you to make a wise choice, either from one of your own litters or from among dogs you have seen that appear suitable.

The greatest care should be taken in the selection of your own stud dog. He must be of true type and highest quality as he may be responsible for siring many puppies each year, and he should come from a line of excellent dogs on both sides of his pedigree which themselves are, and which are descended from, successful producers. This dog should have no glaring faults in conformation; he should be of such quality that he can hold his own in keenest competition within his breed. He should be in good health, be virile and be a keen stud dog, a proven sire able to transmit his correct qualities to his puppies. Need we say that such a dog will be enormously expensive unless you have the good fortune to produce him in one of your own litters? To buy and

Ch. Londonderry's Aladdin, by Ch. Londonderry's Oliver ex Ch. Londonderry's Curtain Call, completing his title in September 1979. "Laddie" finished in four consecutive shows and is the sire of two champions with a number more "pointed" and on their way. Owner-handled by Lee Cord, Londonderry Kennels, Sayville, NY.

use a lesser stud dog, however, is downgrading your breeding program unnecessarily since there are so many dogs fitting the description of a fine stud whose services can be used on payment of a stud fee.

You should *never* breed to an unsound dog or one with any serious standard or disqualifying faults. Not all champions by any means pass along their best features; and by the same token, occasionally you will find a great one who can pass along his best features but never gained his championship title due to some unusual circumstances. The information you need about a stud dog is what type of puppies he has produced and with what bloodlines and whether or not he possesses the bloodlines and attributes considered characteristic of the best in your breed.

If you go out to buy a stud dog, obviously he will not be a puppy but rather a fully mature and proven male with as many of the best attributes as possible. True, he will be an expensive investment, but if you choose and make his selection with care and forethought, he may well prove to be one of the best investments you have ever made.

Of course, the most exciting of all is when a young male you have decided to keep from one of your litters due to his tremendous show potential turns out to be a stud dog such as we have described. In this case he should be managed with care, for he is a valuable property that can contribute inestimably to his breed as a whole and to your own kennel specifically.

Do not permit your stud dog to be used until he is about a year old, and even then he should be bred to a mature, proven matron accustomed to breeding who will make his first experience pleasant and easy. A young dog can be put off forever by a maiden bitch who fights and resists his advances. Never allow this to happen. Always start a stud dog out with a bitch who is mature, has been bred previously, and is of even temperament. The first breeding should be performed in quiet surroundings with only you and one other person to hold the bitch. Do not make it a circus, as the experience will determine the dog's outlook about future stud work. If he does not enjoy the first experience or associates it with any unpleasantness, you may well have a problem in the future.

Your young stud must permit help with the breeding, as later there will be bitches who will not be cooperative. If right from the beginning you are there helping him and praising him whether or not your assistance is actually needed, he will expect and accept this as a matter of course when a difficult bitch comes along.

Things to have handy before introducing your dog and the bitch are

Int. Ch. Hollypines Briarwood Bearcat, by Ch. Colegren's Mr. Hemlock ex Ch. Briarwood Bearcat, owned by Dick and Lillian Lincoln, Tijeras, New Mexico.

Ch. Foyscroft Triple Mitey Migit, by Ch. Kings Creek Triple Threat ex Ch. Pixshire's One and Only, 13″ bitch, finishing her title at Springfield Kennel Club in 1978. Co-owned by the authors, Marcia Foy and Anna K. Nicholas; one of eleven champions bred by Marcia Foy from Triple Threat and One and Only.

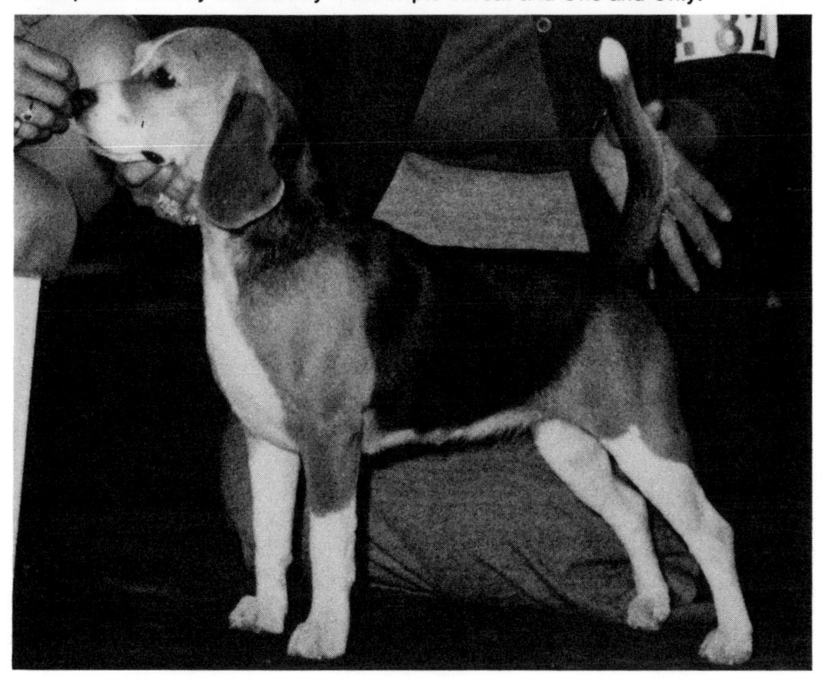

Ch. Teloca Patches On Target, C.D., 13″ dog, by Ch. Teloca's Puddin' An' Tame, C.D. ex Ch. Centurian's Jingle. Owned by Patsy A. Grant and Marie Stuart, the latter handling here to Best of Winners at the 1981 National Beagle Club Specialty under Michele Billings. This dog is the sire of the Best in Show Ch. Teloca Patches Littl' Dickens.

Ch. The Whim's Buckeye, 13″ dog. Buckeye's very impressive record includes Top 13″ Beagle 1970; Top Beagle, both Varieties, 1971 and 1972; and Top Hound in 1972. He is the sire of 97 champions, that include ten Bests in Show, 15 Group winners, six Specialty Bests of Breed; and ten Top Producing Beagles. Marvin Cates handling for Dr. and Mrs. A.C. Musladin, Los Gatos, California, breeders-owners.

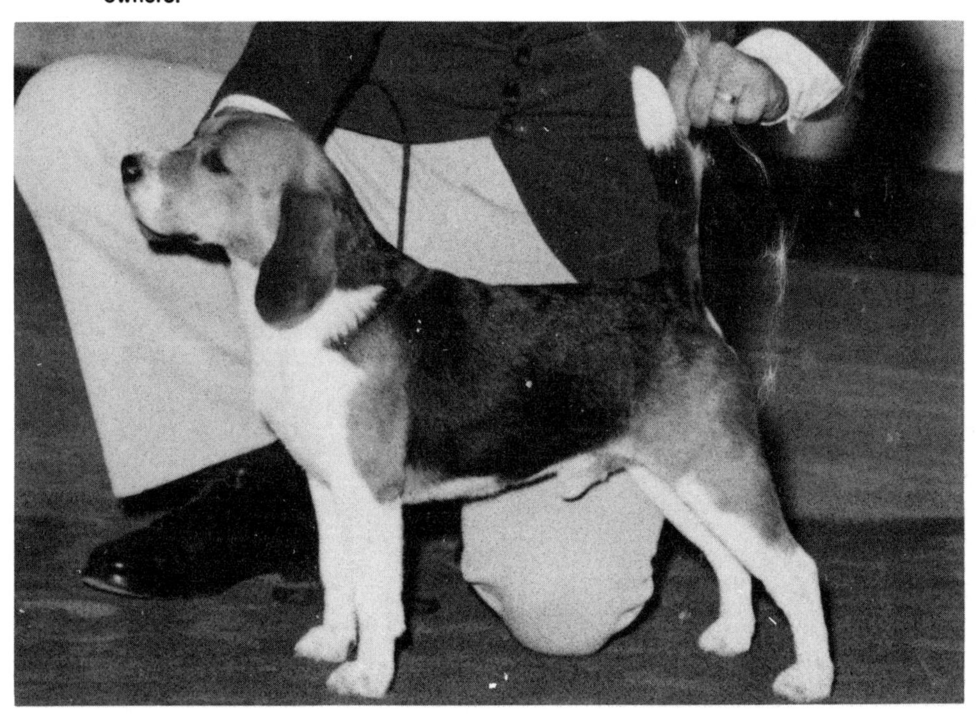

K-Y jelly (the only lubricant which should be used) and a length of gauze with which to muzzle the bitch should it be necessary to keep her from biting you or the dog. Some bitches put up a fight; others are calm. It is best to be prepared.

At the time of the breeding the stud fee comes due, and it is expected that it will be paid promptly. Normally a return service is offered in case the bitch misses or fails to produce one live puppy. Conditions of the service are what the stud dog's owner makes them, and there are no standard rules covering this. The stud fee is paid for the act, not the result. If the bitch fails to conceive, it is customary for the owner to offer a free return service; but this is a courtesy and not to be considered a right, particularly in the case of a proven stud who is siring consistently and whose fault the failure obviously is *not*. Stud dog owners are always anxious to see their clients get good value and to have in the ring winning young stock by their dog; therefore, very few refuse to mate the second time. It is wise, however, for both parties to have the terms of the transaction clearly understood at the time of the breeding.

If the return service has been provided and the bitch has missed a second time, that is considered to be the end of the matter and the owner would be expected to pay a further fee if it is felt that the bitch should be given a third chance with the stud dog. The management of a stud dog and his visiting bitches is quite a task, and a stud fee has usually been well earned when one service has been achieved, let alone by repeated visits from the same bitch.

The accepted litter is one live puppy. It is wise to have printed a breeding certificate which the owner of the stud dog and the owner of the bitch both sign. This should list in detail the conditions of the breeding as well as the dates of the mating.

Upon occasion, arrangements other than a stud fee in cash are made for a breeding, such as the owner of the stud taking a pick-of-the-litter puppy in lieu of money. This should be clearly specified on the breeding certificate along with the terms of the age at which the stud's owner will select the puppy, whether it is to be a specific sex, or whether it is to be the pick of the entire litter.

The price of a stud fee varies according to circumstances. Usually, to prove a young stud dog, his owner will allow the first breeding to be quite inexpensive. Then, once a bitch has become pregnant by him, he becomes a "proven stud" and the fee rises accordingly for bitches that follow. The sire of championship-quality puppies will bring a stud fee of at least the purchase price of one show puppy as the accepted "rule-of-thumb." Until at least one champion by your stud dog has finished, the fee will remain equal to the price of one pet puppy. When his list of champions starts to grow, so does the amount of the stud fee. For a top-producing sire of champions, the stud fee will rise accordingly.

Almost invariably it is the bitch who comes to the stud dog for the breeding. Immediately upon having selected the stud dog you wish to use, discuss the possibility with the owner of that dog. It is the stud dog owner's prerogative to refuse to breed any bitch deemed unsuitable for his dog. Stud fee and method of payment should be stated at this time, and a decision reached on whether it is to be a full cash transaction at the time of the mating or a pick-of-the-litter puppy, usually at eight weeks of age.

If the owner of the stud dog must travel to an airport to meet the bitch and ship her for the flight home, an additional charge will be made for time, tolls, and gasoline based on the stud owner's proximity to the airport. The stud fee includes board for the day on the bitch's arrival through two days for breeding, with a day in between. If it is necessary that the bitch remain longer, it is very likely that additional board will be charged at the normal per-day rate for the breed.

Be sure to advise the stud's owner as soon as you know that your bitch is in season so that the stud dog will be available. This is especially important because if he is a dog being shown, he and his owner may be unavailable owing to the dog's absence from home.

As the owner of a stud dog being offered to the public, it is essential that you have proper facilities for the care of visiting bitches. Nothing can be worse than a bitch being insecurely housed and slipping out to become lost or bred by the wrong dog. If you are taking people's valued bitches into your kennel or home, it is imperative that you provide them with comfortable, secure housing and good care while they are your responsibility.

There is no dog more valuable than the proven sire of champions, Group winners, and Best in Show dogs. Once you have such an animal, guard his reputation well and do *not* permit him to be bred to just any bitch that comes along. It takes two to make the puppies; even the most dominant stud can not do it all himself, so never permit him to breed a bitch you consider unworthy. Remember that when the puppies arrive, it will be your stud dog who will be blamed for any lack of quality, while the bitch's shortcomings will be quickly and conveniently overlooked.

Going into the actual management of the mating is a bit superfluous here. If you have had previous experience in breeding a dog and bitch you will know how the mating is done. If you do not have such experience, you should not attempt to follow directions given in a book but should have a veterinarian, breeder friend, or handler there to help you the first few times. You do not just turn the dog and bitch loose together and await developments, as too many things can go wrong and you may altogether miss getting the bitch bred. Someone should hold the dog and the bitch (one person each) until the "tie" is made and these two people should stay with them during the entire act.

If you get a complete tie, probably only the one mating is absolutely necessary. However, especially with a maiden bitch or one that has come a long distance for this breeding, we prefer following up with a second breeding, leaving one day in between the two matings. In this way there will be little or no chance of the bitch missing.

Once the tie has been completed and the dogs release, be certain that the male's penis goes completely back within its sheath. He should be allowed a drink of water and a short walk, and then he should be put into his crate or somewhere alone where he can settle down. Do not allow him to be with other dogs for a while as they will notice the odor of the bitch on him, and particularly with other males present, he may become involved in a fight.

Pregnancy, Whelping, and the Litter

Once the bitch has been bred and is back at home, remember to keep an ever watchful eye that no other male gets to her until at least the twenty-second day of her season has passed. Until then, it will still be possible for an unwanted breeding to take place, which at this point would be catastrophic. Remember that she actually can have two separate litters by two different dogs, so take care.

In other ways, she should be treated normally. Controlled exercise is good, and necessary for the bitch throughout her pregnancy, tapering it off to just several short walks daily, preferably on lead, as she reaches about her seventh week. As her time grows close, be careful about her jumping or playing too roughly.

The theory that a bitch should be overstuffed with food when pregnant is a poor one. A fat bitch is never an easy whelper, so the overfeeding you consider good for her may well turn out to be the exact opposite. During the first few weeks of pregnancy, your bitch

Dad's First Girl with her litter of six puppies by Ch. Jo Mar's Repeat Performance. Victor Lopez, owner, Lightninridge Beagles, Katonah, New York.

should be fed her normal diet. At four to five weeks along, calcium should be added to her food. At seven weeks her food may be increased if she seems to crave more than she is getting, and a meal of canned milk (mixed with an equal amount of water) should be introduced. If she is fed just once a day, add another meal rather than overload her with too much at one time. If twice a day is her schedule, then a bit more food can be added to each feeding.

A week before the pups are due, your bitch should be introduced to her whelping box so that she will be accustomed to it and feel at home there when the puppies arrive. She should be encouraged to sleep there but permitted to come and go as she wishes. The box should be roomy enough for her to lie down and stretch out but not too large lest the pups have more room than is needed in which to roam and possibly get chilled by going too far away from their mother. Be sure that the box has a "pig rail"; this will prevent the puppies from being crushed against the sides. The room in which the box is placed, either

An all-champion litter by Ch. R.J.B. Sean owned by Dreamland Beagles, Mrs. Vera Lucia Costa, San Paulo, Brazil.

in your home or in the kennel, should be kept at about 70 degrees Fahrenheit. In winter it may be necessary to have an infrared lamp over the whelping box, in which case be careful not to place it too low or close to the puppies.

Newspapers will become a very important commodity, so start collecting them well in advance to have a big pile handy to the whelping box. With a litter of puppies, one never seems to have papers enough, so the higher pile to start with, the better off you will be. Other necessities for whelping time are clean, soft turkish towels, scissors, and a bottle of alcohol.

You will know that her time is very near when your bitch becomes restless, wandering in and out of her box and of the room. She may refuse food, and at that point her temperature will start to drop. She will dig at and tear up the newspapers in her box, shiver, and generally look uncomfortable. Only you should be with your bitch at this time. She does not need spectators; and several people, even though they may be family members whom she knows, hanging over her may upset her to the point where she may harm the puppies. You should remain nearby, quietly watching, not fussing or hovering; speak calmly and frequently to her to instill confidence. Eventually she will settle down in her box and begin panting; contractions will follow. Soon thereafter a puppy will start to emerge, sliding out with the contractions. The mother immediately should open the sac, sever the cord with her teeth, and then clean up the puppy. She will also eat the placenta, which you should permit. Once the puppy is cleaned, it should be placed next to the bitch unless she is showing signs of having the next one immediately. Almost at once the puppy will start looking for a nipple on which to nurse, and you should ascertain that it is able to latch on successfully.

If the puppy is a breech (*i.e.*, born feet first), you must watch carefully for it to be completely delivered as quickly as possible and the sac removed quickly so that the puppy does not drown. Sometimes even a normally positioned birth will seem extremely slow in coming. Should this occur, you might take a clean towel and, as the bitch contracts, pull the puppy out, doing so gently and with utmost care. If, once the puppy is delivered, it shows little signs of life, take a rough turkish towel and massage the puppy's chest by rubbing quite briskly back and forth. Continue this for about fifteen minutes, and be sure that the mouth is free from liquid. It may be necessary to try mouth-to-mouth breathing, which is done by pressing the puppy's jaws open and, using a finger, depressing the tongue which may be stuck to the roof of the mouth. Then place your mouth against the puppy's and blow hard down the puppy's throat. Bubbles may pop out of its nose, but keep on blowing. Rub the puppy's chest with the towel again and try artificial respiration, pressing the sides of the chest together slowly and rhythmically—in and out, in and out. Keep trying one method or the other for at least twenty minutes before giving up. You may be rewarded with a live puppy who otherwise would not have made it.

If you are successful in bringing the puppy around, do not immediately put it back with the mother as it should be kept extra warm. Put it in a cardboard box on an electric heating pad or, if it is the time of year when your heat is running, near a radiator or near the fireplace or stove. As soon as the rest of the litter has been born it then can join the others.

An hour or more may elapse between puppies, which is fine so long as the bitch seems comfortable and is neither straining nor contract-

Sleepy pups from Bayberry Beagles owned by Andy and Carolyn Hayduck.

Littermates Ch. Holiday's Whispering Wind, 15″, and Ch. Holiday's Petite Chablis, 13″, sired by Ch. Foyscroft Red Barn ex Ch. Hearthside's Fancy Ribbons. Breeders, Paul and Arline Buckley. Handlers Sandy Robichaud and Phyllis Wright.

ing. She should not be permitted to remain unassisted for more than an hour if she does continue to contract. This is when you should get her to your veterinarian, whom you should already have alerted to the possibility of a problem existing. He should examine her and perhaps give her a shot of Pituitrin. In some cases the veterinarian may find that a Caesarean section is necessary due to a puppy being lodged in a manner making normal delivery impossible. Sometimes this is caused by an abnormally large puppy, or it may just be that the puppy is simply turned in the wrong position. If the bitch does require a Caesarean section, the puppies already born must be kept warm in their cardboard box with a heating pad under the box.

Once the section is done, get the bitch and the puppies home. Do not attempt to put the puppies in with the bitch until she has regained consciousness as she may unknowingly hurt them. But do get them back to her as soon as possible for them to start nursing.

Should the mother lack milk at this time, the puppies must be fed by hand, kept very warm, and held onto the mother's teats several times a day in order to stimulate and encourage the secretion of milk, which should start shortly.

Assuming that there has been no problem and that the bitch has whelped naturally, you should insist that she go out to exercise, staying just long enough to make herself comfortable. She can be offered a bowl of milk and a biscuit, but then she should settle down with her family. Freshen the whelping box for her with fresh newspapers while she is taking this respite so that she and the puppies will have a clean bed.

Unless some problem arises, there is little you must do about the puppies until they become three to four weeks old. Keep the box clean and supplied with fresh newspapers the first few days, but then turkish towels should be tacked down to the bottom of the box so that the puppies will have traction as they move about.

If the bitch has difficulties with her milk supply, or if you should be so unfortunate as to lose her, then you must be prepared to either hand-feed or tube-feed the puppies if they are to survive. We personally prefer tube-feeding as it is so much faster and easier. If the bitch is available, it is best that she continues to clean and care for the puppies in the normal manner excepting for the food supplements you will provide. If it is impossible for her to do this, then after every feeding you must gently rub each puppy's abdomen with wet cotton to make it urinate, and the rectum should be gently rubbed to open the bowels.

Newborn puppies must be fed every three to four hours around the

5-week-old puppies at Starcrest Kennels. Second from *left,* future Ch. Page Mill Pamela of Starcrest. On the *right,* future Ch. The Bonus Jack of Starcrest. Robert and Louise Merrill, owners, Los Gatos, California.

clock. The puppies must be kept warm during this time. Have your veterinarian teach you how to tube-feed. You will find that it is really quite simple.

After a normal whelping, the bitch will require additional food to enable her to produce sufficient milk. In addition to being fed twice daily, she should be given some canned milk several times each day.

When the puppies are two weeks old, their nails should be clipped, as they are needle sharp at this age and can hurt or damage the mother's teats and stomach as the pups hold on to nurse.

Between three and four weeks of age, the puppies should begin to be weaned. Scraped beef (prepared by scraping it off slices of beef with a spoon so that none of the gristle is included) may be offered in very small quantities a couple of times daily for the first few days. Then by the third day you can mix puppy chow with warm water as directed on the package, offering it four times daily. By now the mother should be

A litter of seven 7-week-old Beagle puppies sired by Danish Ch. Buglair Sundance out of Int. Ch. Interim's Fair Lady Fidget. Bred by Dr. Barbara Rudorf, Germany. Photo courtesy of the Garland Moores, Atwater, California.

kept away from the puppies and out of the box for several hours at a time so that when they have reached five weeks of age she is left in with them only overnight. By the time the puppies are six weeks old, they should be entirely weaned and receiving only occasional visits from their mother.

Most veterinarians recommend a temporary DHL (distemper, hepatitis, leptospirosis) shot when the puppies are six weeks of age. This remains effective for about two weeks. Then at eight weeks of age, the puppies should receive the series of permanent shots for DHL protection. It is also a good idea to discuss with your vet the advisability of having your puppies inoculated against the dreaded parvovirus at the same time. Each time the pups go to the vet for shots, you should bring stool samples so that they can be examined for worms. Worms go through various stages of development and may be present in a

stool sample even though the sample does not test positive in every checkup. So do not neglect to keep careful watch on this.

The puppies should be fed four times daily until they are three months old. Then you can cut back to three feedings daily. By the time the puppies are six months of age, two meals daily are sufficient. Some people feed their dogs twice daily throughout their lifetime; others go to one meal daily when the puppy becomes one year of age.

The ideal age for puppies to go to their new homes is between eight and twelve weeks, although some puppies successfully adjust to a new home when they are six weeks old. Be sure that they go to their new owners accompanied by a description of the diet you've been feeding them and a schedule of the shots they have already received and those they still need. These should be included with the registration application and a copy of the pedigree.

Chapter 20

Traveling with Your Beagle

When you travel with your dog, to shows or on vacation or wherever, remember that everyone does not share our enthusiasm or love for dogs and that those who do not, strange creatures though they seem to us, have their rights, too. These rights, on which we should not encroach, include not being disturbed, annoyed, or made uncomfortable by the presence and behavior of other people's pets. Your dog should be kept on lead in public places and should recognize and promptly obey the commands "Down," "Come," "Sit," and "Stay."

Take along his crate if you are going any distance with your dog. And keep him in it when riding in the car. A crated dog has a far better chance of escaping injury than one riding loose in the car should an accident occur or an emergency arise. If you do permit your dog to ride loose, never allow him to hang out a window, ears blowing in the breeze. An injury to his eyes could occur in this manner. He could also become overly excited by something he sees and jump out, or he could lose his balance and fall out.

Never, ever under any circumstances, should a dog be permitted to ride loose in the back of a pick-up truck. We have noted, with horror, that some people do transport dogs in this manner, and we think it cruel and shocking. How easily such a dog can be thrown out of the truck by sudden jolts or an impact! And we are sure that many dogs have jumped out at the sight of something exciting along the way. Some unthinking individuals tie the dog, probably not realizing that were he to jump under those circumstances, his neck would be broken, he could be dragged alongside the vehicle, or he could be hit by another vehicle. If you are for any reason taking your dog in an open back truck, please

Winners of the National Beagle Club's very first Specialty Show in 1970. *Left*, Ch. Draper's Lemon Drop Daisy Mae, with John D. White, Jr. was Best of Variety 13″ and Best of Opposite Sex to Best in Show. *Right*, Ch. Kings Creek Triple Threat, with Marcia Foy, was Best of Variety 15″ and Best in Show. Triple Threat amassed 271 Group placements, of which 84 were firsts, and saw two of his sons win the National in later years. The judge was John P. Murphy, whose nephew, Desmond Murphy, is now proving a popular and knowledgeable Beagle judge in the family tradition.

have sufficient regard for that dog to at least provide a crate for him, and then remember that, in or out of a crate, a dog riding under the direct rays of the sun in hot weather can suffer and have his life endangered by the heat.

If you are staying at a hotel or motel with your dog, exercise him somewhere other than in the flower beds and parking lot of the property. People walking to and from their cars really are not thrilled at "stepping in something" left by your dog. Should an accident occur,

Ch. Saddlerock Sandman II taking Winners Dog at Westminster in 1977, handled by co-owner Marcia Foy as breeder-owner Isabella Hoopes looks on. Mrs. Hoopes is the famous lady of the Saddlerock Beagles, and "Sandy" is the last of the famous Saddlerocks who played so important a role in Beagle history for half a century.

pick it up with a tissue or a paper towel and deposit it in a proper receptacle; do not just walk off leaving it to remain there. Usually there are grassy areas on the sides of and behind motels where dogs can be exercised. Use them rather than the more conspicuous, usually carefully tended, front areas or those close to the rooms. If you are becoming a dog show enthusiast, you will eventually need an exercise pen to take with you to the show. Exercise pens are ideal to use when staying at motels, too, as they permit you to limit the dog's roaming space and to pick up after him more easily.

Never leave your dog unattended in the room of a motel unless you are absolutely, positively certain that he will stay there quietly and not damage or destroy anything. You do not want a long list of complaints from irate guests, caused by the annoying barking or whining of a lonesome dog in strange surroundings or an overzealous watch dog barking furiously each time a footstep passes the door or he hears a sound from an adjoining room. And you certainly do not want to return to torn curtains or bedspreads, soiled rugs, or other embarrassing evidence of the fact that your dog is not really house-reliable after all.

If yours is a dog accustomed to traveling with you and you are positive that his behavior will be acceptable when left alone, that is fine. But if the slightest uncertainty exists, the wise course is to leave him in the car while you go to dinner or elsewhere; then bring him into the room when you are ready to retire for the night.

When you travel with a dog, it is often simpler to take along from home the food and water he will need rather than buying food and looking for water while you travel. In this way he will have the rations to which he is accustomed and which you know agree with him, and there will be no fear of problems due to different drinking water. Feeding on the road is quite easy now, at least for short trips, with all the splendid dry prepared foods and high-quality canned meats available. A variety of lightweight, refillable water containers can be bought at many types of stores.

If you are going to another country, you will need a health certificate from your veterinarian for each dog you are taking with you, certifying that each has had rabies shots within the required time preceding your visit.

Be careful always to leave sufficient openings to ventilate your car when the dog will be alone in it. Remember that during the summer, the rays of the sun can make an inferno of a closed car within only a few minutes, so leave enough window space open to provide air circulation. Again, if your dog is in a crate, this can be done quite safely. The fact that you have left the car in a shady spot is not always a guarantee that you will find conditions the same when you return. Don't forget that the position of the sun changes in a matter of minutes, and the car you left nicely shaded half an hour ago can be getting full sunlight far more quickly than you may realize. So, if you leave a dog in the car, make sure there is sufficient ventilation and check back frequently to ascertain that all is well.

Chapter 21

Responsibilities of Breeders and Owners

The first responsibility of any person breeding dogs is to do so with care, forethought, and deliberation. It is inexcusable to breed more litters than you need to carry on your show program or to perpetuate your bloodlines. A responsible breeder should not cause a litter to be born without definite plans for the safe and happy disposition of the puppies.

A responsible dog breeder makes absolutely certain, so far as is humanly possible, that the home to which one of his puppies will go is a good home, one that offers proper care and an enthusiastic owner. We have tremendous admiration for those people who insist on visiting (although doing so is not always feasible) the prospective owners of their puppies, to see if they have suitable facilities for keeping a dog, that they understand the responsibility involved, and that all members of the household are in accord regarding the desirability of owning one. All breeders should carefully check out the credentials of prospective purchasers to be sure that the puppy is being placed in responsible hands.

We are certain that no breeder ever wants a puppy or grown dog he has raised to wind up in an animal shelter, in an experimental laboratory, or as a victim of a speeding car. While complete control of such a situation may be impossible, it is at least our responsibility to make every effort to turn over dogs to responsible people. When selling a puppy, it is a good idea to do so with the understanding that should it become necessary to place the dog in other hands, the purchaser will first contact you, the breeder. You may want to help in some way, possibly by buying or taking back the dog or placing it elsewhere. It is not fair just

Ch. Jabrwoki's Hex On You, 13″ bitch, and her sire, Ch. Suntree's Hocus Pocus, each winning its Variety. Hex On You belongs to Shawn and Barbara Robblee; Hocus Pocus, to Bill and Susan Dooley.

15″ Beagle, Ch. Yaupon Row Sailor Boy, C.D.X. is, to our knowledge, the first and only Best in Show winning Beagle in the United States to have earned a C.D.X. as well in Obedience. Bred by Samuel R. Whittaker, Jr., who has bred many famous dogs at his Yaupon Row Kennels, Sailor Boy is owned by Mr. and Mrs. Hugh Peek of Pollok, Texas.

Ch. Foyscroft Triple Dragon Lady, by Ch. Kings Creek Triple Threat ex Ch. Foyscroft True Blue Lou, finishing her title at Albany Kennel Club in 1973 by taking Best of Variety. Dragon's show career included a Winners Bitch at Westminster earlier in that year. Owned and handled by Marcia Foy.

to sell our puppies and then never again give a thought to their welfare. Family problems arise, people may be forced to move where dogs are prohibited, or people just plain grow bored with a dog and its care. Thus the dog becomes a victim. You, as the dog's breeder, should concern yourself with the welfare of each of your dogs and see to it that the dog remains in good hands.

The final obligation every dog owner shares, be there just one dog or an entire kennel involved, is that of making detailed, explicit plans for the future of our dearly loved animals in the event of the owner's death. Far too many of us are apt to procrastinate and leave this very important matter unattended to, feeling that everything will work out or that "someone will see to them." The latter is not too likely, at least not to the benefit of the dogs, unless you have done some advance planning which will assure their future well-being.

Life is filled with the unexpected, and even the youngest, healthiest, most robust of us may be the victim of a fatal accident or sudden illness. The fate of our dogs, so entirely in our hands, should never be left to chance. If you have not already done so, please get together with your lawyer and set up a clause in your will specifying what you want done with each of your dogs, to whom they will be entrusted (after first making absolutely certain that the person selected is willing and able to assume the responsibility), and telling the locations of all registration papers, pedigrees, and kennel records. Just think of the possibilities which might happen otherwise! If there is another family member who shares your love of the dogs, that is good and you have less to worry about. But if your heirs are not dog-oriented, they will hardly know how to proceed or how to cope with the dogs themselves,

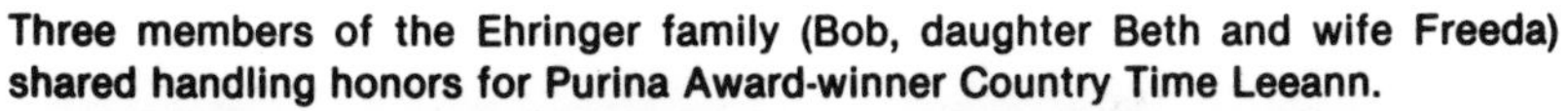

Three members of the Ehringer family (Bob, daughter Beth and wife Freeda) shared handling honors for Purina Award-winner Country Time Leeann.

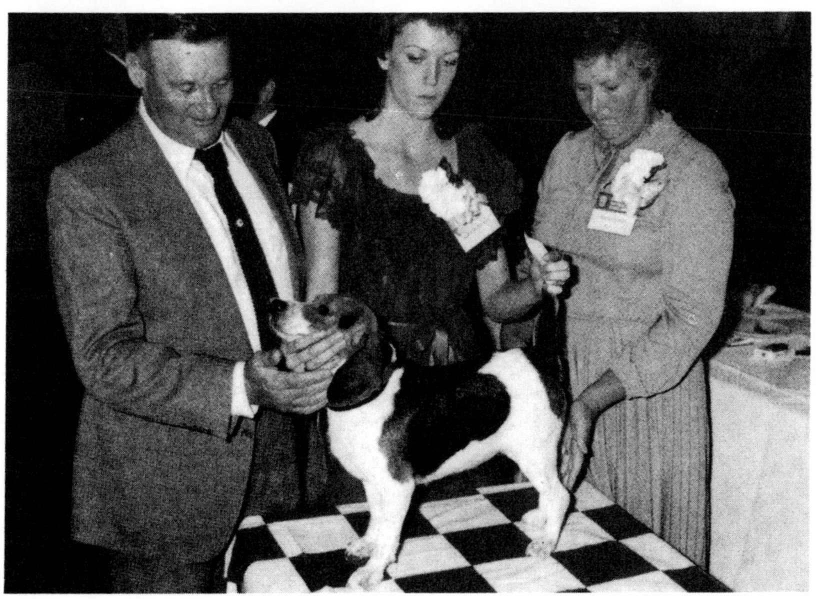

and they may wind up disposing of or caring for your dogs in a manner that would break your heart were you around to know about it.

In our family, we have specific instructions in each of our wills for each of our dogs. A friend, also a dog person who regards her own dogs with the same concern and esteem as we do ours, has agreed to take over their care until they can be placed accordingly and will make certain that all will work out as we have planned. We have this person's name and phone number prominently displayed in our van and car and in our wallets. Our lawyer is aware of this fact. It is all spelled out in our wills. The friend has a signed check of ours to be used in case of an emergency or accident when we are traveling with the dogs; this check will be used to cover her expense to come and take over the care of our dogs should anything happen to make it impossible for us to do so. This, we feel, is the least any dog owner should do in preparation for the time our dogs suddenly find themselves without us. There have been so many sad cases of dogs unprovided for by their loving owners, left to heirs who couldn't care less and who disposed of them in any way at all to get rid of them, or left to heirs who kept and neglected them under the misguided idea that they were providing them "a fine home with lots of freedom." All of us *must* prevent any of these misfortunes befalling our own dogs who have meant so much to us!

Index